BIG FORDS & MERCS

A SOURCE BOOK

EDITED AND ANNOTATED BY

Samuel A. Shields, Jr.

Motorbooks International
Publishers & Wholesalers Inc.
Osceola, Wisconsin 54020, USA

Bookman Publishing/Baltimore, Maryland

Printed in the U.S.A.
Copyright 1984 in U.S.A. by Bookman Dan!, Inc.

ISBN 0-934780-38-2

First Edition
First Printing

Inquiries may be directed to:
Bookman Dan!, Inc.
P.O. Box 13492
Baltimore, Maryland 21203

Book trade distribution by:
Motorbooks International
P. O. Box 2
Osceola, Wisconsin 54020

Contents

Ever since 1903 when Henry Ford built Old 999 and won his first race, Ford has been building high performance machines. And proving them by winning . . . at Bonneville, Pomona, Indianapolis, Riverside and Le Mans. But there's more to Ford performance than a worldwide winning streak. The same Ford engineers who stretch their minds to win on the tracks are involved in designing performance cars and parts you can buy. And if you don't think that makes for winners on the road, look for this sign which marks your Ford Dealer's Performance Corner and let him prove it. It's the place you've got to go to see what's going on!

Preface

Although I have been a Mopar enthusiast since my early years and have written four books on Mopar cars, I have long wanted to write this book on Fords and Mercurys. In 1963 I had an unhappy experience in trying to make a trade on a new Plymouth, and therefore drove down the street and made a very successful trade on a new Ford. Through the following years I have purchased many Fords and Mopars and liked both. My favorite years of Fords are 1963 and 1964.

When I volunteered to write this book, I had a very difficult time deciding which years to cover and finally decided on covering 1957 thru 1970. Nineteen Fifty-Seven was the year when both Ford and Mercury took on a totally new image in styling and began to offer the really high-performance engine options. Nineteen Seventy was the year when the preformance images came to a end.

Being a literature collector and dealer, it was only natural that I would collect literature on the cars as I owned them. For those that I have not owned, I have been able to dive into my business inventory and select the missing items to include in this book.

In 1954 Ford finally broke with tradition and began manufacturing an overhead valve V-8 and in 1955 they took a step forward with a new, more youthful look with the bold side sweep and the wraparound windshield. Ford continued to use the round taillights that they introduced in 1952, and which, for a number of years, was something of a trademark.

Nineteen Fifty-Seven was the year when Ford and Mercury took a bold step forward. Ford in doing so, put one over on Chevrolet. Also, Ford introduced two totally new body styles: the Skyliner retractable and the Ranchero, a car-based pickup.

As Ford and Mercury became more aggressive, they became more involved in racing and in performance-oriented cars. The early-sixties saw the introduction of the high performance 390's. These were replaced with the 406's, then along came the fire-breathing 427's. The 427's put them in the forefront on the NASCAR tracks and on the drag strips.

As the mid-sixties continued, Ford and Mercury not only continued with performance cars, but began pushing hard into the luxury car market. The 1965 LTD was advertised as being as quiet as a Rolls Royce. I owned one of these 1965 Ltd's and, believe me, it was quiet, although I never had a chance to compare it to a Rolls-Royce (unfortunately!).

As the sixties were drawing to a close, Ford switched its performance image from the big cars to the intermediates. Thus, the big Fords and Mercurys became just full-sized luxury cars.

Many of the performance Fords and Mercurys are very desirable collector cars today and should be even more so in the future. I am pleased to see this literature compiled so as to help other literature collectors locate items to fill holes in their collections, to help owners of these cars to know what literature exists on their vehicles and, hopefully, to help future generations to know more about these great cars.

The purpose of a Source Book is to tell the story of a car through the use of the manufacturer's original literature, some of which, as in the case of these cars, may be quite rare. In each chapter, the front covers of the main items are shown in a montage on the first Source Book page and then the important pages from those brochures are reproduced on the following Source Book pages (and keyed to the text at the beginning of each chapter).

I feel especially appreciative of the moral support I have had in writing this and my previous Source Books, and I wish to thank Tom Bonsall and Ed Lehwald of Bookman Publishing for offering me the opportunity to have these books included in the Source Book series. I hope to continue to offer more books to them in the future.

Cuyahoga Falls, Ohio
June, 1984

You're invited to
ACTION TEST

the Endurance and Acceleration
CHAMP

'57 FORD
TWICE AROUND THE WORLD
IN 20 DAYS!

at your **FORD** Dealer's

Ford for 1957 was of a totally new design from the ground up. This new design was so much different from the other cars being produced at the time that Ford was able to out-sell Chevrolet for the first time since the early thirties. Two new body styles were introduced: the Skyliner retractable and the Ranchero, the half-car, half-truck pickup truck. Although the 1957 Ford did not offer any innovative mechanical features, its styling was definitely innovative. The silhouette of the new Ford was much lower than its competition. The front design featured a low-set grille with boldly set headlights. The rear featured large round taillights and small canted fins. Ford, along with most of the auto industry, was engaged quite heavily in auto racing. Ford set records at Bonneville and Daytona. This year also marked the 25th anniversary of Ford's building V-8 engines.

Engines offered were the 223 cid six (1-bbl) rated at 144 hp, the 272 cid V-8 (2-bbl) rated at 190 hp, the 292 cid V-8 (2-bbl) rated at 212 hp, the 312 cid V-8 (4-bbl) rated at 245 hp, the 312 cid V-8 (two 4-bbl) rated at 270 hp, and the 312 cid V-8 (super-charged 4-bbl) rated at 300 hp. Transmissions offered were the 3-speed manual, the 3-speed manual with overdrive and the 3-speed Fordomatic automatic.

Production amounted to 1,653,068 units, with the following model breakdown (sixes and V-8's totals combined). Prices for sixes follow each model in ()'s, with V-8's costing $100 more: CUSTOM 4-dr sedan 68,924 ($2,042), 2-dr sedan 116,963 ($1,991), 2dr bus. coupe 6,888 ($1,889); CUSTOM 300 4-dr sedan 194,877 ($2,157), 2-dr sedan, 160,360 ($2,105), FAIRLANE 4-dr Town sedan 52,060 ($2,286), 2-dr Club sedan 39,843 ($2,235), 4-dr Town Victoria 12,695 ($2,357), 4-dr Club Victoria 44,127 ($2,293); FAIRLANE 500 4-dr Town sedan 193,162 ($2,333), 2-dr Club sedan 93,763 ($2,281), 4-dr Town Victoria 68,550 (42,404), 2-dr Club Victoria 183,202 ($2,339), Sunliner convertible 77,728 ($2,505), Skyliner retractable convertible 20,766 ($2,942) V-8 only; STATION WAGON 2-dr Ranch Wagon 6-pass. 60,486 ($2,301), 2-dr Del Rio 6-pass. 45,105 ($2,397), 4-dr Country Sedan 6-pass. 135,251 ($2,451), 135,251 ($2,451), 4-dr Country Sedan 9-pass. 49,638 ($2,556), 4-dr Country Squire 9-pass. 27,690 ($2,684).

Thirteen exterior colors were offered with two-tones available at extra cost. Interiors were available in many color combinations of vinyl or vinyl and cloth.

Literature offered for 1957 consisted of the full-line color catalogue dated 8/56 with revisions dated 10/56 and 4/57, the Fairlane large color catalogue dated 8/56 with revisions dated 10/56 and 4/57, the Custom series large color catalogue dated 8/56 with revisions dated 10/56 and 4/57, the Station Wagons large color catlogue dated 8/56 and the same dated 10/56, the Station Wagons folder, the engines and transmissions catalogue (see pages 8-9), the "Out of the desert salt flats..." ad reprint from "Life" magazine, folder (see pages 6 and 10-12), the Skyliner retractable large color catalogue, the Skyliner retractable folder dated 4/57 and the Quick Facts booklet (see page 9).

• When your mood says "scat" this 'Bird will skedaddle!

Thunderbird 312
Special V-8

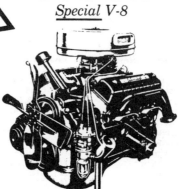

245 hp

- 312-cubic inch displacement
  largest engines in the low-price field

- 9.7 to 1 compression ratio

- 332 ft. lbs. torque at 3200 rpm

- Four-Venturi Carburetor

- Designed to deliver "out-in-front" performance on premium gasoline

There's new **Thunderbird sizzle** in this new Thunderbird 312 Special V-8. With a compression ratio of 9.7 to 1 and a four-venturi carburetor, this engine delivers a brand of GO you'll love. It was originally built for the Thunderbird.*
*With Overdrive or Fordomatic

The world's largest-selling eight!

Available in any model with any transmission: 3-speed, Overdrive or Fordomatic

• Power to keep you out in front of the pack!

Thunderbird 312
Super V-8

270 hp

- 312-cubic inch displacement
  largest engines in the low-price field

- 9.7 to 1 compression ratio

- 336 ft. lbs. torque at 3400 rpm

- Twin 4-Venturi Carburetor

- Designed to deliver "out-in-front" performance on premium gasoline

If you appreciate "out-in-front" performance, then this Thunderbird 312 Super V-8 is for you! Built for the Thunderbird* and featuring twin 4-venturi carburetors, for outstanding acceleration and endurance.
*Optional with any transmission

The world's largest-selling eight!

Available in any model with any transmission: 3-speed, Overdrive or Fordomatic

• Horsepower galore for checkered flag performance!

300 hp

The exclusive Ford Thunderbird 312 Supercharged V-8 will deliver surging 300 horsepower!

• *8.6 to 1 compression ratio*

• *4-venturi carburetor*

• *312-cubic inch displacement*

SPECIFICATIONS OF THE ALL-NEW '57 FORD

IMPORTANT DIMENSIONS (Fordor Sedans)

FORDOMATIC—Combination torque converter and automatic gear train. Three forward gear ratios. Water-cooled (air-cooled with Six engine). No mechanical linkage between engine and drive system.

OVERDRIVE—Economical, extra 4th gear allows 30% lower engine speeds than in 3rd gear. Convenient handle below instrument panel locks Overdrive in or out.

CONVENTIONAL—Three-speed transmission has all-helical gears with tailored-to-engine ratios. Easy, finger-tip control lever. Offers 3 speeds forward plus reverse.

CLUTCH—Semi-centrifugal clutch has full-centrifugal levers for positive clutch engagement. All bearings are oil-impregnated or permanently lubricated.

STEERING—Steering ratio increased to 27 to 1 for easier steering effort. New deep-dish safety steering wheel has 17½-inch diameter.

FUEL TANK CAPACITIES—Fuel tanks on all models have capacities increased to 20 gallons. Center-fill fueling on all models (except station wagons, which have access port on left rear fender).

BRAKES—Giant-Grip, Double-Sealed brakes have 11-inch diameter—180-sq. in. lining area for all sedans, 191 sq. in. for station wagons. Brake pedal is the suspended type. Master cylinder is mounted on front face of dash.

All dimensions in inches	'57 CUSTOM	'57 FAIRLANE	'56 CUSTOMLINE
Length (over-all)	201.7	207.7	198.5
Width (maximum)	77.0	77.0	75.9
Height (maximum—with design load)	57.2	56.2	60.4
Wheelbase	116.0	118.0	115.5
Tread Front	59.0	59.0	58.0
Tread Rear	56.4	56.4	56.0
Head Room Front	34.8	33.8	34.9
Head Room Rear	33.5	34.5	33.9
Shoulder Room Front	57.6	57.3	57.0
Shoulder Room Rear	57.0	57.0	56.8
Leg Room Front	44.3	43.1	44.3
Leg Room Rear	42.1	41.0	41.9

The specifications contained herein were in effect at the time this folder was approved for printing. The Ford Division of Ford Motor Company reserves the right to discontinue models at any time, or change specifications or design, without notice and without incurring obligation.

PRICES: Some items referred to in this folder are at extra cost. For the price of model and equipment desired, consult an authorized Ford Dealer.

FORD Division of FORD MOTOR COMPANY • **Dearborn, Michigan**

Litho in U.S.A.

ONLY SPEED LINES SHOW as a 1957 Ford hurtles past photo-electric cells to set Salt Flat records.

THE LONGEST LEFT TURN IN HISTORY

The new 1957 Ford hurtles over the Salt Flats at fantastic 108.16 mph for 50,000 hot miles

This is the true story of a classic endurance test. It involves 27 men, two stock 1957 Ford cars, and 458 National and International records for automobile performance. But what happened in twenty blazing September days in Utah also involves every American who owns, or drives, or rides in cars.

THE LONGEST left turn in history began on a desert of salt at 1:50 p.m. on Sunday, September 9, 1956.

As the United States Automobile Club (USAC) timer flagged the start of the run, two Fords flashed past the two batteries of photo-electric cells and dwindled swiftly into black specks on the blinding white salt.

Once the cars had disappeared on the first

lap, those who were left lit cigarettes and relaxed. One said: "How can I do my work if I keep my fingers crossed for the next couple of weeks?" They all looked at the landscape; for a while there would be nothing else to do.

Except to watch the Fords go by. And by. And by again. Five thousand times.

The landscape that the cars whispered over is a special kind of hell. Bonneville Salt Flats is one of the deadliest deserts on earth. Nothing can live on it, nothing can grow on it: not an insect, not a weed. It is as desolate as the plains of the moon.

When waterfowl fly each year across the flats, some of them alight unsuspectingly in the brackish puddles, to rest. There they die,

USAC OFFICIAL, John Bodine, one of many on duty 24 hours a day, took his regular shift; verified each record-breaking mile from Mile One to Mile 50,000. Infallible electric clocks were used.

THEY DROVE 5 YEARS INTO TOMORROW

DANNY O'BRIEN, a driver who is such an expert mechanic that he also helped in the swift, slick pit-stop drills. The drivers kept awake on their long grind by munching grapes and cookies. But not one of them gained in weight.

DANNY EAMES, veteran Ford test-driver and crew chief, wore sun glasses to cheat the glare of the noon sun. Each driver whiled away his shift differently; some wrote jokes to throw out at the crews in pit stops.

CHUCK STEVENSON, famous driver, who won the Mexican road race two years in succession, wraps against the cold. They took solid punishment: endless circling turned the slick salt to bone-crushing potholes.

their plumage fouled by the greasy, sticky salt. The "Flats," stretch over 3,000 square miles of western Utah. The famous race-track section is 200 square miles of crystalline salt; hard as concrete, without dust, pure white, smooth.

The sky is blue, the salt is white, the nearby mountains are a dead dun brown, the far mountains purple, the farthest mountains blue. These are the colors of Bonneville, just as they have been for some 70,000 years. At dawn the salt is pink, at sunset the salt is gold.

The mountains around the ancient lake bed are as brutal, as savagely forbidding as the vast white sheet of salt—and almost as dead; they grow only sagebrush and tumbleweeds, and are populated only by rattlesnakes and little darting horned toads.

All summer long the dry thin mountain air heats to 100 degrees in the day; when the sun plunges behind the mountains the temperature drops swiftly to 50 degrees or less.

Through the blazing heat of day, through the biting cold of night, through nature's temperature torture, the Fords piled up the miles.

The Flats have had almost no history through the slow centuries: the dead salt turned back all travelers. In 1846 the ill-fated Donner party dragged their caravans of dying oxen slowly across the bitter 90 miles: the tracks of those covered wagons are still clearly rutted in the salt, undisturbed for a century. The Flats defied the railroads until 1900, and the highway builders until 1920. But already by 1914 the Flats had been discovered as the ideal place to test a car's performance and endurance. The nearby town of Wendover began to make automobile news all over the world.

INTO this harsh science-fiction landscape, shortly after Labor Day this year, came a crew of human beings of different talents.

Twelve of them were veteran drivers, race and performance-test champions.

Fifteen were pit men, mechanics with an odd assortment of skills. They are the best men in the world at doing things for which there is practically no call, such as filling the gas tank of a car in less than 17 seconds.

The rest were observers, cameramen—and most importantly, USAC and Federation Internationale de Automobile officials.

The test had been carefully and deliberately designed to measure the sheer endurance, the absolute stamina of a completely new kind of automobile—the 1957 Ford. The Ford management had coldly decided to make the test in the most difficult possible way.

Official rules, standards and procedures, were to be honored to the exact letter.

There was to be no leeway from start to finish, no margins, no allowances. *Every second, including all pit stops, was to be counted.*

THE USAC AND FIA men who were supervising the entire test, had to be at the track 24 hours a day, as long as the run continued. Four officials had to be in the Timing Shack. In three little sun-baked huts around the rim of the 10-mile track were three "spotters" endlessly reporting as the cars zipped past their stations.

The clock was the enemy of the cars whirling over the salt. It's not even a clock, but an electrical machine without moving parts—*accurate to within 1/1000 of a second.*

Outside the Time Shack stood two facing batteries of photo-electric cells, one on each side of the track. Each time a car passed between these cells, the timing device in the shack automatically imprinted on paper the exact thousandth of a second.

Once the timer clicked into action, as it did on September 9, nothing could be done until the men and the steel gave up, fatigued beyond endurance. It ticked away all the seconds in the pit, all the seconds of high noon and full moon, the heat and the chill, the time to eat and sleep.

And at every pit stop an eagle-eyed official had to record the temperature in the sun, in the shade, and on the salt every hour, as well as the wind velocity, for a complete record of weather conditions.

THE monotony began. The pit crews had a dull time. They are so fantastically expert that they can complete a full pit stop in as little as 17 seconds. This leaves them with 59 minutes and 43 seconds to kill until the next pit stop.

The cars whirled on over the ten miles of salt all that Sunday afternoon, on the long gradual left turn that seemed endless.

In the afternoons, in the steady mirages of the Salt Flats, the mountains often seem to hang suspended, six feet off the ground. And so did the cars—floating softly, silently, swiftly, high above the brilliant white desert of salt.

Especially swiftly.

FOR the most severe rule of all was the true basis of the test: the cars had to go at high speeds in order to break the records they were after. The way to torture a car most hideously is to keep it at high speed until it melts or snaps or erodes or falls apart.

These speeds were truly high. The first 24 hours were run at over 120 miles per hour, then the cars were throttled down to a running speed of over 110 m.p.h.

The blue-and-white Ford flicked by. Then the black-and-yellow. Again and again. The records began to fall, slowly at first. Each hour meant 110 miles of driving, or 11 times around the ten-mile track. Every two or three hours a substitute driver swung into each car.

The sun dropped out of sight, the moon floated up. The little smudge pots were lighted along the inner circle of the track, the tiny yellow flames flickering as the cars swooshed by into the velvet desert dark.

The pit men drank coffee and smoked and read, sunbathing by day, working in sweaters at

NIGHT PIT STOPS had to be serviced just as swiftly as the daytime halts. The veteran service crews gassed, oiled and watered the cars in as little as 17 seconds of hot work.

THE GLITTERING NEW FORDS soon became salt-crusted as they whisked silently over the most perfect racing surface in the world. But the 50,000-mile endurance test, run under the most rigid rules ever, permitted no time for polish or prettying-up.

night. They couldn't play cards—the important hands always come up just before a pit stop.

The time went on. Sunday became Monday. Tuesday and Wednesday went by. Still the cars were floating silently over the salt at 110 miles per hour. Then it was Thursday and Friday and pretty soon Sunday again—the cars had run a week at this torturing, furious speed.

And along went another Monday, another Tuesday—and the records were still falling.

Time and monotony and fatigue play tricks on human beings. Once a driver went right through the pit at 110 miles an hour. Once one of the pit men idly splashed a paper cup full of water at the windshield of the car as it passed. But water is a solid lump when struck at 110 miles an hour—the water went right through the windshield. The glass was taped up. The car rolled on.

A pit stop works like this: while the car is still slowing down, with the engine turned off, one mechanic hits the front fender with a piece of metal to ground all electricity. Another, already running behind with gas hose in hand, begins squirting gasoline through the air into the hole of the tank while the car is still moving. By this time the hood is up, a mechanic is checking the oil, another is checking the plugs and the carburetor, and the car has run over lifts to allow other men to get below and check the suspensions, the driveshaft, the springs and the gears. It seems a moment only—and then the car has leaped away again.

Gradually the pit stops grew more tense. How long could the Fords go on with no change except oil and gas and water? How long could steel—and men—endure?

The second Wednesday passed, and Thursday. The sun came up, blazed, sank; the moon came up, the desert was chill, they drank coffee and drove and drove and drove, and still the Fords were ramming around that gigantic left turn at 110 miles per hour.

The drivers carried lots of food. The monotony of this kind of driving grinds the nerves. They ate grapes—one grape at a time, a couple of grapes each lap, trying to make it only one grape per lap. They would write notes as they rode, little jokes to throw out at the pit stops.

The second week dragged slowly, mile by mile, hour by hour. Now everyone was tense. The records had fallen in clusters.

WHAT was all this proving? What good is all this speed?

The real answer came from Crew Chief Danny E. Eames during the grind: "No one should go this fast except racing drivers—and then only on race tracks.

"This kind of test is designed to improve the breed of cars, to test their durability. We're not after mere speed.

"The big thing is to torture the engine, the chassis, the body, and all the thousands of parts at high speed for tremendous distances. Here we've got an all-new car, a new kind of Ford, and we wanted to prove to ourselves, as well as to the American people, just what we had.

"And there it is, running like a streak, running perfectly after 30,000 miles at over 110 miles per hour. Still sweet. Still smooth.

"This is better than fine-car performance. This is a damned fine automobile."

AND still the two Fords whirled on over the salt, salt that was no longer smooth, but deeply pitted with bone-crushing potholes. Hitting them again and again—and again—at this furious, grinding speed was a fiendish test of running gear, of body, of chassis—and of men.

Finally, on September 28, at 8:10 p.m., Ford Car No. 1 reached the impossible goal: 50,000 miles at an average of 108.16 miles per hour, including all pit stops.

Car No. 2 finished a few hours later, averaging over 107 miles per hour—both cars still running

sweetly, both ready to continue for thousands of miles more.

But no need to. They had broken all the records from one kilometer and one mile to 50,000 miles—including 30 of the top possible class of records—the "world unlimited" class.

Everyone shook hands. The drivers, the pit men, the officials, the observers, photographers and TV cameramen. They unhooked the clock, and left the salt to bleach as it has through the centuries.

THUS ended the longest left turn in history, quietly, undramatically.

Just as a matter of interest, previous to this test, the same two Fords warmed up with a 1957 Ford convertible on the famous Bonneville straightaway. They showed their get-up-and-go by smashing 57 national acceleration records.

By the time the Fords left Bonneville, the record book was rewritten . . . with 458 new national and international records listed for the New Kind of Ford.

There is only one thing left. Shake hands with your Ford dealer. He'll introduce you to a car identical in every tiny respect with the two cars that have just done the impossible. And he has them in 19 different models, on two different wheelbases. And with your choice of engines, all the way from the Mileage-Maker Six, the economy champion, to the Thunderbird Super V-8s.

This is the New Kind of Ford, the car with the Mark of Tomorrow.

**FORD DIVISION
FORD MOTOR COMPANY**

FORD GOES FIRST IN ENDURANCE

1957 Mercury

Mercury for 1957 was a total departure from previously built Mercurys. It was called "America's first production dream car," having copied much of it's basic design after an earlier dream car. The styling was bold, creative and distinctive. It definitely was not a copy of other cars.

This new Mercury offered many new features. The power seat that "remembered," the power-boost fan, the "Keyboard Control" with push-button transmission selection, neutral start button and parking brake operation. Noteworthy was the fact that the Mercury was the pace car at the 1957 Indianapolis 500 race.

The engine availability consisted of the 312 cid V-8 (4-bbl) rated at 255 hp, the 368 cid V-8 (4-bbl) rated at 290 hp and the 368 cid V-8 (dual 4-bbl) rated at 335 hp. The transmissions offered were the 3-speed manual, the 3-speed manual with overdrive and the 3-speed Merc-O-Matic automatic.

Production amounted to 285,722 units, with the individual models breakdown as follows. Prices follow each model in ()'s: MONTEREY 4-dr hdt. sedan, 22,475 ($2,763), 4-dr sedan 53,839 ($2,645), 2-dr hdt. coupe 42,199 ($2,693), 2-dr sedan 33,982 ($2,576),

convertible 5,003 ($3,005); MONTCLAIR 4-dr hdt. sedan 21,156 ($3,317), 4-dr sedan 19,836 ($3,188), 2-dr hdt. coupe 30,111 ($3,236), convertible 4,248 ($3,430); TURNPIKE CRUISER 2-dr hdt. coupe 7,291 ($3,758), 4-dr hdt. sedan 8,305 ($3,849), convertible 1,265 ($4,103); STATION WAGONS 2-dr Commuter 6-pass. 4,885 ($2,903), 2-dr Voyager 6-pass. 2,283 ($3,403), 4-dr Commuter 6-pass. 11,990 ($2,973), 4-dr Colony Park 6-pass. 7,386 ($3,677), 4-dr Commuter 8-pass. 5,752 ($3.070), 4-dr Voyager 8-pass. 3,716 ($3,403).

Fifteen exterior colors were offered. Interiors were available in an unlisted number of colors in vinyl or vinyl and cloth.

Literature offered for 1957 consisted of the full-line small color folder, the full-line small color mailer folder, the full-line large color folder (see specs on page 16), the full-line large color folder, revised to show quad headlights, dated 11-56, the Station Wagons color catalogue, the Quick Facts booklet (see pages 14-15), and a Monterey 4-dr sedan color card.

NEW THERMO-MATIC CARBURETOR
WITH DUAL AIR INTAKES

Both new V-8's feature a new Thermo-Matic Carburetor with unique dual air intakes that automatically select and deliver either . . . cool, outside air . . . heated, under-the-hood air . . . or, a mixture of both—for top engine efficiency. Compare this "all-weather" system with competitive "compromise" systems which are designed and adjusted to "get-by" by using only the air available under the engine hood. Furthermore, Mercury's system will provide the correct temperature for efficient fuel-air mixing with the higher octane fuels of the future.

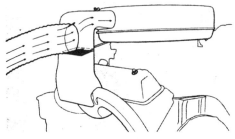

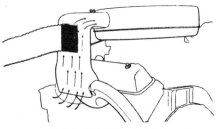

ON SUMMER DAYS

When engine compartment air is above 80-degrees F. outside air comes in through a "cold air duct" in the grille. Competitive systems pull in hot, thin air from directly under the hood. Mercury's cooler air increases usable power by as much as 11%—improves performance and gas mileage . . . prevents vapor lock and sluggish operation.

ON WINTER DAYS

When engine compartment air is below 60-degrees F. the cold air duct is closed off and all air coming to the carburetor is heated around the exhaust manifold. Prevents pre-warmup icing stalls in traffic . . . and improves gas mileage by as much as 3 miles per gallon during warm-up period. This system is another Mercury exclusive in its field.

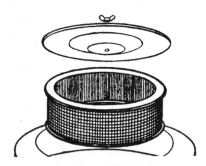

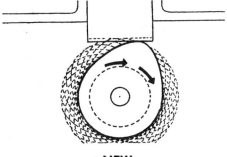

SUPER-PROTECTIVE
CARBURETOR AIR FILTER

Contains thousands of square inches of special filter paper to remove all foreign matter from incoming air before it reaches the engine. Easy for service man to clean . . . just remove cartridge and shake dust and dirt out. Lasts up to 20,000 miles.

NEW
HIGH-LIFT CAMSHAFT

Increases the deep breathing efficiency of Mercury's powerful new V-8's by providing wide openings for the big overhead valves. Contributes to smoother idling, high torque output for normal driving, and high performance at top engine speeds.

NEW
HIGH COMPRESSION RATIO

Mercury's two great engines with their ultra-high compression ratios squeeze more power from today's high octane fuels . . . afford reserve to accommodate even higher powered future fuels. High-turbulence combustion chambers afford more complete burning.

IMPROVED
MERC-O-MATIC DRIVE

Teamed with Mercury's new Keyboard Control is the most versatile and convenient automatic transmission in its field . . . Merc-O-Matic Drive. Improved for still faster, smoother response, it's standard on Montclairs, Colony Park and Voyager models.

PERFORMANCE

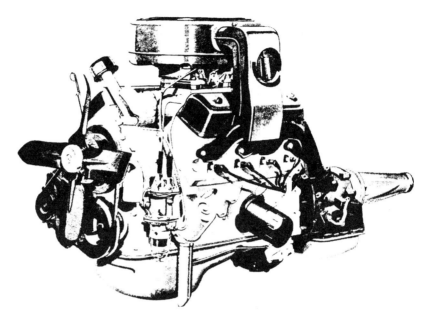

UP TO 290 HP

...the most spectacular performance in Mercury history

For 1957 The Big M offers 2 sensational, ultra-high compression V-8's . . . the most powerful in Mercury history. The advanced-design, high-performance SAFETY-SURGE engine with 255 horsepower, 9.75 to 1 compression ratio, is standard. Available as an option is the magnificent TURNPIKE CRUISER engine, with 290 horsepower, 368 cu. in. displacement, 9.75 to 1 compression ratio. As a standard exclusive feature on Montclairs, Colony Park and Voyager station wagons with the SAFETY-SURGE V-8, you get Mercury's unique Power-Booster Fan that saves up to 17 horsepower other cars waste. You find outstanding engineering advances in these great new engines—a number of them described below. Whichever engine you choose, you enjoy the most spectacular performance you've ever known in a Mercury.

SPECIFICATIONS

	Turnpike Cruiser Engine	Safety-Surge Engine
TYPE	Overhead-valve, 90-degree V-8, deep-block construction	
HORSEPOWER RATING	290 @ 4600 rpm	255 @ 4600 rpm
TORQUE RATING	405 lb.-ft. @ 2800 rpm	340 lb.-ft. @ 2600 rpm
COMPRESSION RATIO	9.75 to 1	9.75 to 1
DISPLACEMENT, PISTON	368 cubic inches	312 cubic inches
BORE & STROKE	4.0 x 3.66 in.	3.8 x 3.44 in.
CARBURETOR	Thermo-Matic 4-barrel, downdraft design with dual float chambers	
CARBURETOR AIR INTAKE	Dual intakes, thermostatically controlled for hot or cold air	
SPARK CONTROL	Combination centrifugal-vacuum control	
AIR FILTER	Super-protective paper type filter	
LUBRICATION SYSTEM	Full Pressure	
ELECTRICAL SYSTEM	12-volt	

Models

MONTCLAIR SERIES: Phaeton Sedan, Phaeton Coupe, Convertible, 4-door Sedan. MONTEREY SERIES: Phaeton Sedan, Phaeton Coupe, Convertible, 4-door Sedan, 2-door Sedan. STATION WAGON SERIES: Colony Park 4-door, 9-passenger; Voyager 4-door, 9-passenger and 2-door, 6-passenger; Commuter 4-door, 9-passenger, 4-door, 6-passenger and 2-door, 6-passenger.

Engine

BASIC CONSTRUCTION: Advanced short-stroke, low-friction design. One-piece 90° V-8 block with deep skirt crankcase. Precision-molded alloy iron crankshaft with 5 steel-backed copper-lead main bearings. Rubber floated vibration damper. Autothermic closed type pistons in the Safety-Surge V-8; Autothermic slipper skirt type in Turnpike Cruiser V-8. Two compression and one oil ring. Overhead free-flow intake and exhaust.

SIZE AND RATING: The 1957 Mercury offers two mighty engines: The 255 horsepower Safety-Surge V-8 with 312 cubic inch displacement, 3.8 in. bore and 3.44 in. stroke, 9.75 to 1 compression ratio; 290 horsepower Turnpike Cruiser V-8 with 368 cubic inch displacement, 4.0 in. bore and 3.66 in. stroke, 9.75 to 1 compression ratio.

FUEL SYSTEM: A four-barrel Thermo-Matic carburetor with temperature controlled dual air intakes and super-protective air filter is standard on both engines. Automatic choke and idling control. Mechanical diaphragm type fuel pump. Fuel tank capacity 20 gallons. Woven plastic type fuel tank filter.

ELECTRICAL SYSTEM: 12 volt system. Low cut-in speed, high-capacity 30-ampere generator with automatic current and voltage regulation. 12-volt, 6-cell, 66-plate battery. High torque, 12-volt "Folo-Thru" starter.

IGNITION SYSTEM: High speed single breaker-arm distributor with combination centrifugal-vacuum spark advance control. Weatherproof ignition with high-tension wiring and anti-fouling 18mm spark plugs.

LUBRICATION SYSTEM: Controlled full-pressure lubrication with full-flow, disposable oil filter. Rotor type oil pump. Directed-flow crankcase ventilation. Oil capacity 6 quarts with filter change—5 quarts without.

OVERHEAD VALVES: Free-turning, rotating type valves with integral valve guides. Chrome steel intake valves have a diameter of 1.925 in. on the Safety-Surge V-8; 2.01 in. on the Turnpike Cruiser V-8. Austenitic steel exhaust valves have a diameter of 1.515 in. on Safety-Surge V-8; 1.64 in. on Turnpike Cruiser V-8. Silent, chain-driven camshaft.

COOLING SYSTEM: Pressurized series-flow cooling system with centrifugal-type high-capacity water pump. Full length water jackets. Positive action choke-type thermostat. Low-speed 4-blade silent fan. Coolant capacity, with optional heater: 21 quarts in Safety-Surge V-8; 24 quarts in Turnpike Cruiser V-8.

EXHAUST SYSTEM: Overhead free-flow manifold with rear outlets. Dual exhaust standard on Montclair and station wagon models except Commuter Station Wagons; optional on Monterey models, except convertible.

POWER BOOSTER FAN: Temperature controlled clutch, completely automatic, variable speed. Idles when not needed for cooling. (On Montclairs, Colony Park, Voyagers, with Safety-Surge engine only.)

Power Train

MERC-O-MATIC DRIVE: Combination of fluid torque converter with a 3-speed planetary gear train. Multiplies engine torque more than 5 times. Fluid heat exchanger cooling. Mechanical Keyboard Control controls driving operations. Oil capacity 10½ quarts.

CONVENTIONAL TRANSMISSION: Selective gear type with three speeds forward, one reverse. All gears helical. Constant mesh second gear. Oil capacity 3¼ pints.

OVERDRIVE TRANSMISSION: 3-speed selective-type gear transmission with planetary gear train providing 4th forward gear (.72 to 1 ratio). Oil capacity 4½ pints.

CLUTCH: (With conventional and overdrive transmissions.) Dry, non-centrifugal disc-type. Diameter clutch face, 10½-inch. Suspended pedal.

REAR AXLE: Hypoid gears with straddle-mounted pinion gear. Rear axle ratios 3.70 or 3.89 to 1 with conventional transmission or overdrive; 2.91 or 3.22 to 1 with Merc-O-Matic.

Chassis

FRAME: Rigid ladder-type, double-drop design with welded box-section side rails and 5 cross-members. Internally and externally reinforced. Extra-strength reinforcements for convertible models.

FRONT SUSPENSION: Independent ball-joint front suspension of swept-back design. Suspension arm back sweep—20° lower, 0° upper. Suspension arm tilt—upward 3° for both upper and lower arms. Silent-block rubber bushings. Helical coil springs. Full-cushion hydraulic shock absorbers. One-piece front torsion-bar stabilizer. Auxiliary rubber compression springs.

REAR SUSPENSION: Splay-mounted long-leaf type rear springs —55 inches long. Auxiliary rubber compression springs. Compression-type rear shackles. Hotchkiss Drive. Full-cushion hydraulic shock absorbers, sea-leg mounted.

STEERING: Ball and rack type gear with 54 recirculating ball bearings. Steering shaft straddle-mounted between anti-friction bearings. Equal-length tie-rods. Overall steering ratio, 27 to 1 manual, and 24 to 1 with optional power steering.

BRAKES: Internal expanding, hydraulic self-energizing type. 11-inch brake drum. With 312-cubic-inch engine, 212.12 sq. inch total braking area. With 368-cubic-inch engine and all station wagon models, 233.44 sq. inch total area.

PARKING BRAKE: Independent mechanical parking brake operating rear brakes. Toe-set pedal.

WHEELS AND TIRES: Riveted steel wheels, 14-inch diameter. 6-inch rims. Tubeless tires, 8.00 x 14 in. on Montclair, Monterey closed models; (8.00 x 14 or 8:50 x 14 in. on other models.)

Body

DIMENSIONS: Overall length 211.1 in., Overall height 56.4 in., Overall width 76.9 in.; Hiproom (f) 63.5 in., (r) 63.5 in., Headroom (f) 39.1 in., (r) 38.3 in., Legroom (f) 46.5 in., (r) 45.1 in. (Dimensions are for 4-door sedans.)

STRUCTURE: Welded steel body. Center-fill gas tank. Baked enamel finish. Front-hinged hood. Counterbalanced hood and rear deck. Double-panel door construction. Safety door locks on all doors. Two-stop front doors. One-piece windshield and rear window. Up to 1178 sq. in. windshield area, and up to 4122 sq. in. total window area.

VENTILATION: High-level cowl ventilation. Adjustable vent windows on all doors.

MAJOR OPTIONS*: Merc-O-Matic with Keyboard Control†, Power Booster Fan†, Touch-O-Matic Overdrive, power steering, power brakes, Power Seat That Remembers, 4-way power seat, power windows, power lubrication, Dream-Car spare carrier, tinted windows, white sidewall tires, Climate-Master air conditioner and heater, padded instrument panel, sun visors and seat belts.

*Optional at extra cost.　　　　†Standard on some models.

These specifications were in effect at the time this literature was approved for printing. Mercury Division of Ford Motor Company, Detroit, Michigan, reserves the right to discontinue or change at any time, specifications or design without incurring any obligation.

1958 Ford

Although retaining the basic body of the 1957, Ford did a total redesign for 1958. The front offered a bolder look by featuring quad headlights, a larger, lower grille and a fake hood air inlet. The side trim was longer and more pronounced. The rear featured a four taillight design, a new concept at the time. Ford based their advertising on the fact that the car had circled the world in an endurance test.

Engines offered were the 223 cid six (1-bbl) rated at 145 hp, the 292 cid V-8 (2-bbl) rated at 205 hp, the 332 cid V-8 (2-bbl) rated at 240 hp, the 332 cid V-8 (4-bbl) rated at 265 hp and the 352 cid V-8 (4-bbl) rated at 300 hp. Transmissions offered were the 3-speed manual, the 3-speed manual with overdrive, the 2-speed Fordomatic automatic and the 3-speed Cruise-O-Matic automatic.

Production amounted to 950,053 units with the following model breakdown (sixes and V-8's totals combined). Prices for sixes follow each model in ()'s, with V-8's costing $137 more: CUSTOM 300 4-dr sedan 163,368 ($2,119), 2-dr sedan 173,441 ($2,065), 2-dr bus. coupe 4,062 ($1,977); FAIRLANE 4-dr Town Sedan 57,490 ($2,250), 4-dr Town Victoria 38,366 ($2,196); 4-dr Town Victoria 5,868 ($2,394), 2-dr Club Victoria 16,416 ($2,329); FAIRLANE 500 4-dr Town Sedan 105,698 ($2,403), 4-dr Club Sedan 34,041

($2,349), 4-dr Town Victoria 36,059 ($2,474), 2-dr Club Victoria 80,439 ($2,410), Sunliner convertible 35,029 ($2,625), Skyliner retractable convertible 14,713 ($3,138 V-8 only); STATION WAGONS 2-dr Ranch wagon 34,578 ($2,372), 4-dr Ranch wagon 32,854 ($2,426), 2-dr Del Rio 12,687 ($2,478), 4-dr Country Sedan, 6-pass. 68,772 ($2,532), 4-dr Country Sedan, 9-pass. 20,702 ($2,639), 4-dr Country Squire 15,020 ($2,769).

Twelve exterior colors were offered with two-tones optional at extra cost. Interiors were available in many color combination of vinyl or vinyl and cloth.

Literature offered for 1958 consisted of the full-line color folder dated 9-57, with revisions dated 10-57, 12-57, and 4-58 (see specs on page 19); the Fairlane large color catalogue dated 9-57 with revisions dated 10-57 and 12-57; the Custom series large color catalogue dated 9-57 with revisions dated 10-57 and 12-57; the Station Wagons large color catalogue dated 9-57 with revisions dated 10-57 and 12-57; the Station Wagons color folder dated 9-57; the engines and transmissions catalogue (see page 18), the "The car that went around the world...." catalogue (see page 20), the "Round the world" map color folder; and the Accessories color catalogue. The Ford was also included in the full-line press kit.

1958 FORD FAIRLANE and FAIRLANE 500

There's nothing newer in the world than the 58 FORD

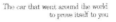

The car that went around the world to prove itself to you

1958 FORD CUSTOM 300

Announcing the greatest advance
in V-8 design in 25 years . . .

FORD'S new INTERCEPTOR V-8's
with PRECISION FUEL INDUCTION

For 1958 Ford presents three engines that are new from fan blade to flywheel—the matchless Interceptor V-8's!

These new engines feature the most important advance in V-8 design in 25 years—an advance that gives you more power on *less* gasoline—*Precision Fuel Induction!*

These Interceptor engines have *machined* combustion chambers (instead of rough cast) to polish off every bit of power from every molecule of fuel . . . larger displacements . . . higher compression ratios (up to 10.2 to 1) . . . higher horsepower (up to 300 strong) . . . higher torque and more compact design.

After each V-8 is assembled, it is electronically balanced while running under *its own power* before being mounted in the car. It is equal in smoothness to the most expensive engines built—yet you get it at the low Ford price!

Interceptor 352 Special V-8
with Precision Fuel Induction

So efficient it gets more out of gasoline than _ever_ before!

Here is the finest engine ever produced by Ford, the world's largest and most experienced builders of V-8 engines. Delivering a mighty 300 horsepower, this all-new, 4-barrel Interceptor 352 Special delivers its maximum useful thrust at normal everyday driving speeds. And thanks to Precision Fuel Induction, it runs smoother, more quietly and with greater fuel economy than any engine in its class! Here, indeed, is an engine destined to bring a new high level of performance to the American Road.

Available for all Fairlane 500 and Station Wagon models

Feature Facts

Exteriors and Interiors: A total of 13 exciting new body colors are available, all of gleaming, durable, baked-on enamel. All models come in Single Color or stunning new Style Tone, as well as Conventional Two Tone on Fairlane 500's. Country Club trim is available on Fairlane models only. Ribbed gold anodized aluminum molding optional on Custom 300, Country Sedans and Del Rio Ranch Wagon models. Interiors are beautifully upholstered with long-lasting leather-grained vinyl, woven plastic or nylon fabrics including exclusive new tweed pattern, in colors to harmonize with exteriors. See the complete selection at your Ford Dealer's.

Engines: *145-hp Mileage Maker Six* — 223-cu. in. displ.; 3.62" bore x 3.60" stroke; 8.6 to 1 comp. ratio; regular fuel; manual choke. (For all models except Skyliner.)

205-hp Ford 292 V-8 (Optional on all models) — 292-cu. in. displ.; 3.75" bore x 3.30" stroke; 9.1 to 1 comp. ratio; regular fuel; low-silhouette 2-venturi carburetor, automatic choke.

New 240-hp Interceptor 332 V-8 (Optional on Fairlane 500 and Station Wagons) — 332-cu. in. displ.; 4.00" bore x 3.30" stroke; 9.5 to 1 comp. ratio; regular fuel; low-silhouette 2-venturi carburetor, automatic choke; self-adjusting hydraulic valve lifters.

New 265-hp Interceptor 332 Special V-8 (Optional on Fairlane 500 and Station Wagons) — 332-cu. in. displ.; 4.00" bore x 3.30" stroke; 9.5 to 1 comp. ratio; regular fuel; low-silhouette 4-venturi carburetor, automatic choke; self-adjusting hydraulic valve lifters.

New 300-hp Interceptor 352 Special V-8 (Optional on all models)—352-cu. in. displ.; 4.00" bore x 3.50" stroke; 10.2 to 1 comp. ratio; premium fuel; low-silhouette 4-venturi carburetor, automatic choke; self-adjusting hydraulic valve lifters.

Engine Features: For greater economy and longer life all engines have short-stroke, low-friction, deep-block design; free-turning overhead valves; Super-Filter air cleaner; full-pressure lubrication; Full-Flow oil filter; 12-volt electrical system; turbo-action 18-mm. spark plugs. V-8 engines are electronically balanced under own power for optimum smoothness. All Interceptor engines have Precision Fuel Induction for superior performance and economy.

Transmissions: *3-speed* with gear ratios tailored to each engine. Optional: *Overdrive* with automatic 4th gear. *Fordomatic Drive* with smooth-acting torque converter and three forward gears for normal or fast starting. *New Cruise-O-Matic* high performance automatic with two selective drive ranges for smooth 1-2-3 full-power getaway or 2-3 gradual acceleration and axle ratio of 2.69 to 1 for fuel economy (with Special V-8's only).

Suspension: Smoother-acting Angle-Poised, 4-way ball-joint front and variable-rate, outboard-mounted rear suspension. Shock absorbers front and rear.

Ford-Aire Suspension: Complete air cushion system for the utmost in smooth, soft riding, with automatic leveling valves to maintain constant car height, under all load conditions. (Optional on Fairlane, Fairlane 500 and Station Wagon models with Interceptor V-8's and automatic transmissions.)

Steering: Magic-Circle recirculating-ball type for smoother, easier steering. Lifeguard deep-center steering wheel.

Other Available Equipment: Lifeguard padded instrument panel, cushioned sun visors. Ford seat belts. I-Rest tinted safety glass. SelectAire or PolarAire Conditioner, including tinted glass (V-8's only). Manually operated 4-way front seat. Heavy-duty springs (for wagon models). Whitewall tires. Fuel-vacuum pump for positive-action windshield wipers.

Prices: All Power Assists and Accessories as well as some of the items illustrated or referred to in this folder are at extra cost. For the price of the model with the equipment you desire, see your Ford Dealer.

Comparative information in this folder was obtained from authoritative sources, but is not guaranteed. The specifications contained herein, were in effect at the time this folder was approved for printing. Ford Division of Ford Motor Company reserves the right to discontinue models at any time, or change specifications or design, without notice and without incurring obligation.

58 FORD IN HERAT, AFGHANISTAN

The car that went around the world
to prove itself to you

58 F⊕RD

PROVED AND APPROVED AROUND THE WORLD

1958 Mercury

The 1958 Mercury continued with the same basic design as the 1957, but with minor design changes to distinguish it.

The engine availabilty for 1958 consisted of the 312 cid V-8 (4-bbl) rated at 235 hp, the 383 cid V-8 (4-bbl) rated at 312 hp, the 383 cid V-8 (4-bbl) rated at 330 hp, the 430 cid V-8 (4-bbl) rated at 360 hp and the 430 cid V-8 (triple 2-bbl) rated at 400 hp. The transmissions offered consisted of the 3-speed manual, the 3-speed manual with overdrive, the 3-speed Merc-O-Matic automatic and the 3-speed Multi-drive Merc-O-Matic automatic.

Production amounted to 133,271 units, with individual model breakdown as follows. Prices follow each model in ()'s: MEDALIST 4-dr sedan 10,982 ($2,617), 2-dr sedan 7,750 ($2,547); MONTEREY 4-dr hdt. sedan 6,909 ($2,840), 4-dr sedan 28,892 ($2,721), 2-dr hdt. coupe 13,693 ($2,769), 2-dr sedan 10,526 ($2,652), convertible 2,292 ($3,081); MONTCLAIR 4-dr hdt. sedan 3,609 ($3,365, 4-dr sedan 4,801 ($3,365), 2 dr hdt.

coupe 5,012 ($3,284), 2-dr Turnpike Cruiser 2,864 ($3,498), 4-dr Turnpike Cruiser 3,543 ($3,597), convertible 844 ($3,536); PARKLANE 4-dr hdt. sedan 5,241 ($3,944), 2-dr hdt. coupe 3,158 ($3,867), convtible 853 ($4,118); STATION WAGON 2-dr Commuter 6-pass. 1,912 ($3,035), 2-dr Voyager 6-pass. 568 ($3,535), 4-dr Commuter 6-pass. 8,601 ($3,105), 4-dr Colony Park 6-pass. 4,474 ($3,201), 4-dr Commuter 9-pass. 4,227 ($3,201), 4-dr Voyager 9-pass. 2,520 ($3,635).

Seventeen exterior colors were offered. Interiors were available in an unlisted number of color combinations of vinyl or vinyl and cloth.

Literature offered for 1958 consisted of the full-line small color catalogue unrevised and revised (see specs on page 24), the full-line show color folder unrevised and revised, and the Station Wagons color catalogue. The Mercury was also included in the full-line press kit.

MAJOR SPECIFICATIONS — 1958 MERCURY

ENGINES

MONTEREY AND COMMUTER MODELS: 312-hp, 383 cubic inch displacement. Torque rating, 405 lb-ft. Compression ratio 10.5 to 1.

MONTCLAIR, VOYAGER AND COLONY PARK: 330-hp, 383 cubic inch displacement. Torque rating, 425 lb-ft. Compression ration 10.5 to 1.

PARK LANE SERIES: 360-hp. 430 cubic inch displacement. Torque rating, 480 lb-ft. Compression ratio 10.5 to 1. Dual exhaust. Assembled with Multi-Drive Merc-O-Matic. Also, optional at extra cost for Turnpike Cruiser models.

SUPER MARAUDER: 400-hp. 430 cubic inch displacement. Compression ratio 10.5 to 1. Three 2-barrel carburetors. Available as special order option with Multi-Drive Merc-O-Matic for all 1958 Mercury models.

BASIC CONSTRUCTION: One-piece V-8 block. In-block combustion chambers. Water-cooled intake manifold. Cool-Power Design eliminates hot spots. Aircraft-type low-friction pistons. Cylinder bore, 4.3 in. Piston stroke 3.3 in. for 383 cu. in. engines and 3.7 in. for 430 cu. in. versions.

FUEL SYSTEM: Low-silhouette 4-barrel Thermo-Matic carburetor. Dual temperature-controlled carburetor air intakes. Dry-type carburetor air filter.

ENGINE LUBRICATION: Full-pressure lubrication with simplified oil line pattern. Internally mounted rotor-type pump. Capacity, 5 quarts. Forced-air crankcase ventilation.

ELECTRICAL: 12-volt system. High-capacity dual-drive generator with low cut-in speed. High torque "Folo-Thru" starter. Combination centrifugal-vacuum spark advance control. Front-mounted distributor. Battery sizes—66-plate battery for vehicles with conventional or overdrive transmission; 78-plate battery with Merc-O-Matic transmission.

OVERHEAD VALVES: Free-turning, rotating type valves. Intake valve-head diameter 2.08 inches with 383 cu. in. engines; 2.14 inches with 430 cu. in. versions. Exhaust valve-head diameter 1.77 in.

REAR AXLE: Hypoid gears with straddle-mounted pinion gear. Rear axle ratio is 2.69 to 1 with 312-hp and 330-hp engines, and 2.91 to 1 with 360-hp and 400-hp engines. All air conditioned vehicles have 2.91 to 1 rear axles. With conventional transmission or overdrive, the rear axle ratio is 3.56 to 1.

CHASSIS

FRAME: Ladder-type with outward curved side rails, and 5 cross-members. Side rails internally and externally reinforced. Extra-strength x-member for convertible frames.

FRONT SUSPENSION: Independent ball-joint front suspension with swept-back design. Permanently lubricated threaded bushing for upper suspension arms. 10-coil front springs. Full-cushion hydraulic shock absorbers. Rubber-mounted, linkless front torsional stabilizer bar.

REAR SUSPENSION: Splay-mounted leaf-type rear springs. 55-inch long springs all models, except Park Lane, 60 inches. Compression-type shackles. Full-cushion shock absorbers.

COOLING SYSTEM: 3-stage cooling with 21½ quart capacity (with optional heater). 3 thermostats adjust cooling capacity to needs.

EXHAUST SYSTEM: Center-outlet exhaust manifold with extra-large passages. Dual exhaust standard on Park Lane models.

POWER TRAIN

MERC-O-MATIC TRANSMISSION: Combination of fluid torque converter and 3-speed planetary gear train. Mechanical Keyboard Control drive selector. Multi-Drive Merc-O-Matic (standard in Park Lane) affords choice of low-gear or intermediate-gear starts. Oil capacity 10¾ quarts.

CONVENTIONAL TRANSMISSION: Selective gear type with three speeds forward, one reverse. All gears helical. Constant-mesh second gear. Overdrive with 4th forward speed (.72 to 1 ratio) optionally available for Monterey and Commuter models.

STEERING: Ball and rack type gear. Steering shaft straddle-mounted. Over-all steering ratio 31.0 to 1 manual, 24.0 to 1 with optional power.

BRAKES: Internal-expanding, hydraulic type, with self-adjusting brake linings. 11-inch drum. Brake shoe width—3 in. front, 2½ in. rear. Total braking area 233.4 sq. in. Independent mechanical parking brake. Step-on parking brake pedal.

BODY

SEDAN DIMENSIONS: Wheelbase 122 inches, except Park Lane, 125 in. Over-all length 213.2 in., except Park Lane, 220.2 in. Over-all height Monterey and Montclair models 56.6 in.; Park Lane, 56.8 in. Over-all width, 81.0 in. Hip room (f) 61.3 in., (r) 62.9 in. Effective headroom (f) 39.0 in., (r) 38.3 in. Effective leg room (f) 46.2 in., (r) 44.9 in.

STRUCTURE: Welded steel body. Front-hinged hood. Combination bumper-grille. Double-panel door, hood, and deck lid construction. Safety door locks. Two-stop front doors. Dual headlamps. High-level outside air intakes on cowl. Windshield area 1169 sq. in. except Turnpike Cruiser, 1312 sq. in. Total sedan window area, 3991 sq. in.

MAJOR OPTIONS*: Merc-O-Matic with Keyboard Control†, Power-Booster Fan; power steering†; power brakes†, automatic power seat, 4-way power seat, heater-defroster, heater-defroster-air conditioner, overdrive, power-operated windows, power lubrication, tinted windows, nylon tires†, whitewall tires, padded instrument panel†, padded sun visors and seat belts, Air Cushion Ride, dual exhaust†, Super Marauder V-8 engine.

*Optional at extra cost. †Standard on some models.

Mercury Division of Ford Motor Company, Dearborn, Michigan, reserves the right to discontinue or change, at any time, model specifications or design without incurring obligation.

1959 Ford

Nineteen Fifty-Nine saw the marriage between the Ford and the Thunderbird and the beginning of the Galaxie. Ford again gave Chevrolet a hard time in the sales department. Ford offered a really balanced look without the gaudiness of the Chevrolet. The Galaxie was truly an elegant car. This was the last year for the Skyliner retractable.

Engines offered were the 223 cid six (1-bbl) rated at 145 hp, the 292 cid V-8 (2-bbl) rated at 200 hp, the 332 cid V-8 (2-bbl) rated at 225 hp and the 352 cid V-8 (4-bbl) rated at 300 hp. Transmissions available were the 3-speed manual, the 3-speed manual with overdrive, the 2-speed Fordomatic automatic and the 3-speed Cruise-O-Matic automatic.

Production amounted to 1,390,724 units, with the following model breakdown (sixes and V-8's combined). Prices for sixes follow each model in ()'s, with V-8's costing $118 more: CUSTOM 300 4-dr sedan 249,553 ($2,273), 2-dr sedan 228,573 ($2,132); FAIRLANE 4-dr Town Sedan 64,663 ($2,411), 2-dr Club Sedan 35,126 ($2,357); FAIRLANE 500 4-dr Town Sedan 35,670 ($2,530), 2-dr Club Sedan 10,141 ($2,476), 4-dr Town Victoria 9,308 ($2,602), 2-dr Club Victoria 23,892 ($2,537); GALAXIE 4-dr Town Sedan 183,108 ($2,582), 2-dr Club Sedan 52,848 ($2,528), 4-dr Town Victoria 47,728 ($2,654), 2-dr Club Victoria 121,869 ($2,589), Sunliner 12,915 ($2,839), Skyliner retractable convertible 45,868 ($2,957 V-8 only); STATION WAGON 2-dr Ranch Wagon 45,558 ($2,567), 4-dr Ranch Wagon 67,339 ($2,634), 2-dr Country Sedan 6-pass. 8,663 ($2,678), 4-dr Country Sedan 6-pass. 94,601 ($2,745), 4-dr Country Sedan 9-pass. 28,881 ($2,829), 4-dr Country Squire 9-pass. 24,336 ($2,958).

Thirteen exterior colors were offered with two-tones available at extra cost. Interiors were in offered in a number of colors in combinations of cloth and vinyl.

Literature offered for 1959 consisted of the small color catalogue dated 9/58 and the same dated 10/58 (see specs on page 24), the large color catalogue dated 9/58 and dated 10/58, the "Pocket facts about the new 59 Fords" booklet, and the "Buyers Digest" booklet filled with facts and figures. The full-sized Fords were included in the full-line press kit.

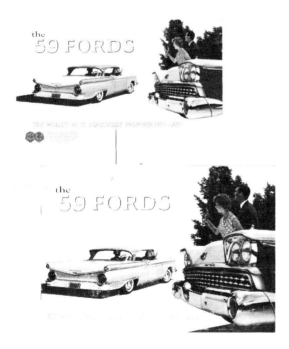

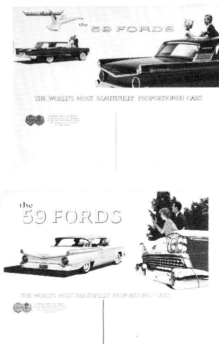

YOU RIDE SILENT, SOLID AND SECURE

. . . and here are some reasons why:

- New Ram-type system for superior body ventilation
- Front-hinged hood has new torsion bar hinge for easier, counterbalanced action
- New larger wrap-around windshield with swept-back pillars for greater visibility
- Five roof cross braces welded to box section rails for high strength and rigidity
- Clear-vision safety glass throughout with much greater area for full-circle visibility
- Front seat safety anchorage locks track structure to the chassis frame. Seat adjusts through 5" to 11 positions and is placed for improved seating posture
- Thick, resilient foam padding in front seat for greater comfort
- Silent-Grip body mounts to soak up road shock and noise

- Larger rocker panels and stronger double-ribbed floor pan with five sturdy cross members welded to bottom for increased rigidity
- Ford's husky frame bows out a full foot wider midway so passengers ride within the safety of heavy frame side rails
- Larger wrap-around glass in back window gives better rear visibility
- New torsion bar hinging of the deck lid provides better counterbalancing, more trunk capacity. Opening weatherproofed with rubber seals and rain trough
- Domed ribbed wheelhousings supply solid foundation for roof rails, back panel and deck lid hinges
- The best insulation in Ford's field includes a half inch of fibrous sound-absorption material in the roof, one inch of glass fibre, felt and finish board on dash

NEW POWER . . . WHERE YOU CAN <u>USE</u> IT!

Mileage Maker Six is the only *modern* Six offered today. Its short-stroke, low-friction design makes possible 145-horsepower with *low* operating economy. In the last two Mobilgas Economy Runs, this Six delivered the most miles per gallon in Class A! Uses *regular* gas, too!

Thunderbird 352 Special V-8 is one of 3 great V-8's for '59. Gives unusual responsiveness in the middle speed range: between 30 and 70 mph. This is power you can *use*! Team it with Ford's great Cruise-O-Matic Drive and you'll enjoy all the gas savings of "built-in" overdrive economy!

4 GREAT TRANSMISSIONS

Fordomatic Drive is an all-new satin-smooth automatic with more durable, simplified design. Normally needs no periodic service. Priced low to banish "stick shifting" forever!

Cruise-O-Matic Drive gives you two separate driving ranges: "D1" for all normal driving with brisk, smooth starts . . . "D2" for gentle, sure-footed starts in snow or mud.

Conventional Drive—Here is the *easiest*, quietest manual shifting ever developed. To give you the utmost in economy, gear ratios are tailored to each engine. A lively performer!

Overdrive saves on gas while it saves your engine! Automatic 4th gear lets your engine loaf at 35 mph while you actually do 50 mph. Saves up to 15% on gasoline, too!

SPECIFICATIONS

Exteriors and Interiors: A total of 13 exciting body colors are available in amazing new Diamond Lustre Finish. All models come in Single Color; also in Conventional Two Tone or Style Tone color combinations except the Country Squire. Interiors are beautifully upholstered with ribbed and new metallic leather-grained vinyls, woven plastic or nylon fabrics, in colors to harmonize wth exteriors. See complete selection at your Ford Dealer's.

Engines: 145-hp *Mileage Maker Six*—223-cu. in. displ.; 3.62" bore x 3.60" stroke, 8.4 to 1 comp. ratio; regular fuel; manual choke. (For all models except Skyliner.)

200-hp *Thunderbird 292 V-8* (Standard V-8 on all models)—292-cu. in. displ.; 3.75" bore x 3.30" stroke; 8.8 to 1 comp. ratio; regular fuel; low-silhouette 2-venturi carburetor; automatic choke.

225-hp *Thunderbird 332 Special V-8* (Optional on all models)—332-cu. in. displ.; 4.00" bore x 3.30" stroke; 8.9 to 1 comp. ratio; premium fuel; low-silhouette 2-venturi carburetor; automatic choke.

300-hp *Thunderbird 352 Special V-8* (Optional on all models)—352-cu. in. displ.; 4.00" bore x 3.50" stroke; 9.6 to 1 comp. ratio; premium fuel; low-silhouette 4-venturi carburetor; automatic choke.

Engine Features: For greater economy and longer life all engines have short-stroke, low-friction, Deep-Block design; free-turning overhead valves; Super-Filter air cleaner; full-pressure lubrication; vacuum-booster fuel pump; Full-Flow oil filter; 12-volt electrical system; Turbo-Action 18-mm. spark plugs and an exhaust system featuring a new aluminized muffler. Every V-8 engine is electronically balanced while operating under its own power for extra smoothness. Special V-8's feature zero-lash hydraulic valve lifters for quietness and Precision Fuel Induction for superior performance and economy.

Transmissions: 3-speed with gear ratios tailored to each engine. Optional: *Overdrive* with automatic 4th gear. *New Fordomatic*

Drive with torque converter and simplified planetary gear set for smooth, responsive, automatic 2-speed operation. In "D" range it provides brisk, smooth starts in low. Available with all engines. *Cruise-O-Matic Drive*, a high-performance automatic with two selective drive ranges—smooth 3-speed operation in "D1" range, starting in low for solid full-power getaways or smoother 2-speed operation in "D2" range, starting in intermediate for gentle, gradual acceleration on ice, snow or loose gravel and specially tailored gas-saving rear axle ratios for "built-in" overdrive economy. Available with Special V-8's only.

Suspension: Smooth-acting Swept-Back, Angle-Poised, Ball-Joint front with new link-type stabilizer and variable-rate, outboard-mounted rear suspension for automatic ride control.

Rear Axle: Hypoid, semi-floating type with exclusive Deep-Offset straddle-mounted pinion for quieter operation, longer life.

Steering: Magic-Circle recirculating-ball type, same as used on the Thunderbird. Lifeguard deep-center steering wheel.

Other Available Equipment: Lifeguard padded instrument panel Cushioned sun visors • Ford seat belts • I-Rest tinted safety glass Manually operated 4-way front seat • Exterior trim package—Tee Ball fender ornaments and bright-metal darts on rear quarter panels (Custom 300) • Interior trim package (Custom 300 and Ranch Wagons) • Sound deadener package • Equa-Lock axle differential Sure-Wipe electric windshield wipers • Backup lights (bulbs and wiring) • Heavy-duty springs (for wagon models) • Whitewall tires.

Prices: All Power Assists and Accessories as well as some of the items illustrated or referred to in this folder are at extra cost. For the price of the model with the equipment you desire, see your Ford Dealer.

Comparative information in this folder was obtained from authoritative sources, but is not guaranteed. The specifications contained herein were in effect at the time this folder was approved for printing. Ford Division of Ford Motor Company reserves the right to discontinue models at any time, or change specifications or design without notice and without obligation.

1959 Mercury

The 1959 Mercury was a continuation of the design theme of the 1957 and 1958 Mercurys, but was a totally new body. Built when "big" meant a luxurious ride and prestige, this Mercury was BIG. The windows were large and offered an excellent view of the road and the scenery.

The engines offered for 1959 consisted of the 312 cid V-8 (2-bbl) rated at 210 hp, the 383 cid V-8 (2-bbl) rated at 280 hp, the 383 cid V-8 (4-bbl) rated at 322 hp and the 430 cid V-8 (4-bbl) rated at 345 hp. The transmissions offered were the 3-speed manual, the 3-speed Merc-O-Matic automatic and the 3-speed Multi-drive Merc-O-Matic automatic.

Production amounted to 150,030 units, with the individual model breakdown as follows. Prices follow each model in ()'s: MONTEREY 4-dr hdt. sedan 11,355 ($2,918), 4-dr sedan 43,570 ($2,832), 2-dr hdt. sedan 17,232 ($2,854), 2-dr sedan 12,694 ($2,768), convertible 4,426 ($3,150); MONTCLAIR 4-dr hdt. sedan 6,713 ($3,437), 4-dr sedan 9,514 ($3,308), 2-dr hdt. coupe 7,375 ($3,357); PARK LANE 4-dr hdt. sedan 7,206 ($4,031), 2-dr hdt. coupe 4,060 ($3,955), convertible 1,257 ($4,206); COUNTRY CRUISER STATION WAGON 2-dr Commuter 6-pass. 1,051 ($3,035), 4-dr Commuter 6-pass. 15,122 ($3,105), 4-dr Colony Park 6-pass. 5,959 ($3,932), 4-dr Voyager 6-pass. 2,496 ($3,793).

Sixteen exterior colors were offered with two-tones available at extra cost. Interiors were available in 34 color combinations of vinyl and cloth.

Literature offered for 1959 consisted of the full-line color folder, the full-line small color catalogue, the "It's time" die cut catalogue shaped like a pocket watch, the accessories catalogue, the "Buyer's Guide" catalogue (see page 32) and the Station Wagons color catalogue. The Mercury was included in the full-line press kit.

AMERICA'S LIVELIEST LUXURY CAR

AMERICA'S LIVELIEST LUXURY CAR

America's Newest V-8's

Mercury offers 4 V-8 engines—one for each series, ranging from the 430 cubic-inch Park Lane engine to the 312 cubic-inch Economy V-8 in the Monterey series.

In new design, performance, raw power and economy, these engines are unmatched by any others in Mercury's field. For example, Oldsmobile has kept the same basic engine design for 11 years; Buick has kept theirs for 7 years. And only Mercury Marauder engines (introduced last year) have the advanced features you see on these pages.

Crankshaft-driven power steering pump

In Mercury, the power steering pump is attached directly to the block and driven by the crankshaft. There is no belt to squeal as in other cars. This pump is designed to last longer, and its placement reduces engine compartment clutter.

Mercury Dual Carburetor Air-Intake System

Dual air intakes on Mercury's Marauder V-8's improve performance, reduce carburetor icing and vapor lock. This system *selects* the air it needs; when engine compartment air is below 60°, the system selects heated air only; between 60° and 80° it selects a mixture of heated and cold air; over 80° it selects only the unheated outside air.

Exclusive in-block combustion

In-block combustion chambers, with fully machined surfaces that defy carbon deposits, sounds very technical—it simply means more even firing because all chambers are the same size. Performance is smoother, more economical. No cars in Mercury's price class offer these advantages.

Exclusive 3-stage cooling

Mercury's engine cooling system operates in three stages, for quicker warm-up and smoother operation from start to stop. No other car in Mercury's field offers this engine advantage.

A totally new car was offered by Ford for 1960. This car was of a far more sleek design than anything else Ford had ever offered. The star of this new fleet was the 2-dr Starliner hardtop. The sleek roof lines of this model matched the sleek lines of the lower body and is now a very desirable collector car. A highlight of the new body was the chrome strip that ran from the parking lights over the fenders to the top of the rear fenders. The taillights were not round, but rather were half-round.

Engines offered for 1960 were the 223 cid six (1-bbl) rated at 145 hp, the 292 cid V-8 (2-bbl) rated at 185 hp, the 352 cid V-8 (2-bbl) rated at 235 hp and the 352 cid V-8 (4-bbl) rated at 300 hp. Transmissions offered were the 3-speed manual, the 3-speed manual with overdrive , the 2-speed Fordomatic automatic and the 3-speed Cruise-O-Matic automatic.

Production amounted to 891,034 units with the following model breakdown (sixes and V-8's totals combined). Prices follow each model in ()'s, with V-8's costing $113 more: FAIRLANE 4-dr sedan 110,373 ($2,311), 2-dr sedan 93,561 ($2,257), 2-dr bus. coupe 1,733 ($2,170); FAIRLANE 500 4-dr Town Sedan 153,234 ($2,388), 2-dr Club Sedan 91,041 ($2,334); GALAXIE 4-dr Town Sedan 103,784 ($2,603), 2-dr Club Sedan 31,866 ($2,549), 4-dr Town Victoria 104,784 ($2,788); starliner 2-dr hardtop 68,641 ($2,610), sunliner convertible 44,762 ($2,860); STATION WAGONS 2-dr Ranch Wagon 27,136 ($2,586), 4-dr Ranch Wagon 43,872 ($2,656), 4-dr Country Sedan, 6-pass. 59,302 ($2,752), 4-dr Country Sedan 9-pass. 19,277 ($2,837), 4-dr Country Squire 22,237 ($2,968).

Twelve exterior colors were offered with two-tones optional at extra cost. Interiors were offered in many color combinations in cloth and vinyl.

Literature offered for 1960 consisted of the small color folder dated 8-59 with revisions dated 11-59 and 1-60, the large color catalogue dated 8-59 with revisions dated 11-59 and 1-60, the Station Wagons color folder dated 8-59, the "Wonderful new world after dark, A wonderful new world of Fords of '60" full-line color catalogue (featuring womens' fashions), the "Ford Wagon Wonderland" color roto catalogue, and the "Buyer's Digest" booklet filled with facts and figures (see pages 28-30). The full-sized Fords were also included in the full-line press kit.

What to look for in the

FINEST FORDS OF A LIFETIME

Before you finally select your new car, you'll want to know a lot more about it than just what you can see on the surface. Is it built with the care a multi-thousand dollar investment deserves? Does it have the comfort and safety features you and your family should have? What about quality checks? To answer these questions and others, Ford has spent millions on engineering and safety research, new laboratory testing techniques and pioneering in quality audit control. The results . . . from any point of view, from every point of value . . . are the finest built Fords of a lifetime!

The Ford Fairlane 500 (illustrated) is 1960's new Value Leader. Every single new feature you see here is a part of this new and wonderful representative of the Finest Fords of a Lifetime. Consider carefully everything you get in this low-priced car. Match it with any other. You'll agree it's America's top buy!

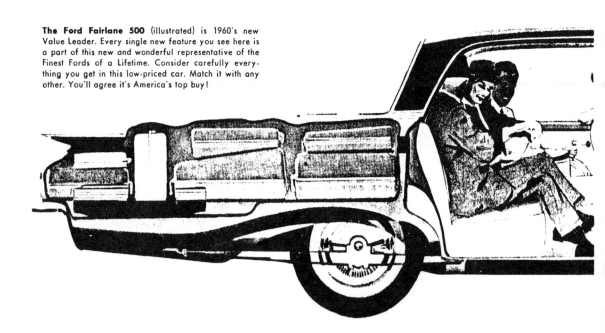

Here's more "built for people" comfort and stretch-out room for six than ever before. In the front and rear seats, the 60 Fords have 5 feet of shoulder room . . . hip room is over 5 feet . . . head room is over 3 feet. It all adds up to Roominess with a capital "R."

Seats are "chair high" so legs are never in an unnaturally cramped position. This means front seat is over 9″ from floor and back seat is over 13″—scientifically correct for long trip or short haul comfort. Seat backs provide a Posture Perfect angle of 23°, the angle that extensive research has shown to be most satisfactory and comfortable while driving.

● Extra-wide front doors are held open in either of *two* positions (two-thirds or all the way) by wonderfully convenient door checks. And Ford's "Automatic Doorman" actually helps you open and close the rear doors.

● All Ford front seats have a thick layer of soft foam padding, standard at no extra cost, for even greater comfort. Beautifully quilted and pleated fabrics are tailor-fitted to Ford's sofa-soft seats.

● Ford's Easy Entrance Windshield Pillars sweep forward to eliminate the dogleg in old-style windshield pillars. With Ford's wider doors, this feature gives you more unobstructed room for easier entry and exit, the most accessible seating in Ford's field.

- It's no strain to load a two-weeks' supply of vacation luggage in Ford's 33.5 cubic foot trunk. Opening is only 27″ above street level for easy lifting. The wide trunk lid opens effortlessly with new torsion bar hinges. Spare tire is out of the way but easy to reach.

- Each Ford model for 1960 has its own tailored-to-weight rear suspension system. New king-sized rear springs are **5 feet long** and set nearly 4 inches farther apart to effectively reduce sidesway on curves. Axle is located well forward on the springs to give a levelized, variable-rate suspension and, in addition, to noticeably reduce dip and dive on starts and stops.

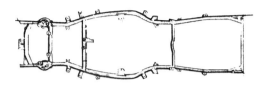

- The new Ford frame is the wide-contoured, safety-type that surrounds the passenger compartment with a rugged ring of steel. It's 50 pounds heavier and 25% stronger than last year's. Frame forms a supremely solid base for the new quality-quiet Ford body and engine.

- New soft ride Tyrex cord tires do away with tire squeal, ride smoother, grip better, last longer.

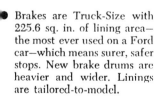

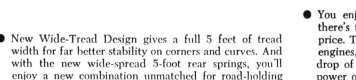

- Brakes are Truck-Size with 225.6 sq. in. of lining area—the most ever used on a Ford car—which means surer, safer stops. New brake drums are heavier and wider. Linings are tailored-to-model.

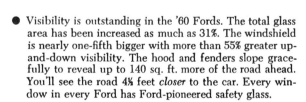

- New Wide-Tread Design gives a full 5 feet of tread width for far better stability on corners and curves. And with the new wide-spread 5-foot rear springs, you'll enjoy a new combination unmatched for road-holding and solid, safety feel!

- A new, convenient parking brake operates quickly, easily by merely pressing handy foot pedal. Hand release is located on instrument panel.

- Visibility is outstanding in the '60 Fords. The total glass area has been increased as much as 31%. The windshield is nearly one-fifth bigger with more than 55% greater up-and-down visibility. The hood and fenders slope gracefully to reveal up to 140 sq. ft. more of the road ahead. You'll see the road 4½ feet *closer* to the car. Every window in every Ford has Ford-pioneered safety glass.

- You enjoy new economy *three* ways, this year. *First,* there's the big-car value you get at the new low Ford price. Then, there's Ford's lower running costs. All Ford engines, for 1960, squeeze more mileage out of every drop of gas. And all Ford engines except the two top-power options *thrive on lower-cost regular!* Ford's new 2-stage Full-Flow Oil Filter lets you go 4000 miles between oil changes. And, *third,* there's Ford's lower upkeep. A big 66-plate battery provides surer starts. All Ford's generators have pre-lubricated, sealed ball bearings front and rear. Aluminized mufflers and tailpipes outlast old type 2 to 1. Beautiful Diamond Lustre Finish lasts and lasts—without waxing *ever!*

Engines: *145-hp Mileage Maker Six*—223-cu. in. displ.; 3.62" bore x 3.60" stroke; 8.4 to 1 comp. ratio; regular fuel; low-silhouette unit-design carburetor; manual choke; full-vacuum spark control; precision-molded crankshaft with four main bearings; new high-capacity rotor-type oil pump; oil capacity, with filter change, 5 qt.

185-hp Thunderbird 292 V-8 (standard V-8 on all models)—292-cu. in. displ.; 3.75" bore x 3.30" stroke; 8.8 to 1 comp. ratio; regular fuel; low-silhouette 2-venturi carburetor, new automatic choke; higher efficiency centrifugal-vacuum spark control; new wedge-type combustion chambers and smaller intake valves for better fuel economy; precision-molded crankshaft, copper-lead main (five) and con. rod bearings; rotor oil pump; oil capacity, with filter change, 6 qt.; Y-type single exhaust (dual on Sunliner).

235-hp Thunderbird 352 V-8 (optional on all models)—352-cu. in. displ.; 4.00" bore x 3.50" stroke; 8.9 to 1 comp. ratio; regular fuel; low-silhouette 2-venturi carburetor, new automatic choke; higher efficiency centrifugal-vacuum spark control; aluminized valves with hydraulic lifters and alternate intake-exhaust valve placement for longest life; precision-molded crankshaft with large journal overlap, copper-lead main (five) and con. rod bearings; rotor oil pump; oil capacity, with filter change, 6 qt.; Y-type single exhaust (dual on Sunliner).

300-hp Thunderbird 352 Special V-8 (optional on all models)—352-cu. in. displ.; 4.00" bore x 3.50" stroke; 9.6 to 1 comp. ratio; premium fuel; low-silhouette 4-venturi carburetor, new automatic choke; higher efficiency centrifugal-vacuum spark control; aluminized valves with hydraulic lifters and alternate intake-exhaust valve placement for longest life; precision-molded crankshaft with large journal overlap, copper-lead main (five) and con. rod bearings; rotor oil pump; oil capacity, with filter change, 6 qt.; dual exhausts.

360-hp Thunderbird 352 Super V-8 (optional on all models)—352-cu. in. displ.; 4.00" bore x 3.50" stroke; 10.6 to 1 comp. ratio; premium fuel; special 4-venturi carburetor; new automatic choke; aluminum intake and low-restriction exhaust manifolds; aluminized valves with solid lifters; dual valve springs and solid retainers; special high-lift camshaft; high-pressure fuel pump; full-centrifugal advance distributor with dual breakers; X-rayed and Magnafluxed crankshaft and connecting rods and pistons; steel-backed copper-lead bearings; dual exhausts. Requires certain heavy-duty equipment: see your Ford Dealer.

Engine Features: For greater economy and longer life, all Ford engines have Short Stroke, low-friction design; Deep-Block construction; new Thunderbird-type Cross-Flow cooling system with separate top reserve tank; 12-volt electrical system; weatherproof ignition with new Static-Ban constant resistance wiring and air-cooled distributor points; 66-plate, 55 amp-hr battery (78-plate, 65 amp-hr with Special V-8 and automatic transmission); new aluminized muffler with integral tailpipe mounted at rear of frame. All V-8's electronically balanced while operating under their own power for extra smoothness.

Clutch and Manual Transmissions: Semi-centrifugal clutch with full-weighted levers for more positive engagement; suspended pedal. Face diameter—9½" with Six, 10½" with 292 V-8, 11" with 352 V-8's. **3-Speed** has shot-peened fine-pitch helical gears for high strength and quietness; forged bronze synchronizers. Tailored-to-engine ratios (to 1): *Six*—1st 3.09, 2nd 1.92, direct 1.00, rev. 3.67; *292 V-8*—1st 2.78, 2nd 1.61, direct 1.00, rev. 3.38; *352 V-8's*—1st 2.37, 2nd 1.51, direct 1.00, rev. 2.81. **Overdrive** (optional) is above 3-speed plus an automatic 4th gear that cuts in above 27 mph, cuts out below 21 mph (approx.). Downshift to direct by flooring accelerator. Lock-out control on instrument panel. Tailored-to-engine ratios (to 1): *Six and 292 V-8*—1st 2.80, 2nd 1.69, direct 1.00, OD .70, rev. 3.80; *352 V-8's*—1st 2.49, 2nd 1.59, direct 1.00, OD .72, rev. 3.154.

Automatic Transmissions: Torque converter in combination with compound planetary gear set. Effective engine braking in "L" position. Water cooled. Selector lever on steering column, illuminated quadrant. **Fordomatic Drive** (optional with all engines except Super V-8) features simplified design with one clutch assembly, lightweight cast-aluminum construction, minimum servicing (each 24,000 miles). Two forward gear ratios, one reverse (to 1): low 1.75, direct 1.00, rev. 1.50. In "D" range gives brisk, smooth starts in low. New, durable cellulose clutch plates for satin-smooth upshift. Selector sequence P-R-N-D-L.

Cruise-O-Matic Drive (optional with all engines except Six in Sunliner and Super V-8) features two selective drive ranges: "D₁" starting in low for all normal driving, "D₂" starting in intermediate for more sure-footed driving on slippery surfaces. Three forward gear ratios, one reverse (to 1): low 2.40, intermediate 1.47, direct 1.00, rev. 2.00. New 12" converter, increased stall speed and moderately higher axle ratio results in even greater responsiveness without compromising fuel economy. Selector sequence P-R-N-D₂-D₁-L.

Rear Axle: Semi-floating type with deep-offset hypoid gears. Straddle-mounted drive pinion.

Torque-Tailored Axle Ratios (to 1): Standard. (Optional ratios in paren.)

Models	3-Speed	Overdrive	Fordomatic	Cruise-O-Matic
Station Wagons				
Six	3.89	3.89	3.56	3.56
292 V-8	3.89	3.89	3.56	3.56
352 V-8	3.56	3.56	3.10	2.91
352 Special V-8	3.56 (3.89)	3.56 (3.89)	2.91 (3.10)	2.91 (3.10)
All other models				
Six	3.56 (3.89)	3.89	3.56	3.56
292 V-8	3.56	3.89 (3.56)	3.10	3.10
352 V-8	3.56	3.56	2.91	2.91
352 Special V-8	3.56	3.56	2.91 (3.10)	2.91 (3.10)

Optional Equa-Lock Differential Ratios (to 1): Same as standard ratios above, except 3.10 with 352 V-8's and automatic transmissions.

Wide-Contoured Frame: Longer, wider box-section design, with deeper side rails, having 25% higher strength and rigidity. Sunliner has 4 cross members plus x-member, others have 5 cross members. Side rails extend outside passenger area, for better foot room and increased side protection. Silent-Grip body mounts.

Front Suspension: Swept-Back, Angle-Poised Ball-joint type with wide-base coil springs and with rubber bushings in lower arms for softer ride. Threaded, permanently lubricated bushings in upper arms. With all V-8 models and with Six in wagons, front end has link-type, rubber-bushed ride stabilizer to control roll on turns. Internally mounted hydraulic double-acting shock absorbers.

Rear Suspension: All-new, asymmetrical, variable-rate design with rear axle located well forward from center of springs for anti-dive and anti-squat control on braking and acceleration. Extra-long, gentle-rate, leaf-type springs with wide spring base provide a softer, more stable, levelized ride. Outboard mounted. Tension-type shackles. Axle nose bumper. Diagonally mounted hydraulic double-acting shock absorbers.

Steering: Magic-Circle low-friction recirculating-ball type steering gear for easy handling. Protective rear mounting. Anti-friction bearings throughout. Symmetrical linkage. Over-all steering ratio 27 to 1, with power steering 25 to 1. Lifeguard 3-spoke, deep-center steering wheel is color-keyed to instrument panel, has bright metal horn ring. Turning diameter 41 ft.

Brakes: All-new Truck-Size double-sealed, self-energizing hydraulic brakes have suspended pedal, dash-mounted master cylinder. Heavier, wider, grooved 11" diameter composite drums with wider molded linings result in longer life, cooler operation and greater fade resistance. Lining area is 225.6 sq. in. (248.4 sq. in. on station wagons). Foot-operated parking brake with new pull-out release on instrument panel. Optional Swift Sure power brakes have special low pedal and power reservoir tank.

Tires: 4-ply, black, long-lived, quieter riding, soft-tread type tubeless with Tyrex cord. Safety-type rims. Sunliner and station wagons—8.00 x 14 on 5½" rims with all engines. Other models—7.50 x 14 on 5" rims with Six and 5½" rims with 292 V-8; 8.00 x 14 on 5½" rims with 352 V-8's. White sidewall tires optional. For station wagons optional 8.00 x 14 6-ply tires recommended in combination with heavy-duty suspension and heavy-duty rear axle for greater cargo-carrying capacity.

Dimensions (inches): wheelbase 119; tread, front 61, rear 60; height, sedans 55, wagons 56.5; width 81.5; length 213.6; front head room, sedans 38.2, wagons 39.2; rear head room, sedans 37.6, 6-pass. wagons 40.5, 9-pass. wagons 37.4 (2nd seat), 35.8 (3rd seat); front leg room, sedans 45.3, wagons 45.4; rear leg room, sedans 43.3, 6-pass. wagons 40.7, 9-pass. wagons 40.0 (2nd seat), 44.8 (3rd seat); wagon loadspace, back of front seat to end of open tailgate 124.4, closed tailgate 104.1; maximum loadspace width 62.8, height 32.7; wagon rear opening (maximum) 28.9 x 60.7.

Prices: All Power Assists, Optional Equipment and Accessories as well as some of the items illustrated or referred to in this catalog are at extra cost. For the price of the model with the equipment you desire, see your Ford Dealer.

FORD DIVISION, *Ford Motor Company,*

The new Ford Quality Audit system, a Ford first, results in products of highest quality. Quality Audit teams select samples from each shift at every assembly plant for an exhaustive search for any deviations from strict quality standards. This enables assembly operations to check and adhere to this quality control at all times.

1960 Mercury

The 1960 Mercury was a complete departure from the 1959 design. It offered a bold new concept of rounded lines rather sharp edges and, although based on the same basic car, with the same roof lines, that is where the similarity ended.

The engines offered were the 312 cid V-8 (2-bbl) rated at 205 hp, the 383 cid V-8 (2-bbl) rated at 280 hp and the 430 cid V-8 (2-bbl) rated at 310 hp. The transmissions offered were the 3-speed manual the 3-speed Merc-O-Matic automatic and the 3-speed Multi-Drive Merc-O-Matic automatic.

Production amounted to 155,884 units, with the individual model breakdown as follows. Prices follow each model in ()'s: MONTEREY 4-dr sedan 49,594 ($2,730), 4-dr hdt. sedan 9,536 ($2,845), 2-dr sedan 21,557 ($2,631), 2-dr hdt. coupe 15,790 ($2,781), convertible 6,062 ($3,077); MONTCLAIR 4-dr sedan 8,510 ($3,280), 4-dr hdt. 5,548 ($3,394), 2-dr hdt. coupe 5,756 ($3,331); PARK LANE 2-dr hdt. 2,974 ($3,794), 4-dr hdt. sedan 5,788 ($3,794), convertible 1,525 ($4,018); COUNTRY CRUISER STATION WAGON 4-dr Commuter 6-pass. 14,949 ($3,127), 4-dr Colony Park 6-pass. 7,411 ($3,837).

Fifteen exterior colors were offered with 36 two-tones offered at extra cost. Interiors were available in an unlisted number of color combinations of vinyl and cloth.

Literature offered for 1960 consisted of the small color catalogue (see page 32), the large color catalogue, the Station Wagons color folder, and the "Buyer's Guide" booklet. The Mercury was also included in the full-line press kit.

STANDARD EQUIPMENT ON ALL 1960 MERCURYS

- Self-Adjusting Brakes • Directional Signals • Back-Up Lights • Safety Steering Wheel
- Padded Garnish Mouldings • 3-Speed Electric Wipers • Safety Glass in Every Window
- Foam Front-Seat Cushion • Disposable Carburetor Air Cleaner • Disposable Fuel Filter
- Full-Flow Oil Filter • 8.00 x 14 or 8.50 x 14 Tyrex Cord Tires • Dual Fender Ornaments
- Aluminized Muffler • Teflon Bearings in Ball-Joint Front Suspension • Super-Enamel

MAJOR SPECIFICATIONS (4-Door Hardtop Models)

Over-all Dimensions

Wheelbase . . . . 126.0″
Wheel tread, front and rear . . . . 60.0″
Over-all length . . . . 219.2″
Over-all width . . . . 81.5″
Over-all height (design load) . 55.8″/56.1″

Trunk Compartment

Capacity with spare tire . . . . 31.5 cu. ft.
Capacity without spare tire . . . . 34.5 cu. ft.

Passenger Space

Front head room* . . . . 38.5″
Rear head room* . . . . 37.1″
Front leg room* . . . . 46.2″
Rear leg room* . . . . 43.0″
Front hip room . . . . 62.5″
Rear hip room . . . . 62.8″
Front shoulder room . . . . 60.5″
Rear shoulder room . . . . 60.8″

*Effective Dimension

1960 MERCURY ENGINE-TRANSMISSION COMBINATIONS

Series	Displacement Bore & Stroke	Horsepower Torque	Compression Ratio	Transmission
MONTEREY & COMMUTER	312 cu in. 3.8″ x 3.44″	205-hp 328 ft-lbs	8.9 to 1	3-speed manual Merc-O-Matic†
MONTEREY & COMMUTER (Opt.)	383 cu in. 4.30″ x 3.30″	280-hp 405 ft-lbs	8.5 to 1	Merc-O-Matic† Multi-Drive†
MONTCLAIR & COLONY PARK	430 cu in. 4.30″ x 3.70″	310-hp 460 ft-lbs	10.0 to 1	Merc-O-Matic Multi-Drive†
PARK LANE	430 cu in. 4.30″ x 3.70″	310-hp 460 ft-lbs	10.0 to 1	Multi-Drive

†Optional at extra cost

BODY FEATURES: Rigidized body construction—with double-panel hood, deck lid and doors. Compound windshield. Safety-Sweep windshield wipers. Cross-flow ventilation. Safety steering wheel. **Exterior finish**—baked Super-Enamel in 15 colors; 36 two-tones.

POWER TRAIN: Overhead valve V-8 engines in three sizes. 12-volt electrical system. Combination vacuum-centrifugal spark control. Full-pressure lubrication. Gas-saving 2-bbl carburetors. Self-cleaning 18mm spark plugs. The 383- and 430-cu in. engines have in-block combustion chambers; 3-stage cooling; water-jacketed intake manifold; hydraulic valve lifters; step-top pistons. **Merc-O-Matic:** Combination of fluid torque converter and 3-speed planetary gear set. 5-position selector lever. Multi-Drive Merc-O-Matic with 6-position selector lever and dual drive ranges. **Conventional transmission:** Selective gear type with 3 forward speeds. **High-economy rear axles** with 2.71 to 1 or 2.91 to 1 ratios with 383- or 430-cu in. engines.

CHASSIS FEATURES: Ladder-type frame—with bowed box-girder side-rails. X-type center reinforcement for convertible frame. **Front suspension:** Swept-back ball-joint design with anti-dive. Helical-coil springs. Full-cushion shock aborbers. Link-type front torsion-bar stabilizer. **Steering:** Ball and rack-type with 54 recirculating balls. Over-all steering ratios—29.1 to 1 for Monterey and Commuter; 31.1 to 1 for Montclair and Colony Park; 20.5 to 1 with power steering. **Rear Suspension:** Splay-mounted leaf-type rear springs—60″ long, 6-leave springs, except station wagons (7). Compression-type rear spring shackles. Hotchkiss drive. **Self-adjusting Brakes:** 11-inch brake drums with full-circle ribs for extra cooling. Brake width 3″ (f), 2½″ (r). Total lining area—233.1 sq in.

MAJOR OPTIONS: Air-blending heater-defroster; combination air conditioner-heater with Climate Dial Control; independent air conditioner; power steering; power brakes; 4-way power seat; power window lifts; transistorized radio; belt-driven windshield washer; trunk compartment lock release; tinted windshield and windows; padded instrument panel; floor-anchored safety belts.

1961 Ford

The 1961 Ford won the Centro per L'Alta Moda Italiana for functional expression of CLASSIC BEAUTY, an honor to be proud of. Although retaining the same basic design as the 1960 models, the front end had a much bolder look, with the headlights now set at the edge of the fenders. The grille ran between the lights, and the tops of the fenders were rounded. The rear fenders sported a very small fin, with the traditional round taillights between the fins and the bumper.

Engines offered were the 223 cid six (1-bbl) rated at 135 hp, the 292 cid V-8 (2-bbl) rated at 175 hp, the 352 cid V-8 (2-bbl) rated at 220 hp and the 390 cid V-8 (4-bbl) rated at 300 hp. Transmissions offered were the 3-speed manual, the 3-speed manual with overdrive, the 2-speed Fordomatic automatic and the 3-speed Cruise-O-Matic automatic.

Production amounted to 791,801 units, with the following model breakdown (sixes and V-8's totals combined). Prices for sixes follow each in ()'s, with V-8's costing $116 more: FAIRLANE 4-dr Town Sedan 66,924 ($2,315), 2-dr Club Sedan 97,208 ($2,261); FAIRLANE 500 4-dr Town Sedan 98,917 ($2,430), 2-dr Club Sedan 42,468 ($2,376); GALAXIE 4-dr Town Sedan 141,823 ($2,590), 2-dr Club Sedan 27,780 ($2,536), 4-dr Town Victoria 30,342 ($2,778), 2-dr Club Victoria 75,437 ($2,597), 2-dr Starliner hdt; 29,669 ($2,597), Sunliner convertible 44,614 ($2,847); STATION WAGON 2-dr Ranch Wagon, 6-pass; 12,042 ($2,586), 4-dr Ranch Wagon, 6-pass. 30,292 ($2,656), 4-dr Country Sedan, 6-pass. 46,311 ($2,868), 4-dr Country Sedan, 9-pass. 16,356 ($2,972), 4-dr Country Squire, 6-pass. 16,961 ($2,941), 4-dr Country Squire 9-pass. 14,657 ($3,011).

Thirteen exterior colors were offered with two-tones optional at extra cost. Interiors were offered in many color combinations of cloth and vinyl.

Literature offered for 1961 consisted of the full-line color folder dated 8-60 (see specs on page 36), the large color catalogue dated 8-60, the "ABC's of the '61 FORD" facts book, and the "Belive it or not" B&W facts booklet, the "Buyer's Digest" booklet, filled with facts and figures. Ford, along with other popular-priced makes (Chevy, Plymouth, Studebaker, etc.) marketed special police options in this era and many of the early "civilian" high performance packages were outgrowths of these police packages. The 1961 Ford police cars catalogue is included here for that reason (see pages 34-35). The full-sized Fords were also included in the full-line press kit.

and Emergency Vehicles

1961 FORDS

The Power-Packed Top of the Ford Line
'61 FORD POLICE INTERCEPTOR V-8

For sheer power and scorching performance, the '61 Ford Fairlane 2-door or 4-door with Police Interceptor V-8 Package is in a class by itself. On the next page you'll find details about the exclusive, blazing, new Interceptor 390 V-8 engine.

As the headliner of Ford's '61 Police Cars, the Interceptor V-8 Sedan is designed for the most rugged and demanding police duty . . . for situations where only absolute peak power will do the job . . . where roadability and handling and built-to-take-it toughness *must* be supreme. Compared with two other prominent-make police cars, the Interceptor V-8 Sedan has more glass area, better forward visibility and wider tread . . . all vital for safer, more efficient police operation.

Radiators are huskier for '61, with heavier brackets, thicker tubes and added reinforcements. Universal joints have new, self-aligning needle bearings with increased grease capacity. Brakes are self-adjusting, linings are thicker. Steering is up to 25% easier with a new 30-to-1 ratio. Grilles have 2½-times-thicker aluminum anodizing. Live-rubber Silent-Grip body mounts contribute to gentler, smoother ride. Lifeguard steering wheel, door locks and safety-swivel rearview mirror are standard.

Below is a list of the equipment included in the Police Interceptor V-8 Package, together with available options.

EQUIPMENT INCLUDED IN POLICE INTERCEPTOR V-8 OR POLICE CRUISER V-8 PACKAGE

Manual 3-Speed Transmission
Extra-Cooling Radiator
Extra-Cooling Fan Pulley
Heavy-Duty Springs
Heavy-Duty Shock Absorbers
Fade-Resistant Brakes
Lubricated Driveshaft

Heavy-Duty Seats
Foam Rubber Padding in Front Seat Cushion
Certified Calibration Speedometer (2-miles-per-hour increments)
Heavy-Duty Floor Mats
MagicAire Heater
Heavy-Duty Battery

HIGHLY RECOMMENDED OPTIONS
(PAO—Pre-Approved Items)

15" Nylon Tires and Wheels
Hi-Speed & Handling Package (besides heavy-duty springs, includes heavy-duty, extra-control shocks and heavy-duty stabilizer bar)
Padded Instrument Panel and Two Padded Sun Visors (with vinyl trim)
Front Seat Belts (for driver)

OTHER OPTIONS
RPO—Monthly Schedule Items

*Electric Windshield Washer
Electric Windshield Wipers, 2-Speed
*Radio—Console Range
*Self-Regulating Electric Clock
I-Rest Tinted Glass (all-round)
*Backup Lights

Overdrive Transmission
Cruise-O-Matic Transmission (Heavy-Duty with Interceptor V-8)
Optional Axle Ratios (see specifications)
*Swift Sure Power Brakes
Master-Guide Power Steering
Safety Package "A"—padded instrument panel and sun visors (standard trim)
Front Seat Belts (driver and passenger)
4-Way Manually Operated Front Seat
Power Front Seat
Power-Lift Door Windows

PAO—Pre-Approved Items

Brown, Green or Red All-Vinyl Upholstery and Trim
Bucket Seats, Front (for maximum effective head room)
Rear Arm Rests (4-Dr. model)
Ash Receptacle in Front Seat-Back (4-Dr. model)
15" Rayon Tires and Wheels
Equa-Lock Differential (with Thunderbird 390 Special V-8)

This all-new '61 Interceptor 390 V-8 is the hottest engine Ford has ever offered. It's available to Law Enforcement Agencies . . . *and to no one else.* It offers lightning acceleration and blazing power like no other engine on the road! The Interceptor V-8 features special high-lift camshaft; solid tappets; high-performance intake and exhaust valve springs with dampers and solid valve spring retainer; forged steel exhaust valves; low-restriction exhaust system with header-type manifolds and low back-pressure mufflers.

Other features are precision-molded, alloy-iron crankshaft; Deep-Block construction; short-stroke design; super-fitted aluminum alloy pistons; high-performance oil pump; vacuum-booster type fuel pump and in-line fuel filter; positive full-pressure lubrication; Full-Flow oil filter with 2-phase depth-type filtration bed; freer-breathing air cleaner; large-sized copper-lead main and connecting rod bearings; positive crankcase ventilation and fume control; and each engine is electronically mass-balanced while operating under its own power. These, and the Interceptor's numerous other features, add up to brute power that's smooth, dependable and long lived.

The Mighty New 330-hp INTERCEPTOR 390 V-8 ENGINE

Displacement	390 cu. in.
Horsepower @ RPM	330 @ 5000
Torque (lbs-ft) @ RPM	427 @ 3200
Compression Ratio (to 1)	9.6
Bore x Stroke (inches)	4.05 x 3.78
Carburetor	Four-Barrel
Exhaust	Low-Restriction Dual

Ford's Powerful New Police CRUISER V-8
...featuring the 300-hp Thunderbird 390 Special V-8

The Police Cruiser V-8 is designed for those whose needs do not quite call for Interceptor power, but who still want commanding V-8 performance and the utmost in rugged dependability. The Cruiser is identical to the Interceptor in every way ('61 Fairlane 2-door or 4-door with included package equipment and available options listed below) except that the Cruiser is powered with Ford's brand-new Thunderbird 390 Special V-8. See Page 12 for details of this mighty Thunderbird V-8, second only to the Interceptor V-8 in power.

Roof Light Wiring—single or double strand (with hole in roof)
Generator Option (40-amp. low cut-in)
*Radio—Full Tone Manual
Radio Noise Suppression
*Inside Non-Glare Mirror
Door Mirror
I-Rest Tinted Glass (windshield only)

DSO—Special Order Items

Generator Options—40- or 60-amp. low cut-in and 50- or 60-amp. HD (see generator chart on Page 9) and Alternator-Rectifier Systems: 50- or 60-amp. Std. or HD and 100-amp. HD.
Charge Indicator Gauge
Oil Pressure Gauge
1¾" I.D. Conduit for Radio Cable
Ventilation and Radio Mounting Base in Luggage Compartment for Radio Equipment

Spare Tire Relocation (to accommodate radio equipment)
Suppression Spark Plugs with Non-Suppressed Ignition Wiring
Roof Lights, Sirens and Controls (specify manufacturer and location required on car)
Simultaneous Flashing Parking and Taillights
Simultaneous Flashing Red Grille Lights and Taillights
Spotlamp—Cowl Mount without Mirror (specify red flashing or clear sealed beam)
Spotlamp—Door Mount with Mirror (specify red flashing or clear sealed beam)
*Body Mount Mirrors
Pace-Type Speedometer with Special Needle Stop (specify mounting on steering column or instrument panel)
Canvas Seat Covers with Rifle Pocket
Glove Compartment Light
Luggage Compartment Light
Map Light

Hand Throttle
Single-Key Locking System (one key for all locks in fleet)
Electric Window Regulators for Front Windows Only
Ceramic Fuel Filters

DEALER INSTALLED ITEMS

Parking Brake Warning Light
Bumper Guards, Front and/or Rear
Deluxe Rear Antenna
Plus many other customary accessories
*Also Dealer Installed

EXPLANATION OF TERMS

RPO—Regular Production Option. Available without delay in production.

PAO—Pre-Approved Option. Available in limited quantities, slight delays possible.

DSO—Domestic Special Order. Specific procurement, with time necessary to fill order.

1961 FORD OPTIONS AND ACCESSORIES

 CONSOLE RANGE RADIO. A moderately priced transistorized car radio of unusual power and fidelity. Designed to provide quality reception even in country driving. Five push buttons give you preset station choices.

 MAGICAIRE HEATER. So famous for its all-season usefulness that it's a "must" with nearly all new Ford owners. Combines with Ford's cowl-top air intake to utilize freshest, cleanest air in heating, defrosting, ventilating.

 MASTER-GUIDE POWER STEERING takes up to 85% of the work of steering out of your hands, makes parking a breeze. You still retain all-important "feel" of the road.

SWIFT SURE POWER BRAKES reduce braking effort as much as 45%. Low pedal means less foot travel from accelerator to brake. Especially appreciated in tight city traffic with its stop-and-go driving.

 POWER FRONT SEAT is an infinite position, posture-control seat with synchronized tilting back. Toggle switch in left-seat side shield picks position you like best smoothly, effortlessly.

 POWER LIFT WINDOWS make raising, lowering windows as simple as pointing your finger. Individual controls at all windows; master control at driver's position. Fifth button enables driver to "lockout" all windows except his own.

PLUS . . . Lifeguard Safety Options (padded sun visors, padded instrument panel, seat belts, rear door safety locks) • SelectAire Conditioner • Electric Clock* • Spotlight/Mirror • Sport Spare Wheel Carrier • Bumper Guards • Backup Lights* • Windshield Washer • Electric Windshield Wipers • Polar-Aire Conditioner • 4-Way Manual Tilt Front Seat • I-Rest Tinted Glass • Parking Brake Signal • Anti-Fume Crankcase Ventilation System (std. on 300-hp V-8) • Equa-Lock Differential • Luggage Rack (wagons) • Full Wheel Covers • Wheel Trim Rings • Choice of Four Body-Mounted Rearview Mirrors • Locking Gas Cap • Full Tone Manual Radio • Inside Non-Glare Mirror • Rocker Panel Trim • Rear Fender Shields and many other items.

*Standard on Galaxies and Country Squires

SPECIFICATIONS

EXTERIORS AND INTERIORS: A total of 13 exciting body colors are available in amazing Diamond Lustre Finish. All models come in single color or in two-tone colors, except the Sunliner and Country Squires. Interiors are beautifully upholstered with patterned, morocco-grained and metallic vinyls, woven plastic or nylon fabrics, in colors to harmonize with exteriors.

ENGINES: 135-hp *Mileage Maker Six* (standard on all models)—223-cu. in. displ.; 3.62" bore x 3.60" stroke; 8.4 to 1 comp. ratio; regular fuel; unit-design single-venturi carburetor; manual choke; free-turning overhead valves; single exhaust.

175-hp *Thunderbird 292 V-8* (optional on all models)—292-cu. in. displ.; 3.75" bore x 3.30" stroke; 8.8 to 1 comp. ratio; regular fuel; 2-venturi carburetor; automatic choke; free-turning overhead valves; Y-type single exhaust (dual on Sunliner).

220-hp *Thunderbird 352 Special V-8* (optional on all models)—352-cu. in. displ.; 4.00" bore x 3.50" stroke; 8.9 to 1 comp. ratio; regular fuel; 2-venturi carburetor; automatic choke; free-turning overhead aluminized valves with hydraulic lifters for automatic valve adjustment; Y-type single exhaust (dual on Sunliner).

300-hp *Thunderbird 390 Special V-8* (optional on all models)—390-cu. in. displ; 4.05" bore x 3.78" stroke; 9.6 to 1 comp. ratio; premium fuel; 4-venturi carburetor; automatic choke; new Anti-Fume crankcase ventilation system; free-turning overhead aluminized valves with hydraulic lifters for automatic valve adjustment; dual exhausts. *375-hp Thunderbird 390 Super V-8* with 10.6 to 1 comp. ratio also available for all models except wagons. This high-performance engine has many special components and requires certain heavy-duty chassis equipment. For details, see your Ford Dealer.

ENGINE FEATURES: For greater economy and longer life all engines have Short Stroke, low-friction, Deep-Block design; Super-Filter air cleaner; vacuum booster and fuel pump; 2-phase Full-Flow oil filter; Cross-Flow cooling system and 180° thermostat; 12-volt electrical system, Turbo-Action 18-mm. spark plugs; single muffler all-aluminized (dual mufflers of aluminized and stainless steel) mounted at rear of frame. All V-8's electronically mass-balanced while operating under their own power for extra smoothness.

TRANSMISSIONS: Manual *3-speed* with gear ratios tailored to each engine, or optional *Overdrive* with automatic 4th gear. *Fordomatic Drive* (optional for all engines except 390 V-8's), a 2-speed automatic featuring simplified design, light weight, minimum servicing. In "D" range gives brisk, smooth starts in low. *Cruise-O-Matic Drive* (optional for all engines except Six and Super V-8), a high-performance automatic featuring new cast-aluminum converter housing and minimum servicing. Has two selective drive ranges—smooth 3-speed operation

in "Drive" starting in low for all normal driving, or 2-speed in alternate drive position starting in intermediate for gradual acceleration on slippery surfaces. New vacuum control provides smoother, more precise operation (eliminates linkage adjustment).

FRAME: Strong, wide-contoured, box-section design with more flexible inner channel for softer, more luxurious ride. Side rails extend outside passenger area for increased side protection.

SUSPENSION: Smooth-acting Swept-Back, Angle-Poised, Ball-Joint front suspension. Ball joints packed with special 30,000-mile grease retained by full life seals. Link-type, rubber-bushed stabilizer on all V-8 models plus Six in wagons. Asymmetrical, variable-rate, outboard-mounted rear suspension for anti-dive and anti-squat. Extra-long, gentle-rate leaf springs with wide spring base provide a soft, stable, levelized ride. Heavy-duty suspension available for wagons.

REAR AXLE: Hypoid, semifloating type with exclusive Deep-Offset straddle-mounted drive pinion for quieter operation, longer life. Optional: Equa-Lock differential; heavy-duty axle for wagons.

BRAKES: All-new, self-adjusting Truck Size double-sealed, self-energizing hydraulic. Brakes adjust automatically when applied while car is moving backwards. Grooved 11" diameter composite drums with thicker molded linings for longer life, cooler operation and greater fade resistance. Lining area is 212.5 sq. in. (on wagons 233.8 sq. in.).

STEERING: Precision-control low-friction, recirculating-ball type, with new higher ratio (30 to 1) for easier steering. New flexible coupling in steering shaft insulates steering wheel for greater driver comfort. New nylon bearings in linkage packed with special 30,000-mile grease and sealed. Lifeguard 3-spoke, deep-center steering wheel, color-keyed to instrument panel, with horn ring.

WARRANTY: Ford Motor Company warrants to its dealers, and its dealers, in turn, warrant to their customers as follows: That for 12 months or for 12,000 miles, whichever comes first, free replacement, including related labor, will be made by dealers, of any part with a defect in workmanship or materials. Tires are not covered by the warranty; appropriate adjustments will continue to be made by the tire companies. Owners will remain responsible for normal maintenance service and routine replacement of maintenance items such as filters, spark plugs, condensers, ignition points and wiper blades.

PRICES: All Power Assists, Optional Equipment and Accessories as well as some of the items illustrated or referred to as optional or available in this folder are at extra cost. For the price of the model with the equipment you desire, see your Ford Dealer.

 The Ford Quality Audit system, a Ford first, results in products of highest quality. Quality Audit Teams select samples from each shift at every assembly plant for an exhaustive search for any deviation from strict quality standards. This enables assembly operations to check and adhere to this quality control at all times.

Comparative information in this folder was obtained from authoritative sources, but is not guaranteed. The specifications contained herein were in effect at the time this folder was approved for printing. Ford Division of Ford Motor Company reserves the right to discontinue models at any time, or change specifications or design without notice and without obligation.

FORD DIVISION, *Ford Motor Company*

The 1961 Mercury again was a totally new car. This time it shared many components with Ford. Since there had been a recession in the late-fifties and there was a swing toward smaller cars, Mercury downgraded the car slightly and lowered the prices.

The engines offered were the 223 cid six (1-bbl) rated at 135 hp, the 292 cid V-8 (2-bbl) rated at 175 hp, the 352 cid V-8 (2-bbl) rated at 220 hp, and the 390 cid V-8 (4-bbl) rated at 300 hp. The transmissions available were the 3-speed manual, the 3-speed manual with overdrive, the 3-speed Merc-O-Matic automatic and the 3-speed Multi-drive Merc-O-Matic automatic.

Production amounted to 66,966 units, with the model breakdown as follows. Prices follow each model in ()'s: METEOR 600 4-dr sedan (production not available, $2,587), 2-dr sedan 18,117 ($2,533);

METEOR 800 4-dr sedan (production not available, $2,765), 2-dr sedan 35,005 ($2,711), 2-dr hdt. (production not available, $2,772), 4-dr hdt. (production not available, $2,837); MONTEREY 4-dr sedan 22,881 ($2,869); 2-dr hdt. 10,942 ($2,876), 4-dr hdt. 9,252 ($2,941), convertible 7,053 ($3,126); STATION WAGON 4-dr Commuter, 6-pass. 8,951 ($2,922), 4-dr Colony Park, 6-pass. 7,887 ($3,118).

Fifteen exterior colors were offered. Interiors were offered in a number of color combinations of vinyl or cloth and vinyl.

Literature offered for 1961 consisted of the small color catalogue, the large color catalogue (see page 38), the Station Wagons color folder, the "Buyer's Guide to '61 cars" booklet, and the accessories catalogue. The big Mercurys were also included the full-line press kit.

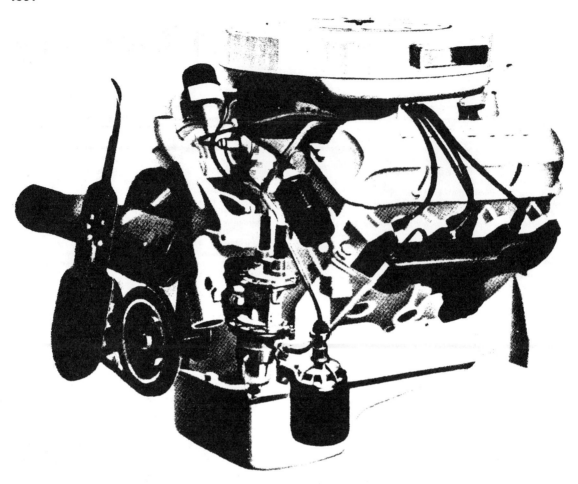

You have a choice of two engines and two transmissions to suit your power tastes. Both engines are designed for the utmost in smooth, efficient performance with scientifically engineered wedge-shaped combustion chambers, deep block construction and overhead valves. A carburetor air filter . . . and disposable fuel filter good for 12,000 miles before replacement—all standard —add to long, dependable engine life. Choose from the *Mercury Marauder "352"* with mighty power to whet the appetite of any driving enthusiast. Or the optional *Mercury Marauder "390"*. For top performance, this is it! With the "352", the Single Range Merc-O-Matic transmission is *standard equipment*. Dual Range Merc-O-Matic is teamed with the "390" to provide maximum acceleration and performance. It is optional on the "352". Mercury's first power-transfer rear axle for all '61 models, gives equal driving force to both rear wheels.

1962 Ford

The "Lively Ones" was the motto for 1962, and to ensure that this was a true statement, Ford offered a group of engines that really moved these cars along. The styling retained much of the appearance from 1961 while taking on a much cleaner look. The front remained similar to 1961. The rear end featured a smoothly sloping deck lid with neatly recessed taillights.

Early in the model run you could purchase 390 cid V-8 with 401 hp. Mid-year this engine was replaced by the 406 cid V-8 with 405 hp.

Engine availability consisted of the 223 cid six (1-bbl) rated at 138 hp, the 292 cid V-8 (2-bbl) rated at 170 hp, the 352 cid V-8 (2-bbl) rated at 220 hp, the 390 cid V-8 (4-bbl) rated at 300 hp, the 390 cid V-8 (4-bbl) rated at 375 hp, and the 390 cid V-8 (three 2-bbl) rated at 401 hp, both early production, and mid-year the 406 cid V-8 (4-bbl) rated at 385 hp, and the 406 cid V-8 (three 2-bbl) rated at 405 hp. Transmissions offered were the 3-speed manual, the 3-speed manual with overdrive, the 2-speed Fordomatic automatic and the 3-speed Cruise-O-Matic automatic.

Production amounted to 746,370 units, with the following model breakdown (sixes and V-8's totals combined). Prices for sixes follow each model in ()'s, with V-8's costing $109 more: GALAXIE 4-dr Sedan 115,594 ($2,507), 2-dr Sedan 54,930 ($2,453); GALAXIE 500 4-dr Town Sedan 174,195 ($2,667), 2-dr Club Sedan 27,824 ($2,613), 4-dr Town Victoria 30,778 ($2,739), 2-dr Club Victoria 87,562), Sunliner convertible V-8 only 42,646 ($3,033); GALAXIE 500XL V-8 2-dr Club Victoria 28,412 ($3,108), Sunliner convertible 13,183 ($3,358); STATION WAGON 4-dr Ranch Wagon 6-pass. 33,674 ($2,733), 4-dr Country Sedan 6-pass. 47,635 ($2,829), 4-dr Country Sedan 9-pass. 16,562 ($2,933), 4-dr Country Squire 6-pass. 16,144 ($3,018), 4-dr Country Squire 9-pass. 15,666 ($3,088).

Thirteen exterior colors were offered with twenty-four two-tones available at extra cost. Interiors were offered in many color combinations of cloth and vinyl.

Literature offered for 1962 consisted of the full-line color folder dated 8-61, 9-61 and 2-62, the Galaxie color catalogue dated 8-61 and 2-62 (see specs on page 50), the "live it up..." color folder, "The Mountain that comes to you..." color mailer catalogue, the "Break Through!" color mailer catalogue, the Ford Owner Newsletter "Meet the new lively ones" color mailer catalogue (see pages 40-41), the Ford Owner Newsletter supplement color mailer catalogue, the accessories color folder, the "Important facts about your 1962 Ford high performance 406," owners manual supplement (see pages 42-47), the full-line color selections folder, and the "Buyer's Digest" booklet, filled with facts and figures (see pages 48-49). The Galaxies were also included in the full-line press kit.

1962

Here are brand-new Fords with grand-new features . . . cars with flair to spare . . . cars that let you steal the spotlight—whether you're spending a day at the beach . . . or a night on the town . . . happy-go-lucky cars that will put you in the mood for ball games and barbecues . . . hay rides and sleigh rides . . . ski trips and ocean dips. And their fast-moving finery is yours at Ford prices—so you *don't* have to be a millionaire to drive like one. Leading the parade is . . .

The lively New Galaxie 500/XL!

... that XL is pronounced "excel"—for when this car shows you what lively means (with a 405-hp Thunderbird V-8, for example), not even the most expensive autos in Canada can match its performance. But you don't even have to start the engine to get that gala Galaxie feeling. Just sit in the car. The sporty console-mounted stick shift (with either 4-speed gear box or Cruise-O-Matic) ... the foam-cushioned bucket seats ... the Thunderbird-type console ... the very atmosphere can quicken your pulse. ● Luxury touches are as plentiful as sun tans on the beach. Plush, specially blended nylon-rayon carpeting not only goes wall-to-wall ... but continues right up on lower sections of doors and side panels. Rear seats, like front seats—both cushions and backs—have 100% molded-foam padding. Instrument panel and sun visors are foam-padded, too. High luster, pleated vinyl upholstery ... two-tone steering wheel ... elegant, bright chrome trim—luxury touches wherever you look—all tell you you're going first class—all the way. ● Being a Galaxie, the XL is a smooth-running craft of outstanding quality—as quiet as moonlight on the water (and just as beautiful). And you get more time to live it up—because you're not tied down by frequent (and expensive) service stops. Galaxie brings you Twice-a-Year Maintenance—needs routine servicing only once every six months or 6,000 miles. ● It doesn't matter whether you prefer to make tracks with the top up or down—there are both a hardtop ... and a convertible to choose from. Come on in—the driving's fine.

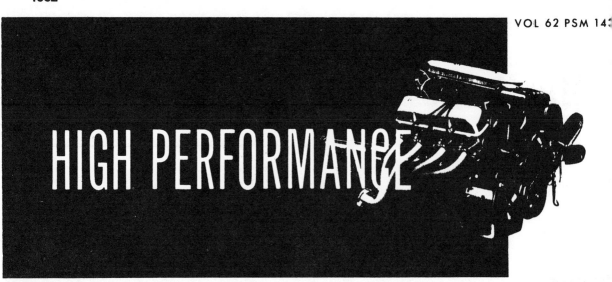

HIGH PERFORMANCE

1962-63 406 V-8 HIGH PERFORMANCE ENGINE SPECIFICATIONS

Bore...4.13 in.
Stroke..3.78 in.
Firing order: 1-5-4-2-6-3-7-8

	4-V	3 2-V
Maximum B.H.P.	385 @ 5800 RPM	405 @ 5800 RPM
Maximum Torque	444 @ 3400 RPM	448 @ 3500 RPM

Compression Ratio: Nominal 10.9:1
                  Maximum 11.4:1
Camshaft, Part No. C2AE-6250-A

Intake opens...24°BTC
Intake closes..72°ABC
Duration...276°
Exhaust opens...72°BBC
Exhaust closes..24°ATC
Duration...276°
Valve overlap..48°

SPECIAL DRAG RACING COMPONENTS

PART NO.	DESCRIPTION	PART NO.	DESCRIPTION
C1AW-4209-E	5.83 Gear Set	C2AZ-8600-A	Fan Blade (5 blade)
WAB-4209-C	5.67 Gear Set	B9MM-8600-E	Fan Blade Assembly 4 blades
WAB-4209-D	5.43 Gear Set		18.5 dia.
WAB-4209-E	5.14 Gear Set	C1AA-8600-E	Fan Blade Assembly 4 blades
WAB-4209-F	4.86 Gear Set		14.0 dia.
WAB-4209-G	4.71 Gear Set	C2AZ-8A616-A	Fan Drive (Clutch)
WAB-4209-H	4.57 Gear Set	B9JE-9441-B	Gasket—Intake Manifold to
WAB-4209-J	4.29 Gear Set		Cylinder Head
WAB-4209-K	3.40 Gear Set	C0AE-9A435-B	Spacer—Exhaust Manifold
B9TE-6500-A	Tappet, Barrel Type	C1AZ-18097-A	Shock Absorbers—Rear
B8A-6565-C	Push Rod	C2AZ-19580-D	Rear Axle Lubricant
C2AZ-8546-A	Fan Spacer*	*Used with C2AZ-8A616-A (only)	

1962-63...406 CU. IN. HIGH PERFORMANCE ENGINE

PARTS LIST

The following is a complete engine and chassis part listing to service the 406 cubic inch high performance and super high performance engine.

For convenience in quickly locating particular parts, the following list is arranged in an ascending numerical order. The designation (#) denotes that the part is applicable to the 6-V only.

C1AA-2263-A	Tube Assy.—Frt. Wheel Brake—R.H.
C1AA-5246-H	Pipe Assy.—Muffler Inlet—R.H. (Conv. only)
C1AA-5246-K	Pipe Assy.—Muffler Inlet
C1AA-5248-C	Pipe Assy.—Muffler Inlet—L.H. (Conv. only)
C0AA-5A289-A	Resonator Assy. (Conv. only)
C2AE-6007-E	Engine Assy.—4-V without Emission Reduction (350-A)
C2AE-6007-E	Engine Assy.—4-V with Emission Reduction (E-350-A)
C2AE-6007-E	Engine Assy.—6-V without Emission Reduction (351-A) #
C2AE-6007-E	Engine Assy.—6-V with Emission Reduction (E-351-A)
C2AZ-6009-B	Engine Assy.—Cylinder Block and Crankshaft
C2AZ-6010-A	Block Assy.—Cylinder
C0AE-6023-D	Pointer—Timing
C2AZ-6049-A	Head Assy.—Cylinder
C2AZ-6051-A	Gasket—Cylinder Head
C1AE-6065-A	Bolt—Cylinder Head—Long
C1AE-6065-C	Bolt—Cylinder Head—Short
C1AE-6B068-A	6-V Kit #
C2AE-6108-K	Piston (4.13 Dia.)
C1AE-6135-B	Pin—Piston
C1AE-6140-A	Retainer—Piston Pin
C2AZ-6200-A	Rod Assy.—Connecting
C1AE-6211-M	Bearing—Connecting Rod—.020 U.S.
C1AE-6211-N	Bearing—Connecting Rod—.030 U.S.
C2AZ-6211-H	Bearing—Connecting Rod—Red
C2AZ-6211-J	Bearing—Connecting Rod—Blue
C2AZ-6211-K	Bearing—Connecting Rod—.002 U.S.
C2AZ-6211-L	Bearing—Connecting Rod—.010 U.S.
C2AZ-6211-R	Bearing—Connecting Rod—.040 U.S.
C0ME-6212-A	Nut—Connecting Rod
C2AZ-6214-A	Bolt—Connecting Rod
C2AE-6250-A	Camshaft
B8A-6256-A	Sprocket—Camshaft
B8A-6261-AA	Bearing—Camshaft Front
B8A-6262-AA	Bearing—Camshaft Center
B8A-6263-AA	Bearing—Camshaft Rear
B8A-6267-AA	Bearing—Camshaft Front Intermediate
B8A-6268-A	Chain—Timing
B8A-6270-AA	Bolt—Crankshaft Main Bearing Cap
C2AZ-6303-B	Crankshaft
B8A-6306-A	Sprocket—Crankshaft
B8A-6310-A	Slinger—Crankshaft Oil
C1AZ-6312-A	Damper Assy.—Crankshaft Vibration
C1AE-6333-A	Bearing—Crankshaft Main Front—Red
C1AE-6333-B	Bearing—Crankshaft Main Front—Blue
C1AE-6333-C	Bearing—Crankshaft Main Front—.002 U.S.
C1AE-6333-D	Bearing—Crankshaft Main Front—.010 U.S.
C1AE-6333-E	Bearing—Crankshaft Main Front—.020 U.S.
C1AE-6333-F	Bearing—Crankshaft Main Front—.030 U.S.
C1AE-6336-B	Seal—Crankshaft Rear Main Bearing Cap
C1AE-6337-A	Bearing—Crankshaft Center—Red
C1AE-6337-B	Bearing—Crankshaft Center—Blue
C1AE-6337-C	Bearing—Crankshaft Center—.002 U.S.
C1AE-6337-D	Bearing—Crankshaft Center—.010 U.S.
C1AE-6337-E	Bearing—Crankshaft Center—.020 U.S.
C1AE-6357-F	Bearing—Crankshaft Center—.030 U.S.
B9TE-6500-A3	Tappet—Valve
C2AZ-6505-A	Valve—Exhaust Std.
C2AZ-6505-C	Valve—Exhaust .015 O.S.
C2AZ-6505-D	Valve—Exhaust .030 O.S.
C0AE-6507-N	Valve—Intake Std.
C0AE-6507-R	Valve—Intake .015 O.S.
C2AZ-6513-A	Spring Assy.—Valve Damper
C2AZ-6514-A	Retainer—Valve Spring
B8A-6518-A	Key—Valve Spring Retainer
C1SE-6524-A	Baffle—Valve Springs Oil
C1AE-6A527-A	Bolt—Valve Rocker Arm Shaft Support
C1DE-6A527-A	Bolt—Valve Rocker Arm Shaft Support
C2AZ-6531-A	Support—Valve Rocker Arm Shaft
B8A-6563-A	Shaft—Valve, Rocker Arm
B8A-6564-B	Arm Assy.—Valve Rocker
B8A-6565-C	Rod—Valve Push
B8A-6571-B	Seal—Intake Valve Stem
C2AZ-6571-A	Seal—Exhaust Valve Stem
C1SE-6582-B	Cover Assy.—Valve Rocker Arm R.H.
C1SZ-6582-A	Cover Assy.—Valve Rocker Arm L.H.
B9AE-6584-C	Gasket—Valve Rocker Arm Cover
B8A-6587-A	Spring—Valve Rocker Arm Locating
C1AE-6600-C	Pump Assy.—Oil
B8AZ-6A618-A	Shaft—Oil Pump Intermediate
C0AE-6622-E	Screen and Cover Assembly—Oil Pump
B8A-6626-A	Gasket—Oil Pump Cover to Inlet Tube Flange
B8A-6629-A	Ring—Oil Pump Inter. Shaft Retain
B9AZ-6A630-A	Baffle—Crankcase Vent. Push Rod Valley
C1AE-6A630-A	Crankcase Vent Duct Assy.
C0AE-6A631-A	Crankcase Vent Oil Separator Element
C1AE-6A632-A	Crankcase Vent Oil Separator Gasket
C1AE-6A632-A	Gasket—Crankcase Vent. Tube Adapt.
C0AE-6A633-A	Crankcase Vent Oil Separator Element Retainer
C0AE-6A636-A	Gasket—Oil Filter Adaptor to Cyl. Block

1962-63...406 CU. IN. HIGH PERFORMANCE ENGINE

PARTS LIST

B8A-6659-A	Gasket—Oil Pump to Cyl. Block
C1AE-6A664-R	Hose—Crankcase Vent. Tube
C1AE-6A664-S	Hose—Crankcase Vent. Tube (5" long)
C1AE-6A665-H	Adaptor Assy.—Crankcase Vent. Tube
C2AE-6A666-A	Valve Assy.—Crankcase Ventilation#
C0ME-6670-A	Spring—Oil Pump Relief Valve (Rear of Cylinder Block)
B9AE-6674-B	Plunger—Oil Pump Relief Valve (Rear of Cylinder Block)
C0AE-6675-F	Pan Assy.—Oil (7 qt.)
C1AE-6675-F	Pan Assy.—Oil (6 qt.)
C1AE-6700-B1	Seal Assy.—Crankshaft Front—Oil
C2AZ-6701-A	Seal—Crankshaft Rear—Oil
C1AE-6A706-A	Connector Assy.—Crankcase Vent. Tube
C2AZ-6A706-B	Connector Assy.—Crankcase Vent. Tube
C0AE-6710-C	Gasket—Oil Pan
C1AZ-6731-A	Filter Assy.—Oil
C2AE-6750-A	Indicator Assy.—Oil Level*
C2AZ-6750-B	Indicator Assy.—Oil Level*
B8A-6754-A	Tube Assy.—Oil Level Indicator
C2AZ-6758-E	Tube—Crankcase Ventilation
C2AZ-6758-F	Tube—Crankcase Ventilation
C2AE-6759-C	Tube—Crankcase Ventilation#
C1AE-6759-F	Tube—Crankcase Ventilation
C0AE-6763-A	Pipe Assy.—Oil Filler
C0AE-6881-A	Adapter Assy.—Oil Filter
C0AA-7550-B	Disc Assy.—Clutch
B7A-7561-A	Hub
8A-7580-A	Bearing
C2AZ-8501-B	Pump Assy.—Water
B5A-8546-A	Spacer—Fan
C2AZ-8546-A	Spacer—Fan
C0AE-8555-A	Tube Water By-Pass
C1MZ-8600-D	Fan Assy.
C2AZ-8600-A	Fan (5-blade)
C2AZ-8A616-A	Fan Clutch
B7Q-9155-A	Filter Assy.—Fuel
C0AE-9180-A	Bracket—Fuel Filter Mounting
C1AE-9A274-F	Fuel Filter Outlet Tube Assy.
C1AE-9D280-A	Carb. Fuel Block Tube Assy. (Fuel Manifold)#
B7TZ-9B281-A	Clip—Fuel Filter Bracket
C1AE-9D281-E	Carburetor Fuel Hose—5.08" Long (Rear)#
C1AA-9291-L	Tube—Fuel Tank to Pump
C0AE-9350-E	Pump Assy.—Fuel
C1AE-9424-E	Intake Manifold Assy.#
B9AE-9A424-A	Intake Manifold Seal—Rear
B9AE-9A425-A	Intake Manifold Seal—Front
C0AE-9A427-B	Valve Assy.—Exhaust Control
C2AZ-9430-C	Manifold Assy.—Exhaust R.H.
C2AZ-9431-C	Manifold Assy.—Exhaust L.H.
*Use with C1AE-6675-F	

B9AE-9441-A	Intake Manifold to Cylinder Head Gasket (2 req'd.)
B9JE-9441-B	Gasket—Int. Manifold to Cyl. Head (Manifold Heat CLOSED)
C2AZ-9441-A	Gasket—Int. Manifold to Cyl. Head (Manifold Heat OPEN)
C1AE-9447-C	Carburetor to Intake Manifold Gasket (3 req'd.)#
C0AA-9450-A	Gasket—Exhaust Manifold to Exhaust Pipe
C1AE-9510-AM	Carburetor Assy. (Holley 4V)
C1AE-9510-AU	Carburetor Assy. (2 req'd.) (Secondary)#
C1AE-9510-AV	Carburetor Assy. (Primary)#
C0AE-9A589-A	Spacer—Carburetor to Intake Manifold
C1AZ-9590-G	Kit—Carburetor Gasket (Holley 4V)
C0AE-9600-K	Cleaner Assy., Carb. Air
C0AE-9601-C	Element Assy.—Carburetor Air Cleaner
EDJ-9601-A	Air Cleaner Element Assy.#
C1AE-9654-A	Air Cleaner to Carburetor Gasket (3 req'd.)#
C1AE-9A702-A	Accelerator Shaft to Bellcrank Rod
C1AE-9724-A	Bellcrank Assy.
C1AE-9772-A	Bellcrank to Carburetor Rod
C1AE-9819-B	Tube—Thermostatic Choke Control Outlet
C1AE-9819-C	Thermostat Choke Control Outlet Tube
C1AE-9B841-A	Carburetor Throttle Rod—Front
C1AE-9B842-A	Carburetor Throttle Rod—Rear
C1AE-9865-A	Insulator—Thermos. Choke Contr. Outlet Tube
C1AE-9865-B	Heat Tube Insulator
B6A-12029-B	Coil Assy.—Ignition (12 V)
B8S-12043-B	Strap Assy.—Ignition Coil
C0AF-12127-K	Distributor Assy.
FDS-12171-A	Arm & Brkt. Assy.—Distr. Breaker
B7A-12191-B	Spring—Distributor Wt. Secondary
B8QH-12192-C	Spring—Distributor Wt. Primary
FEW-12298-A	Wire Assy.—Coil to Distr.—High Tension
C2AZ-12405-A	Spark Plug—Autolite (BF601)
C2AZ-12405-B	Spark Plug—Autolite (BTF1)
B8A-12405-A	Spark Plug—Autolite (BF-42)
C0AF-12405-B	Spark Plug—Autolite (BF-32)
B7A-18599-B	Elbow—Hot Water Heater Connector
C1AF-18599-A	Hot Water Heater Connection Elbow
34079-S8	Throttle Bar Lock Nut (#10-32) (2 req'd.)
351089-S	Nut—5/16-24 (12 req'd.)
351253-S8	Washer .20" ID x .44" OD—(2 req'd.)*
353610-S	Pin—Retainer (2 req'd.)*
357940-S	Ferrule—¼" Compression**
357980-S	Nut—7/16 Hex**
372146-S	Throttle Connecting Pin Nut #8-32
375416-S8	Clamp—8/16 Hose (6 req'd)
375780-S	Clip—Rod to Accelerator Shaft
376410-S	Elbow—Crankcase Vent. Tube #
*Attach carburetor throttle rods to carburetor	
**To attach heat tube to carburetor #6 V only	

HIGH PERFORMANCE ACCESSORIES

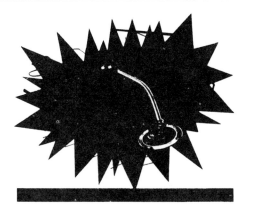

3-SPEED FLOOR SHIFT CONVERSION KIT C2AZ-7A082-A

Combine extra-fast shifting with trouble-free linkage plus "high-performance" with this new 3-Speed Floor Shift Conversion Kit, C2AZ-7A082-A. This "three-for-thrust" kit includes many extras not found in other kits— including a chrome retainer ring, rubber boot, dummy shifter tube, and a sheet metal cover. It is available for all 1960-63 352, 390 C.I.D. engines.

ENGINE DRESS-UP KIT C1AZ-6980-A

Eight chrome-plated parts "customize" and dress-up your 1961-63 390 C.I.D. engine. The easy-to-clean durable parts are precision designed for quick installation and removal. This kit, C1AZ-6980-A, contains the following items:

Air Cleaner Cover	Fuel Filter
Valve Cover—Right Hand	Oil Level Indicator
Valve Cover—Left Hand	Fan Guard
Oil Breather Cap	Master Brake Cylinder Cover

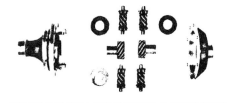

LOCKING DIFFERENTIAL C2AZ-4880-A

This locking differential is for use in 1962-63 models with 390 and 406 C.I.D. engines. It is particularly suited to racing since it is designed to give in-line faster starts and true solid-axle performance on the straightaway, without power loss on the curves.

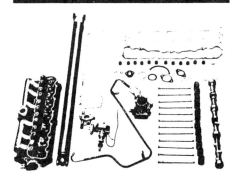

HIGH PERFORMANCE KIT FOR FALCON C2DZ-6B068-A

The completeness of this high performance Falcon Kit adds sparked performance to the 140 and 170 C.I.D. Falcon engines. It provides durability during sustained high-speed highway driving. This kit, Part Number C2DZ-6B068-A, offers that "extra punch" when needed for passing and attaining higher top speeds.

NEW LIGHT-WEIGHT BODY COMPONENT KIT

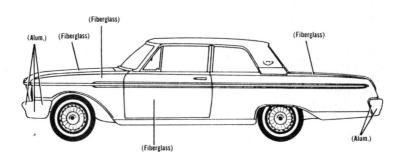

A <u>must</u> installation on cars used in competitive events where every "shaved" pound means extra speed. This new light-weight kit allows an approximate 164 pound weight reduction for Galaxie standard sedans and convertibles. For stock 1962 Galaxies with a 406 engine and a 4-speed transmission, this means a 4% decrease in total curb weight. Aluminum structural parts and fiberglass skin keep the Galaxie lean and in ready racing form. Replaceable parts are pre-fitted for quick installation.

KIT FOR 1962 GALAXIE SEDAN
PART NO. C2AZ-6200012-A

KIT CONTAINS:

1 ea.	C2AB-16005-6-S	Fender Assy. R.H. & L.H. (Fiberglass)
1	C2AB-16610-F	Hood Assy. (Fiberglass)
1 ea.	C2AB-17A867-8-C	Arm—Rear Bumper, Outer R.H. and L.H. (alum.)
1 ea.	C2AB-17787-8-A	Arm—Rear Bumper, Inner R.H. and L.H. (alum.)
1 ea.	C1AB-17A820-1-A	Brace—Front Bumper, Outer (alum.)
1	C2AB-17757-A	Bar—Front Bumper, Impact (alum.)
1 ea.	C2AB-17A971-2-A	Arm—Front Bumper, Inner R.H. and L.H. (alum.)
1 ea.	C2AB-6220200-1-A	Door Panel Assy., Outside R.H. and L.H. (Fiberglass)
1	C2AB-6240110-D	Door Assy.—Luggage Compartment (Fiberglass)

KIT FOR 1962 GALAXIE CONVERTIBLE
PART NO. C2AZ-7600012-A

KIT CONTAINS:

1 ea.	C2AB-16005-6-S	Fender Assy. R.H. and L.H. (Fiberglass)
1	C2AB-16610-F	Hood Assy. (Fiberglass)
1 ea.	C2AB-17A867-8-C	Arm—Rear Bumper, Outer R.H. and L.H. (alum.)
1 ea.	C2AB-17787-8-A	Arm—Rear Bumper, Inner R.H. and L.H. (alum.)
1 ea.	C1AB-17A820-1-A	Brace—Front Bumper, Outer (alum.)
1	C2AB-17757-A	Bar—Front Bumper, Impact (alum.)
1 ea.	C2AB-17A971-2-A	Arm—Front Bumper, Inner R.H. and L.H. (alum.)
1 ea.	C2AB-7620200-1-A	Door Panel Assy.—Outside R.H. and L.H. (Fiberglass)
1	C2AB-6240110-D	Door Assy.—Luggage Compartment (Fiberglass)

PRECISION TACHOMETERS FOR HIGH PERFORMANCE ENGINES

SUN TACHOMETER KIT . . . ALL 8 CYLINDER MODELS

Tachometer Kit
C2RZ-17A326-A

Mounting Bracket Kit
C2RZ-17368-A

The new Tachometer Kit, C2RZ-17A326-A, containing the tachometer head, transmitter, light and flange, is designed to register exact engine efficiency.

An additional Mounting Bracket Kit, C2RZ-17368-A, is also available. This kit contains a chrome-finish tachometer housing, brackets for mounting in or below the instrument panel, or on the steering column, an adjustable steering column clamp, and a rubber protector pad.

ROTUNDA TACHOMETERS . . . ALL 6 OR 8 CYLINDER MODELS

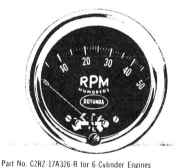

Part No. C2RZ-17A326-B for 6-Cylinder Engines

Part No. C2RZ-17A326-C for 8-Cylinder Engines

New low cost tachometers with the name R O T U N D A proudly displayed on the dial faces are also available for all 6 and 8 cylinder engines. The moisture and dustproof chrome housings have been designed and engineered for long-life and accurate readings.

A two-wire hook-up provides easy installation. Universal mounting of the tachometers eliminates restriction on placement. They may be located on or inserted in the instrument panel, attached to the steering column by means of a bracket, or positioned in the console.

Each Rotunda tachometer has a permanent magnet and a mounting cup. A diffused red neon light is directed downward over the dial, illuminating the face and calibrations. This is an extra visibility convenience item for "grey" days and night time driving. When this red neon light flashes, it indicates that the engine is not functioning properly.

PRODUCTS OF *Ford* MOTOR COMPANY

DAYTONA REPORT:

An unqualified A-OK to Ford's new Thunderbird 406 High Performance V-8

On November 17, 1961, professional driver Curtis Turner stepped into a brand-new '62 Galaxie, slipped it into first, shifted quickly, smoothly up through the gears and ran it *flat out* for 600 miles!

The event was an endurance test. The place was the famed 2½-mile International Speedway at Daytona Beach. The speeds exceeded 150 miles per hour (faster than the winning average at the 1961 Indianapolis 500 mile). The performance was made possible through Ford's 4-speed transmission and the new Thunderbird 406 High-Performance V-8, one of the 12 powerplants in Ford's regular line-up for 1962.

The 4-speed transmission had been tested and proved months before (including a red-hot run up Pikes Peak). But, for the new Thunderbird 406 engine, this was the climax of months of planning, calculating, building and testing by a group of dedicated engineers.

How much power do **you** need?

Obviously, everyone doesn't need or desire the performance of the Thunderbird 406.

Ford builds it for those who want top explosive power. The 406 is a specialized engine, and the Daytona Beach run is simply another example of the rigorous testing given to all Ford products.

Most drivers don't have to worry about power. They don't really need much. Economy is uppermost in *their* minds. On the other hand, there is a sizable number of motorists across the country who have special driving conditions to contend with. They *need* power —lots of it. And there are still others who want both economy *and* power.

Until recent years, all these people would probably have used the same engine, because most manufacturers offered little choice. And because that engine had to be a compromise, one driver often got more power than he could use, while another just as often got less than he needed.

Contrast this virtual absence of choice with what's available today! In the '62 line of Fords there are 50 different power teams (a power team is the combination of engine, transmission and rear axle). The choice ranges from the Falcon 85-horsepower Six with standard 3-speed column shift up to the Thunderbird 406 Super High-Performance 405-horsepower V-8 with 4-speed floor shift . . . and there are 48 variations in between!

"But," you may ask, "why should I worry about the transmission and axle ratio? Doesn't an engine produce all the power for my car?" You're right . . . up to a certain point. The engine *does* produce all the power, but it is not practical to build an internal combustion engine large enough to develop all the driving force you need for starting, accelerating, etc. It's the job of the transmission and the rear

axle to multiply the driving force to satisfy these requirements.

Certainly, in choosing a power team for your new car you will want to start by picking the engine. The right engine for you will be determined by many different factors, including the type of car you buy, the kind of use you will give it, the type of terrain you will drive it over, and what your own personal driving tastes happen to be. The chart below gives the basic specifications for each of the 12 different Ford engines for 1962.

Picking a transmission

Basically, there are two kinds of transmissions —manual and automatic—with variations on these. With manual, the driver must decide when to shift gears. With automatic, the transmission itself senses the need to change ratio and does so automatically, at just the right instant. Here's some information on the types of transmissions available in '62 Fords:

3-Speed Manual: Standard "straight stick" type. Good economy and excellent acceleration. Standard on all Fords except Thunderbirds.

Overdrive: 3-speed manual combined with an automatic 4th speed or "overdrive" gear that cuts in automatically when accelerator pedal is released at speeds above 27 miles per hour. Engine speed is reduced about 30%, resulting in substantial gas savings, quieter operation, longer engine life.

Fordomatic: Fully automatic, 2-speed geared transmission combined with a fluid torque converter. Provides quiet, smooth, efficient no-shift driving at low cost.

Cruise-O-Matic: Fully automatic, 3-speed geared transmission combined with a fluid torque converter. In normal driving, car always starts in low gear, shifts automatically to intermediate gear and then to high for smoothest starts, fastest acceleration and most efficient operation. For easy starting on ice or wet, slippery pavement, you can start in intermediate range.

4-Speed Manual: Floor-mounted shift lever. Offers more rapid acceleration because of an additional gear ratio. Engine speed can be maintained more closely to the maximum horsepower output of the engine because the gear ratios are more closely spaced.

4-speed manual transmission proved perfect partner for Thunderbird 406 High-Performance V-8's dazzling Daytona performance.

1962 FORD ENGINES

ENGINE	CU. IN. DISPL.	MAX. HP @ RPM	MAX. TORQUE @ RPM	BORE & STROKE (IN.)	COMP. RATIO	CARB. TYPE	FUEL REC'MD
FALCON							
Falcon Six‡....................	144	85 @ 4200	134 @ 2000	3.50 x 2.50	8.7:1	1-bbl.	Reg.
170 Special Six....................	170	101 @ 4400	156 @ 2400	3.50 x 2.94	8.7:1	1-bbl.	Reg.
FAIRLANE							
Fairlane Six‡....................	170	101 @ 4400	156 @ 2400	3.50 x 2.94	8.7:1	1-bbl.	Reg.
Challenger V-8....................	221	145 @ 4400	216 @ 2200	3.50 x 2.87	8.7:1	2-bbl.	Reg.
Challenger 260 V-8....................	260	164 @ 4400	258 @ 2200	3.80 x 2.87	8.7:1	2-bbl.	Reg.
GALAXIES & WAGONS							
Mileage Maker Six‡....................	223	138 @ 4200	203 @ 2200	3.62 x 3.60	8.4:1	1-bbl.	Reg.
Thunderbird 292 V-8....................	292	170 @ 4200	279 @ 2200	3.75 x 3.30	8.8:1	2-bbl.	Reg.
Thunderbird 352 Special V-8....................	352	220 @ 4300	336 @ 2600	4.00 x 3.50	8.9:1	2-bbl.	Reg.
Thunderbird 390 Special V-8....................	390	300 @ 4600	427 @ 2800	4.05 x 3.78	9.6:1	4-bbl.	Prem.
Thunderbird 406 High-Performance V-8‡‡....................	406	385 @ 5800	444 @ 3400	4.13 x 3.78	11.4:1	4-bbl.	Super Prem.
Thunderbird 406 Super High-Performance V-8‡‡....................	406	405 @ 5800	448 @ 3500	4.13 x 3.78	11.4:1	6-bbl.	Super Prem.
THUNDERBIRD							
Thunderbird 390 Special V-8‡....................	390	300 @ 4600	427 @ 2800	4.05 x 3.78	9.6:1	4-bbl.	Prem.
Thunderbird 390 Sports V-8....................	390	340 @ 5000	430 @ 3200	4.05 x 3.78	10.5:1	6-bbl.	Prem.

‡Denotes standard equipment; other engines are optional at extra cost
‡‡Available only on Galaxie and Galaxie/500 and only with optional 4-speed or Overdrive transmission

SPECIFICATIONS

The Ford Quality Control system, a Ford first, results in products of highest quality. All manufactured parts pass rigid dimensional, laboratory and durability tests. Quality Control teams also select samples from each shift at every assembly plant for an exhaustive search for any deviations from strict engineering specifications.

ENGINES: 138-hp *Mileage Maker Six* (standard)—223-cu. in. displ.; 3.62″ bore x 3.60″ stroke; 8.4 to 1 comp. ratio; regular fuel; single-venturi carburetor; manual choke; aluminized valves with mechanical automatic adjusters; precision-molded crankshaft with four main bearings; oil capacity, with filter change, 5 qt.; single exhaust.

170-hp Thunderbird 292 V-8 (optional)—292-cu. in. displ.; 3.75″ bore x 3.30″ stroke; 8.8 to 1 comp. ratio; regular fuel; 2-venturi carburetor; automatic choke; precision-molded crankshaft, copper-lead main (five) and con. rod bearings; oil capacity, with filter change, 6 qt.; Y-type single exhaust (dual on Sunliner).

220-hp Thunderbird 352 Special V-8 (optional)—352-cu. in. displ.; 4.00″ bore x 3.50″ stroke; 8.9 to 1 comp. ratio; regular fuel; 2-venturi carburetor; automatic choke; aluminized valves with hydraulic lifters for automatic valve adjustment; precision-molded crankshaft, copper-lead main (five) and con. rod bearings; oil capacity, with filter change, 6 qt.; Y-type single exhaust (dual on Sunliner).

300-hp Thunderbird 390 Special V-8 (optional)—390-cu. in. displ.; 4.05″ bore x 3.78″ stroke; 9.6 to 1 comp. ratio; premium fuel; 4-venturi carburetor; automatic choke; aluminized valves with hydraulic lifters for automatic valve adjustment; precision-molded crankshaft, copper-lead main (five) and con. rod bearings; oil capacity, with filter change, 6 qt.; dual exhausts. ***375-hp Thunderbird 390 High-Performance V-8*** with 10.6 to 1 and ***401-hp Thunderbird 390 Super High-Performance V-8*** with 11.1 to 1 comp. ratios also available for all models except wagons. For details, consult your Ford Dealer.

ENGINE FEATURES: For greater economy and longer life, Ford engines have Short Stroke, low-friction design; Deep-Block construction; Free-Turning overhead intake and exhaust valves; Super-Filter air cleaner with reusable element; high-capacity in-line 30,000-mile fuel filtering system; Rotunda Full-Flow disposable-type oil filter; Cross-Flow cooling system with separate top reserve tank and 180° Positive-Action thermostat; new 30,000-mile or 2-yr. permanent antifreeze; 12-volt electrical system; weatherproof ignition with Static-Ban constant resistance wiring and air-cooled distributor points; triple-seal 18-mm. Turbo-Action spark plugs; 66-plate, 55 amp-hr battery (78-plate, 65 amp-hr with Special V-8's and automatic transmissions); single muffler all-aluminized (dual mufflers of aluminized and stainless steel) with aluminized integral tailpipe(s) mounted at rear of frame. All V-8's electronically balanced for extra smoothness.

CLUTCH and MANUAL TRANSMISSIONS: Semi-centrifugal clutch with full-weighted levers for more positive engagement; suspended pedal. Face diameter —9½″ with Six, 10½″ with 292 V-8, 11″ with 352 Special and all 390 V-8's. **3-Speed** transmission has new clutch interlock in low and reverse; ratios (to 1): **Six**—1st 3.20, 2nd 1.85, direct 1.00, rev. 3.88; **292 V-8**—1st 2.78, 2nd 1.61, direct 1.00, rev. 3.38; **352 Special and all 390 V-8's**—1st 2.37, 2nd 1.51, direct 1.00, rev. 2.81. **4-Speed** transmission (optional) has floor-mounted "short stick," available with 352 Special and all 390 V-8's; ratios (to 1): 1st 2.36, 2nd 1.78, 3rd 1.41, direct 1.00, rev. 2.42. **Overdrive** (optional) is same as above 3-speed plus an automatic 4th gear that cuts in above 28 mph, cuts out below 21 mph (approx.). Downshift to direct by flooring accelerator. Lockout control on instrument panel. Tailored-to-engine ratios (to 1): **Six and 292 V-8**—1st 2.80, 2nd 1.69, direct 1.00, OD .70, rev. 3.80; **352 Special and all 390 V-8's**—1st 2.49, 2nd 1.59, direct 1.00, OD .72, rev. 3.15.

AUTOMATIC TRANSMISSIONS: Torque converter in combination with compound planetary gear set. Effective engine braking in "L" position. Liquid cooled. Selector lever on steering column, illuminated quadrant on instrument panel. **Fordomatic Drive** (optional with all engines except 390 V-8's) features simplified design, lightweight cast-aluminum construction, minimum servicing.

Two forward gear ratios, one reverse (to 1): low 1.75, direct 1.00, rev. 1.50; converter (stall) 2.6 with Six and 292 V-8, 2.5 with 352 Special V-8. In "D" range gives brisk, smooth starts in low. New vacuum control provides smoother shifting, minimum servicing. Selector sequence P-R-N-D-L. **Cruise-O-Matic Drive** (optional with all engines except Six and High-Performance V-8's) features lightweight construction with cast-aluminum converter housing. Two selective drive ranges: "Drive" (green dot) starting in low for all normal driving, or alternate drive position (white dot) starting in intermediate for more sure-footed driving on slippery surfaces. Three forward gear ratios, one reverse (to 1): low 2.40, intermediate 1.47, direct 1.00, rev. 2.00; converter (stall) 2.1. Vacuum control provides smooth, precise and permanently coordinated-with-engine shifting, minimum servicing. Selector sequence P-R-N-DRIVE-L.

REAR AXLE: Semi-floating type with deep-offset hypoid gears. Straddle-mounted drive pinion. **Torque-Tailored Axle Ratios (to 1): Conventional Drive —3-Speed Manual:** Wagons 3.89 with Six and 292 V-8, 3.56 with Special V-8's; Other Models: 3.56 with all engines; **4-Speed Manual:** 3.56 with 352 Special V-8 and all 390 V-8's. **Overdrive**—3.89 with Six or 292 V-8, 3.56 with 352 and all 390 V-8's. **Fordomatic Drive**—Wagons: 3.56 with Six and 292 V-8, 3.00 with 352 Special V-8; Other Models: 3.56 with Six, 3.00 with 292 V-8 and 352 Special V-8. **Cruise-O-Matic Drive**—Wagons: 3.56 with 292 V-8, 3.00 with Special V-8's; Other Models: 3.00 with 292 V-8 and Special V-8's. **Optional:** Heavy-duty axle for wagons with higher capacity wheel bearings, larger diameter shafts.

WIDE-CONTOURED FRAME: Strong box-section design with flexible inner channel, new more flexible front cross members and other refinements to reduce road harshness and vibration for safer, more luxurious ride. Sunliner has 4 cross members plus X-member, others have 5 cross members. Side rails extend *outside* passenger area, for better foot room and increased side protection. Silent-Grip body mounts.

FRONT SUSPENSION: Swept-Back, Angle-Poised Ball-Joint type with wide-base coil springs for softer ride, easier steering. With V-8 models and Six in wagons, front end has rubber-bushed ride stabilizer to control roll on turns. Internally mounted shock absorbers.

REAR SUSPENSION: Asymmetrical, variable-rate design with rear axle located well forward from center of springs for anti-dive and anti-squat on braking and acceleration. Extra-long, gentle-rate, leaf-type springs with wide spring base provide a soft, stable, levelized ride. Outboard mounted. Tension-type shackles. Diagonally mounted shock absorbers.

STEERING: Precision-control, low-friction recirculating-ball type steering gear with anti-friction bearings throughout plus high ratio for easier steering. Flexible coupling in steering shaft insulates steering wheel. Symmetrical linkage with nylon bearings in tie-rod and pitman arm pivots are packed with special 30,000-mile grease retained by full life seals. Over-all steering ratio 30 to 1; with power steering, 25 to 1. Turning diameter approx. 41 ft.

BRAKES: Self-adjusting hydraulic brakes of double-sealed, self-energizing design. Brakes adjust automatically when applied while car is moving backwards. Easy-operating suspended pedal. Dash-mounted master cylinder. Grooved 11-inch composite drums for maximum cooling. Total lining area is 234 sq. in. on wagons, 212 sq. in. on other models. Foot-operated parking brake with pull-out release knob on instrument panel. Optional Swift Sure power brakes have special low pedal and power reservoir tank.

TIRES: 4-ply, black, tubeless with Tyrex Rayon cord and Soft-Tread design. Safety-type rims. Wagons—8.00 x 14 on 6″ rims. Other Models—7.50 x 14 on 5½″ rims, except 8.00 x 14 tires on 5½″ rims with combination of Special V-8's with Cruise-O-Matic and air conditioning. White narrow band sidewall tires optional. For wagons optional 8.00 x 14 6-ply tires recommended with heavy-duty suspension and axle options for greater cargo-carrying capacity.

PRICES: All Power Assists, Optional Equipment and Accessories as well as some of the items illustrated or referred to as optional or available in this catalog are at extra cost. For the price of the model with the equipment you desire, see your Ford Dealer.

Comparative information in this catalog was obtained from authoritative sources, but is not guaranteed. The specifications contained herein were in effect at the time this catalog was approved for printing. Ford Division of Ford Motor Company reserves the right to discontinue models at any time, or change specifications or design without notice and without incurring obligation.

PRODUCTS OF MOTOR COMPANY

The 1962 Mercury was basically a carry-over of the 1961 model with the major changes only in the grille and the taillights. The taillights now protruded from the upper rear fender area. The grille now sported horizontal bars. Mid-year saw the introduction of the Monterey S-55. This sporty model featured bucket seats and console.

Engine availablity consisted of the 223 cid six (1-bbl) rated at 138 hp, the 292 cid V-8 (2-bbl) rated at 170 hp, the 352 cid V-8 (2-bbl) rated at 220 hp, the 390 cid V-8 (4-bbl) rated at 300 hp, the 390 cid V-8 (4-bbl) rated at 330 hp, the 406 cid V-8 (4-bbl) rated at 385 hp and the 406 cid V-8 (triple 2-bbl) rated at 405 hp. The transmissions offered were the 3-speed manual, the 3-speed manual with overdrive, the 4-speed manual, the 3-speed Merc-O-Matic automatic, the 3-speed Multi-drive Merc-O-Matic automatic.

Production amounted to 107,369 units, with the model breakdown as follows. Prices follow each model in ()'s: MONTEREY 4-d sedan 18,975 ($2,726),

2-dr sedan 5,117 (42,672), 2-dr hdt. 5,328 (2,733), 4-dr hdt. 2,691 ($2,920), 4-dr Commuter station wagon 8,389 ($2,920); MONTEREY CUSTOM 4-dr sedan 27,591 ($2,965), 2-dr hdt. 10,814 ($2,972), 4-dr hdt. sedan 8,932 ($3,037), 4-dr Colony Park Station Wagon 9,596 ($3,219), convertible 5,849 ($3,222); MONTEREY S-55 2-dr hdt. 2,772 ($3,488), convertible 1,315 ($3,738).

Sixteen exterior colors were offered with 27 two-tones available at extra cost. Interiors were available in black, red, blue, beige and turquoise in vinyl or vinyl and cloth.

The literature offered for 1962 consisted of the Monterey & Comet small color catalogue, and the Comet, Meteor and Monterey small color catalogue, the Monterey large color catalogue unrevised and revised, the Monterey S-55 color folder (see pages 52-53), the "Mercury Power" folder (see page 54), and the "1962 Car Buyers Guide!" booklet. Mercury was included in the full-line press kit.

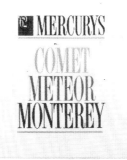

THE S Fifty Five

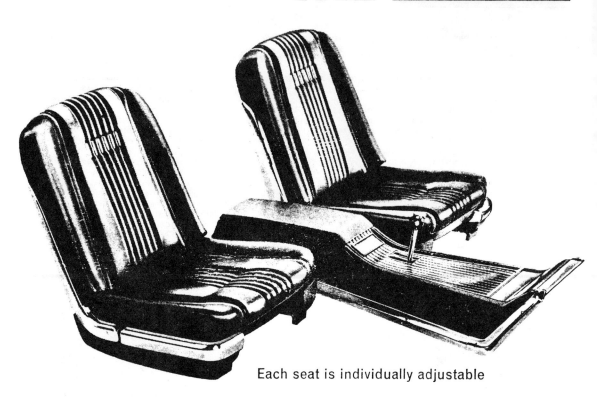

Each seat is individually adjustable

JOINS THE 1962 MERCURY BUCKET-SEAT SIZZLERS

Go Mercury for the best-looking **bucket-seat** buys . . . now in each size! Five luxury models, each with bucket seats, to suit every purse and personality . . . the compact Mercury Comet S-22, smartly ahead of the compact crowd . . . the compact Comet Villager, newest, most luxurious 6-passenger station wagon with optional front bucket seats . . . the new standard-size Mercury Meteor S-33, the beautiful balance between big cars and compacts . . . and, now, for the big-car man, the ultra-luxurious Mercury Monterey *S-Fifty-Five* in convertible or hardtop! See them—try them—and buy the one that suits you best!

Monterey 352 V-8   Monterey 390 V-8

Monterey 292 V-8—Standard V-8 for all 1962 Monterey and Monterey Custom models. The 292-cubic-inch engine is an efficient, thoroughly proved V-8 design with 2-barrel carburetor, mechanical valve lifters and automatic choke.

Monterey 352 V-8—A bigger-engine V-8 option for all Monterey and Monterey Custom models. The Monterey 352 V-8 has hydraulic valve lifters . . . uses regular gas. Costs only $51.50* extra.

Monterey 390 V-8—Puts Monterey right at the front of the high-performance class with 300 horsepower. The 4-barrel carburetor, hydraulic valve lifters, and Mercury's low-maintenance features combine for high performance at moderate cost. The big-displacement Monterey 390 V-8 is available with Multi-Drive Merc-O-Matic or 4-speed manual transmission. Cost for this high-performance engine is only $137.60* more than the standard Monterey 292 V-8.

*Manufacturer's suggested retail prices.

1962 MONTEREY ENGINES

	Monterey 292 V-8	Monterey 352 V-8	Monterey 390 V-8
Displacement	292 cu. in.	352 cu. in.	390 cu. in.
Bore & stroke	3.75" x 3.30"	4.00" x 3.50"	4.05" x 3.78"
Adv. power rating @ rpm	170 hp @ 4200 rpm	220 hp @ 4300 rpm	300 hp @ 4600 rpm
Adv. torque rating @ rpm	279 lb-ft @ 2200 rpm	336 lb-ft @ 2600 rpm	427 lb-ft @ 2800 rpm
Carburetor	2 bbl.	2 bbl.	4 bbl.
Compression ratio	8.8 to 1	8.9 to 1	9.6 to 1
Fuel	Regular	Regular	Premium
Transmissions			
3-speed manual	X	X	
4-speed manual		X	X
Merc-O-Matic	X	X	
Multi-Drive Merc-O-Matic	X	X	X

"Total Performance" became the keynote for 1963 with an increase in engine options to give more go to the pack. The biggest news was the addition of the '63½ Sports Hardtop. This sleek fastback hardtop was enthusiastically accepted. New in the mechanical field was the fully sychronized 3-speed manual transmission. Additional features were the optional T-Bird type swingaway steering column, the simulated wire wheel covers, and the AM-FM radio.

Engines offered were the 223 cid six (1-bbl) rated at 138 hp, the 260 cid V-8 (2-bbl) rated 164 hp, the 289 cid V-8 (2-bbl) rated at 195 hp, the 352 cid V-8 (2-bbl) rated at 220 hp, the 390 cid V-8 (4-bbl) rated at 300 hp, the 406 cid V-8 (4-bbl) rated at 385 hp and the 406 cid V-8 (triple 2-bbl) rated at 405 hp. Both 406's were early in the production. Later in the year production was the 427 cid V8 (dual 4-bbl) rated at 425 hp. Transmissions offered were the 3-speed manual, the 3-speed manual with overdrive, the 4-speed manual, the 2-speed Fordomatic automatic.

Production amounted to 844,534 units, with the following model breakdowns (sixes and V-8's totals combined). Prices follow each model in ()'s with V-8's costing $109 more: FORD 300 2-dr sedan 44,124 ($2,378); 2-dr sedan 26,010 ($2,324); GALAXIE dr sedan 82,419 ($2,507), 2-dr sedan 30,335 ($2,453); GALAXIE 500 4-dr Town Sedan 205,722 ($2,667), 2-dr Club Sedan, 21,137 ($2,613), 4-dr Club Victoria 26,558 ($2,739), 2-dr Club Victoria 49,733 ($2,674), Sports hardtop 100,500 ($2,674), Sunliner convertible 36,867 ($3,033 V-8 only); GALAXIE 500XL (V-8 only) 4-dr Town Victoria 12,596 ($3,333), 2-dr Club Victoria 29,713 ($3,628), Sports hardtop 33,870 ($3,268), Sunliner convertible 18,551 ($3,518); STATION WAGONS Country Sedan, 6-pass. 64,954 ($2,938), 9-pass. 22,250 ($3,042), Country Squire, 6-pass. 19.922 ($3,127), 9-pass. 19,246 ($3,197).

Thirteen exterior colors were offered with two-tones optional at extra cost. Interiors were offered in blue, turquoise, beige, gold, chestnut, red or black in vinyl and cloth or all vinyl on bench seats.

Literature offered for 1963 consisted of the full-line color catalogue dated 8-62 and revised 12-62 and 2-63 (see pages 56-59), the Galaxie color catalogue dated 8-62 and revised 12-62 (see pages 56-59), the "Preview: 1963" color mailer catalogue, the "you've never driven...." color mailer catalogue, the "'63s from Ford" color mailer catalogue, the "Why we called the Police on the carpet" color mailer catalogue, the color selector, the "Total Performance, 1903-1963" catalogue (see pages 69-78), "The story of Ford's Total Performance!" B&W folder, the "1963 Ford facts, figures for high performance, booklet (see pages 60-64), the Buyers Digest, the "From the Raceway.." booklet dealer item (see pages 65-68), the "Ford high performance parts and accessories" folder dealer item, the "Ford engines... Total performance with a purpose" booklet, dealer item), the colors selector folder, and the "Buyer's Digest" booklet, filled with facts and figures. Galaxies were also included in the full-line press kit.

1963 SUPER TORQUE FORD

1963 FORD GALAXIE
GALAXIES · GALAXIE 500'S · GALAXIE 500-XL'S · GALAXIE WAGONS

From the Raceway...

TOTAL PERFORMANCE
1903-1963

TOTAL PERFORMANCE!

GALAXIE 500/XL HARDTOPS

XL stands for "extra lively." Lively in looks, XL hardtops (either the much-talked-about 2-door or the brand-new 4-door) have all the verve of limited-edition foreign offerings that sell for thousands more. Such lively luxuries as leathery vinyl trim, bucket front seats, Thunderbird-inspired command console with either stick shift Fordomatic (std.), Cruise-O-Matic (opt.) or 4-speed manual (opt.). Turn the key and you can have action as lively as you like with the 164-hp Galaxie V-8 (std.), or Thunderbird V-8 options of 220 hp, 300 hp, 385 hp or the big 6-barrel bravo with 405 hp! Try the extra lively going of an XL hardtop with a lusty Thunderbird V-8 just once and you'll never be fully satisfied with anything else.

Galaxie 500/XL Hardtop Standard Equipment

Includes all luxury features listed for Galaxies and Galaxie 500's, pages 4 & 6 plus the following unique 500/XL items:

Choice of All-Vinyl Interiors in Rose Beige, Blue, Black, Red, Turquoise, Chestnut, and Gold

Choice of 13 Diamond Lustre Enamel Exterior Colors

Front Bucket Seats, 100% Foam-Cushioned, Individually Adjustable

Full-Length Command Console

"Bucket-Styled" Rear Seat, Individually Contoured, 100% Foam-Cushioned

Seats, Door and Side Panels Feature Chrome-Mylar Highlights

Color-Keyed, Wall-to-Wall Carpeting

Color-Keyed Instrument Panel with Full-Chromed Controls

Super-Deluxe Arm Rests and Ash Trays, Front and Rear

Bright-Metal Seat Side Shields and Door Lock Buttons

Distinctive Galaxie 500/XL Body Trim

Bright-Metal-Accented Accelerator and Brake Pedals

Automatic Courtesy-Safety Lights in Both Lower Door Panels

Galaxie V-8 164-hp Engine

Two-Speed Fordomatic Drive with Console-Mounted "Sports Stick"

Full Wheel Covers with Simulated "Knock Off" Spinners

Popular Options and Accessories

Choice of Four Thunderbird V-8's from 220 to 405 hp

Dual-Range Cruise-O-Matic Drive with Console-Mounted "Sports Stick" (for all except 406 V-8's)

4-Speed Manual Transmission with Console-Mounted "Sports Stick" (except 260 V-8; required with 406 V-8's)

Choice of 21 Two Tone Paint Combinations

Swing-Away Steering Wheel (in combination with power steering and automatic transmission)

Power Steering—Power Driver's Seat—Power Brakes

SelectAire Conditioner

Tinted Glass—Power Windows

Padded Instrument Panel and Sun Visors—Seat Belts

AM-FM All-Transistor, Push Button Radio —Rear Seat Speakers

Tachometer (0- 8,000 rpm)

Power Pipes (muffler bypass)

See pages 24-27 for Options, Accessories and Power Teams

Basic Specifications

Over-all Length 209.9"
Over-all Width 80.0"
Over-all Height 55.5"
Wheelbase 119.0"
Curb Weight (approx.) 3773 lb.
Trunk Volume 29.9 cu. ft.

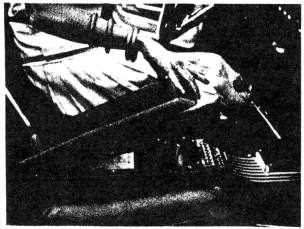

XL Hardtop Interior (above). Who could resist being carried away by this one? The bucket seats are deep foam-cushioned to cradle you in comfort. (Rear seat is "bucket-styled," equally luxurious and comfortable.) Sculptured chrome seat side shields, mylar highlights in seats and side panels, unique carpet-trimmed doors are a few of XL's elegant touches. Another is the XL command console (shown close-up at left). "Action end" up forward is for short-shift sports stick. At rear is a spacious storage compartment for maps, sunglasses, or camera.

GALAXIE 500/XL CONVERTIBLE

XL stands for "extra luxury." Wherever appreciators of the finer things gather and the talk turns to cars, you're sure to hear about the XL Convertible. Here's where Ford stylists, who have created a gorgeous convertible in the Galaxie 500, have even outdone themselves! Add to Galaxie's glamour a dash of sports car spirit—front bucket seats, deeppleated and foam-cushioned . . . full-length command console in between with short-shift "sports stick" . . . bucket-tailored 3-passenger rear seat—ruddy vinyls sparkling with mylar all around. To tailor XL Convertible performance to your preference, take your pick from eight Galaxie power teams. For convertible fanciers, an XL is the *piece de résistance.* And, if you're not already a convertible fancier, an XL can make you one—fast!

Galaxie 500/XL Convertible Standard Equipment

Includes all luxury items listed for Galaxies and Galaxie 500's, pages 4 and 6 plus the following unique 500/XL items:

Choice of Pleated All-Vinyl Interiors in Blue, Turquoise, Chestnut, Gold, Red, Black, and Rose Beige

Choice of 13 Diamond Lustre Enamel Exterior Colors

Front Bucket Seats, 100% Foam-Cushioned, Individually Adjustable

Full-Length Command Console

"Bucket-Styled" Rear Seat, Individually Contoured, 100% Foam-Cushioned

Vinyl 3-Ply Top in Choice of Black, White or Blue

Color-Keyed, Contour-Padded Top Boot with Concealed Fasteners

Seats, Doors and Side Trim Panels Accented with Chrome-Like Mylar

Color-Keyed, Wall-to-Wall Carpeting

Automatic Courtesy-Safety Lights in Both Lower Door Panels

Galaxie V-8 164-hp Engine

Two-Speed Fordomatic Drive with Console-Mounted "Sports Stick"

Full Wheel Covers with Simulated "Knock Off" Spinners

Popular Options and Accessories

Choice of Four Thunderbird V-8's from 220 to 405 hp

Dual-Range Cruise-O-Matic Drive with Console-Mounted "Sports Stick" (for all except 406 V-8's)

4-Speed Manual Transmission with Console-Mounted "Sports Stick" (except 260 V-8; required with 406 V-8's)

Swing-Away Steering Wheel (in combination with power steering and automatic transmission)

Power Steering—Power Driver's Seat— Power Brakes

Tinted Glass—Power Windows

Padded Instrument Panel and Sun Visors—Seat Belts

AM-FM All-Transistor, Push Button Radio —Rear Mount Antenna

Tachometer (0-8,000 rpm)

Power Pipes (muffler bypass)

See pages 24-27 for Options, Accessories and Power Teams

Basic Specifications

Over-all Length 209.9"
Over-all Width 80.0"
Over-all Height 54.5"
Wheelbase 119.0"
Curb Weight (approx.) 3924 lb.
Trunk Volume 27.4 cu. ft.

GALAXIE POWER TEAM

This year those who know their performance are going for Galaxie because Galaxie has the *going* spirit in every one of its 19 power teams! You get livelier response to the throttle . . . a smooth surge of power in every speed range. In Thunderbird V-8's, Galaxie V-8 or Six, you get more GO from every gallon—more wheel-turning power from every drop of fuel! And in half of Galaxie's new engines the fuel is familiar, low-price regular!

Akton Olson Miller was chosen as Ford's Performance Advisor because of his distinguished career in the performance field.

Ak is a co-founder of the oldest hot rod club in America—The Road Runners founded in 1937. Also he was instrumental in the establishment of the Southern California Timing Association. This organization, with Ak as president, staged the first hot rod show in America. This show was held in Los Angeles Armory in 1948. He also initiated the first annual Bonneville Speed Trial in 1948.

Ak was also a founder of the National Hot Rod Association, and is currently serving as a Vice President.

Ak has participated in almost every type of performance driving from the Pikes Peak Hill Climb, the Bonneville Speed Trials, and the Mexican Road Race to the Mobil Economy Run.

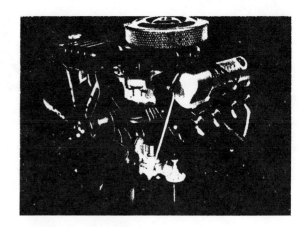

THE FORD
HIGH PERFORMANCE
ENGINE STORY

The current series of Ford high performance engines, the 406 and 427 cubic inch models had their beginning in 1958 when Ford introduced a new line of engines starting with a 332 cubic inch version.

This engine was designed to enable Ford engineers to obtain more displacement than was feasible with the earlier models. It was improved in subsequent years and in 1960 a 352 cubic inch version was introduced, which was the first high performance engine to be offered by Ford Motor Company. It developed 360 horsepower at 6000 rpm.

In 1961 the engine was enlarged to 390 cubic inches and the horsepower increased to 401.

In 1962 the displacement was increased to 406 cubic inches and the engine delivered 405 horsepower.

In 1963 Ford is offering the latest of the current series; the displacement is now 427 cubic inches and the engine develops 425 horsepower at 6000 rpm.

All of this was accomplished by using the same basic block as far as overall dimensions and exterior looks are concerned. However, the story goes much deeper.*

It is generally possible to increase the performance of any given engine by raising the compression ratio to extreme limits, installing cam shafts with wild timing and putting on larger manifolds and carburetion. However, Ford engineers had an additional requirement in mind when they began the development of the 427 and that was reliability compatible with high performance.

Because Ford Motor Company's reputation had to

ride with this high performance engine many thousands of hours were spent developing and testing high performance components that would not only deliver horsepower in the ratio of one hp per one cubic inch, but would also allow the engine to be driven at high sustained speeds for long periods.

To achieve this reliability, special cylinder blocks were made with larger main bearing webbings. Special attention was given to oil supply, oil pressure and oil control areas. Details such as inspection for casting flaws, balancing, etc. were all given high priority. The end result is an engine that has established a strong reputation for reliability and performance but also provides the buyer with a power plant that idles at a moderate speed and has excellent oil control. These facts make the Ford high performance series the best value on the market.

Not only has this engine proven itself in dynamometer testing in Ford's laboratories, but it has proven itself in speed events throughout the nation. Since their introduction in 1960, Ford engines have played a prominent role wherever high performance events have been staged. Their inherent reliability plus high performance has established them as a top contender in these events. We feel our record is one that speaks well for the current series of high performance engines.

We invite you to try the new 1963 high performance Ford and once again capture that lively Ford feeling.

*Each new version of the Ford high performance engine incorporated modifications and improvements in such vital areas as carburetion, lubrication, exhaust manifolding and basic engine durability.

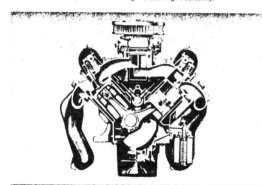

FORD 427 CUBIC INCH HIGH PERFORMANCE ENGINE

FORD HIGH PERFORMANCE ENGINE SPECIFICATIONS

DESCRIPTION	Part No.	
	406	**427**
Bore	4.13 in.	4.23 in.
Stroke	3.78 in.	3.78 in.
Firing order:	1-5-4-2-6-3-7-8 4-V	1-5-4-2-6-3-7-8 4-V
Maximum B.H.P.	385 @ 5800 RPM 6-V 405 @ 5800 RPM 4-V	410 @ 5600 RPM 8-V 425 @ 6000 RPM 4-V
Maximum Torque	444 @ 3400 RPM 6-V 448 @ 3500 RPM	476 @ 3400 RPM 8-V 480 @ 3700 RPM
Compression Ratio:	Nominal 10.9:1 Maximum 11.4:1	Nominal 10.9:1 Maximum 11.5:1
Camshaft, Part No. C2AE-6250-A		
Intake opens	24°BTC	8° 30' ATC*
Intake closes	72°ABC	36° 30' ABC*
Exhaust opens	72°BBC	11° 30' BBC*
Exhaust closes	24°ATC	39° 30' BTC*
Valve overlap	48°	96°
Contact point settings	.019—.021 (dwell angle 33 to 35)	.018—.022 (dwell angle 33 to 35)
Spark Plug Recommendations	Autolite BF32, BF22, BTF1	Autolite BF32, BF22, BTF1
Spark Plug Gap	Street Use: .032 Racing: .025	Street Use .032 Racing: .025
Crank Compression	160 to 200 psi sea level	
Ignition Timing	8°	8°
Valve lash	.025-.028 Hot	.025-.028 Hot
Fuel Pump Pressure	5 to 6 lbs. at 1800 RPM (No Load)	5 to 6 lbs. at 1800 RPM (No Load)
RPM Red Line	6200 RPM	6200 RPM
Carburetor Jets	6-V 2 End 66 Power .038	8-V—Primary 62 Fixed Power .040
Recommended for Quarter Mile	Center 62 2 End 64 Power .042	N/A AT TIME OF PRINTING
Valve Spring Pressure (replace below 70)	80 to 90 lbs. at 1.820 length	80 to 90 lbs. at 1.820 length
Valve Spring compressed to 1.320	255 to 280 lbs.	255 to 280 lbs.

*Figures based on 8-V engine

FORD PERFORMANCE RECORDS FOR 1962-1963

Ford engines are used in a variety of speed contests. The following are some examples of races which Ford has won, all requiring the utmost in reliability and performance:

1962 NASCAR

Darlington Rebel 300—Ford 1, 2 and 3
Charlotte World 600—Ford 1, 3 and 5
Atlanta 500—Ford 1st
Darlington Southern 500—Ford 1 and 3
4-15-62—Wilkesboro, N.C.—Ford—Second
5-12-62—Darlington 500—Ford—First, Second, Third, Sixth
5-27-62—Charlotte 600—Ford—First, Third and Fifth
6-10-62—Atlanta 328—Ford—First
7-4-62—Daytona 500—Ford—Third

7-29-62—Bristol, Tenn.—Ford—Second
9-3-62—Darlington 500—Ford—First, Third and Seventh
9-9-62—Atlanta Rural 150—(Richmond, Va.)—Ford—Third
9-13-62—Augusta, Ga. 100—Ford—First
9-23-62—Martinsville, Va. 250—Ford—First
9-30-62—Wilkesboro, N. C.—Ford—Second
10-14-62—Charlotte, N. C.—Ford—Third

1963 NASCAR

1-20-63 Riverside 500—Ford—First

1962 USAC

During the 1962 season Ford won 10 of the 22 USAC late model stock car races.
USAC awarded the Ford Division of FoMoCo a Manufacturers Award for winning ten out of twenty-two major stock car races.

1962 MARC

MARC awarded the Ford Division of FoMoCo its Manufacturers Championship Trophy for winning twenty-two out of thirty-five stock car races.

Presented here are some of the fastest times posted by winning Fords:
Les Ritchey—San Gabriel, Calif., Class AFX—12:00 e.t.—116.73
Gas Rhonda—Lodi, Calif.,—Class AFX—12:25 e.t.—114.80
Dick Brannan—Indianapolis Dragway—Class AFX—12:40 e.t.—115.65

Phil Bonner—Covington, Ga.—'62 Class AFX—Top Speed 123.90—Nov. '62
Phil Bonner—Dallas, Ga.—'62 Class AFX—e.t. 11:80—Jan. '63
Bob Tasca—Providence R.I.—Northeastern Champion NHRA Classes SSS, AFX, and Street Eliminator—July 1962

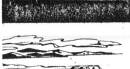

October 1962—a Ford Galaxie experimental 483 cubic inch engine broke 46 national and international speed records—driven by Fred Lorenzen,

Don White and Ralph Moody—average speed for 500 miles—163.85 (10 mile circular track). Best speed obtained 176.978—two-way average: 172.26.

MONTE CARLO RALLYE

Falcon Sprints finished first and second in Class 8 (3000 CC and over) in the 1963 Monte Carlo Rallye.

PIKES PEAK HILL CLIMB —JULY 4, 1962

Stock Division—1962 Ford—Curtis Turner—1st—14.55.5
Stock Division—1962 Ford—Parnelli Jones—3rd—15.02.5
Unlimited Sports Division—Devin/Ford Special—1st Ak Miller—14.29.3

500 Mile Marathon—Salton Sea, California—November 1962. Mike Wallace, first place in a Rayson Craft powered by a 406 Ford—competed against 65 craft powered by all types of engines from outboards to Allison aircraft.

Orange Bowl Regatta—Florida—December 27, 1962—Mike Wallace, first place—9 hour marathon.
Jr. Brummett—established world's records for 1, 2 and 3 hr. closed course—December 27, 1962.

Florida to New York Record Run—Blue Moppie (Bertram Hull, powered by two 406 Fords).
Around Nassau Sweepstakes—(Forest Johnson Hull) powered by 3 Ford 406's—1st place.

All of the above performances were registered with stock Ford high performance engines.

OPTIONAL ITEMS FOR THE QUARTER MILE

For Ford owners preparing their cars for optimum quarter mile performance, we recommend the following optional equipment available through your local Ford dealer:

DESCRIPTION	Part No.	
	406	427
5.83 Gear Set	C1AW-4209-E	
5.67 Gear Set	WAB-4209-C	
5.43 Gear Set	WAB-4209-D	
5.14 Gear Set	WAB-4209-E	
4.86 Gear Set	WAB-4209-F	
4.71 Gear Set	WAB-4209-G	
4.57 Gear Set	WAB-4209-H	
4.29 Gear Set	WAB-4209-J	
3.40 Gear Set	WAB-4209-K	
Tappet, Barrel Type	B9TE-6500-A	
Push Rod	B8A-6565-C	
Fan Spacer*	C2AZ-8546-A	
Fan Blade (5 blade)	C2AZ-8600-A	
Fan Blade Assembly, 4 blades 18.5 dia.	B9MM-8600-E	
Fan Blade Assembly, 4 blades 14.0 dia.	C1AA-8600-E	
Fan Drive (Clutch)	C2AZ-8A616-A	
Gasket—Intake Manifold to Cylinder Head	B9JE-9441-B	
Spacer—Exhaust Manifold	C0AE-9A35-B	
Shock Absorbers—Rear	C1AZ-18097-A	
Rear Axle Lubricant	C2AZ-19580-D	
*Used with C2AZ-8A616-A (only)		
Rotunda Tachometers (6 cyl. eng.)	C2RZ-17A326-B	
(8 cyl. eng.)	C2RZ-17A326-C	
Locking Differential	C2AZ-4880-A	

(427 column): PART NUMBERS NOT AVAILABLE AT TIME OF PRINTING. ALL PARTS AVAILABLE FEB. 15, 1963

LIGHTWEIGHT VEHICLE COMPONENTS

For 1963 Ford is offering a special lightweight vehicle designed for maximum performance in quarter mile events. The car is available as a fastback tudor hardtop model and includes the following special equipment:

- 427 cubic inch high performance engine (425 HP) with aluminum flywheel housing
- 4 speed manual transmission with aluminum case
- 4:11 to 1 rear axle
- Heavy duty suspension and brakes
- 6.70 x 15 4 ply nylon tires
- Aluminum bumpers and bumper brackets
- Lightweight frame
- Fiberglass hood
- Fiberglass front fenders
- Fiberglass doors
- Fiberglass deck lid
- Lightweight floor mats
- Lightweight bucket seats

This vehicle may be purchased through your local Ford dealer by submitting an order for D.S.O. vehicle number AS-225-39D.

In order to obtain maximum performance in quarter mile events we suggest that you add spring clips on the rear springs and add shims to the rear axle pinion nose bumper. In addition your vehicle should be equipped with Ford extra heavy duty shock absorbers (C1AZ-18077-A and C1AZ-18097-A).

OPTIONAL ITEMS FOR SUSTAINED HIGH SPEED

For Ford Owners preparing their cars for sustained high speed usage, we recommend the following optional equipment designed for the harsh punishment this type of usage demands:

DESCRIPTION	Part No.	
	406	427
Oil Seal—Rear Wheel Bearing Inner	C1AA-1177-A	
Spindle R.H.	C0AZ-3102-A	
Spindle L.H.	C0AZ-3103-A	
Rod Assy.—Spindle Arm	C0AA-3280-C	
End—Spindle Arm	C1AA-3289-D	
Rod Assy.—Idler Arm	C0AA-3304-C	
Sleeve Assy.—Drag Link	AG-3310-A	
Brkt.—Idler Arm Mtg.	C0AA-3351-A	
Arm—Idler	C0AA-3355-A	
Bushing—Idler	LF-3357-A	
Arm—Pitman	C0AA-3590-D	
Shaft—Rear Axle R.H.	C0AW-4234-D	
Shaft—Rear Axle L.H.	C0AZ-4235-C	
750 lb./in. Front Spring	AJ-5310-N	
900 lb./in. Front Spring	AJ-5310-R	
1200 lb./in. Front Spring	C2AZ-5310-A	
Stabilizer Bar	C1AA-5482-A	
Insulator	C0AA-5493-A	
Oil Pan—Extra Cooling (7 qt.)	C0AE-6675-F	
Indicator Assy.—Oil level	C0AE-6750-C	
Gasket—Intake Manifold	B9JE-9441-B	
Spacer—Exhaust Manifold	C0AE-9A-435-B	
Fan Blade Assy.	C1AA-8600-E	
Oil Cooler	C1AZ-6A642-A	
Rotunda Tachometer (6 cyl. eng.)	C2RZ-17A326-B	
Rotunda Tachometer (8 cyl. eng.)	C2RZ-17A326-C	
Locking Differential	C2AZ-4880-A	
Transistor Ignition		

(427 column): PART NUMBERS NOT AVAILABLE AT TIME OF PRINTING. ALL PARTS AVAILABLE FEB. 15, 1963

PARTS LIST

The following is a list of the most common parts used when servicing 406 or 427 Ford high performance engines. Most items are interchangeable for all Ford engines from the 332 to the 427 cubic inch units.

DESCRIPTION	Part No. 406	Part No. 427
ENGINE ASSEMBLY COMPLETE	**406**	**427**
Engine Assy.—4V without Emission Reduction (350-A)	C2AE-6007-E	C3AE-6007-H
Engine Assy.—4V with Emission Reduction (E-350-A)	C2AL-6007-E	Standard
Engine Assy.—6V without Emission Reduction (351-A)	C2AE-6007-E	
Engine Assy.—6V with Emission Reduction (E-351-A)	C2AE-6007-E	Standard
ENGINE ASSEMBLY—CYLINDER BLOCK AND CRANKSHAFT	C2AZ-6009-B	C3AZ-6009-K
CYLINDER BLOCK	C2AZ-6010-A	C3AZ-6010-AK
CYLINDER HEAD ASSEMBLY	C2AZ-6049-A	C3AZ-6049-J
Gasket—Cylinder Head	C2AZ-6051-A	C3AZ-6051-B
Bolt—Cylinder Head—Long	C1AE-6065-A	C1AE-6065-A
Bolt—Cylinder Head—Short	C1AE-6065-C	C1AE-6065-C
VALVE TRAIN ASSEMBLY		
Camshaft	C2AE-6250-A	C3AZ-6250-D2
Sprocket—Camshaft	B8A-6256-A	C3AZ-6256-A
Timing Chain	B8A-6268-A	B8A-6268-A
Tappet	B9TE-6500-A3	B9TE-6500-A3
Push Rod	B8A-6565-C	B8A-6565-C
Rocker Arm Assembly	B8A-6564-B	B8A-6564-B
Rocker Arm Shaft	B8A-6563-A	B8A-6563-A
Rocker Arm Locating Spring	B8A-6587-A	B8A-6563-B
Rocker Arm Support Shaft	C2AZ-6531-A	C3AZ-6531-A
Valve Spring and Damper Assembly	C2AZ-6513-A	C3AZ-6513-A
Spring Retainer	C2AZ-6514-A	C3AZ-6514-A
Spring Retainer Key	B8A-6518-A	B8A-6518-A
Valve Spring Oil Baffle	C1SE-6524-A	C1SE-6524-A
Intake Valve Stem Seal	B8A-6571-B	B8A-6571-B
Exhaust Valve Stem Seal	C2AZ-6571-A	
Valve—Exhaust Std.	C2AZ-6505-A	C3AZ-6505-E
Valve—Exhaust .015 O.S.	C2AZ-6505-C	C3AZ-6505-G
Valve—Exhaust .030 O.S.	C2AZ-6505-D	C3AZ-6505-H
Valve—Intake Std.	C0AE-6507-N	C3AZ-6507-E
Valve—Intake .015 O.S.	C0AE-6507-R	C3AZ-6507-G
Valve—Intake .030 O.S.		C3AZ-6507-H
CRANKSHAFT ASSEMBLY		
Crankshaft	C2AZ-6303-B	C3AZ-6303-G
Sprocket—Crankshaft	B8A-6306-A	B8A-6306-A
Slinger—Crankshaft Oil	B8A-6310-A	B8A-6310-A
Damper Assy.—Crankshaft Vibration	C1AZ-6312-A	C2AZ-6312-B
Flywheel Assy.	B8A-6375-A	C3AZ-6375-G
INTAKE MANIFOLD ASSEMBLY—6V	C1AE-9424-E	
Carburetor Assy. (Primary)	C1AE-9510-AV	
Carburetor Assy. (2 req'd) (Sec'n'dy)	C1AE-9510-AU	
Fuel Pump Assembly	C0AE-9350-E	
INTAKE MANIFOLD ASSEMBLY—4V	C1AE-9424-C	C3AZ-9427-J
Carburetor Assy. (Holley 4V)	C1AE-9510-AM	C3AZ-9510-B
Fuel Pump Assy.		C3AE-9350-L
EXHAUST MANIFOLD		
Manifold Assy.—Exhaust R.H.	C2AZ-9430-C	C3AZ-9430-C
Manifold Assy.—Exhaust L.H.	C2AZ-9431-C	C3AZ-9431-F
DISTRIBUTOR ASSEMBLY	C0AF-12127-K	C0AF-12127-K
Ignition Coil (12V)	B6A-12029-B	B6A-12029-B
ENGINE BEARINGS		
Bearing—Connecting Rod—.020 U.S.	C1AE-6211-M	C1AE-6211-M
Bearing—Connecting Rod—.030 U.S.	C1AE-6211-N	C1AE-6211-N
Bearing—Connecting Rod—Red		C1AE-6211-H
Bearing—Connecting Rod—Blue		C1AE-6211-J
Bearing—Connecting Rod—.002 U.S.	C1AE-6211-K	C1AE-6211-K
Bearing—Connecting Rod—.010 U.S.	C1AE-6211-L	C1AE-6211-L
Bearing—Camshaft Front	B8A-6261-AA	C3AZ-6261-A
Bearing—Camshaft Center	B8A-6262-AA	B8A-6262-AA
Bearing—Camshaft Rear	B8A-6263-AA	B8A-6263-AA
Bearing—Camshaft Front Intermed.	B8A-6267-AA	B8A-6267-AA
Bearing—Rear Intermediate	B8A-6270-AA	B8A-6270-AA
Bearing—Crankshaft Main Front—Red	C1AE-6333-A	C1AE-6333-A
Bearing—Crankshaft Main Front—Blue	C1AE-6333-B	C1AE-6333-B

DESCRIPTION	Part No. 406	Part No. 427
	406	**427**
Bearing—Crankshaft Main Front—.002 U.S.	C1AE-6333-C	C1AE-6333-C
Bearing—Crankshaft Main Front—.010 U.S.	C1AE-6333-D	C1AE-6333-D
Bearing—Crankshaft Main Front—.020 U.S.	C1AE-6333-E	C1AE-6333-E
Bearing—Crankshaft Main Front—.030 U.S.	C1AE-6333-F	C1AE-6333-F
Seal—Crankshaft Rear Main Bearing Cap	C1AE-6336-B	To be available
Bearing—Crankshaft Center—Red	C1AE-6337-A	C1AE-6337-A
Bearing—Crankshaft Center—Blue	C1AE-6337-B	C1AE-6337-A
Bearing—Crankshaft Center—.002 U.S.	C1AE-6337-C	C1AE-6337-C
Bearing—Crankshaft Center—.010 U.S.	C1AE-6337-D	C1AE-6337-D
Bearing—Crankshaft Center—.020 U.S.	C1AE-6337-E	C1AE-6337-E
Bearing—Crankshaft Center—.030 U.S.	C1AE-6357-F	C1AE-6357-F
OIL PUMP ASSEMBLY	C1AE-6600-C	C3AZ-6600-A
Pan Assy.—Oil (7 qt.)	C0AE-6675-F	C3AE-6675-A
Pan Assy.—Oil (6 qt.)	C1AE-6675-F	C1AE-6675-F
FLYWHEEL ASSEMBLY		
Plate & Cover Assy.—Clutch Pressure	C1AZ-7563-C	To be available
Disc Assy.—Clutch	C0AA-7550-B	To be available
Flywheel		C3AZ-6375-G
TRANSMISSION ASSEMBLY 4-speed	C2AZ-7003-F	To be available
4-Speed Shift Kit		
3-Speed Floor Shift Conversion Kit	C2AZ-7A082-A	

IN ORDER TO PROVIDE...

427 buyers with a durable high performance vehicle, every Ford equipped with the 427 engine includes a number of special chassis items to take the extra stresses and improved handling to match the horsepower. These components include:

- High capacity clutch
- Heavy-duty transmission
- Larger drive shaft and heavy-duty U-joints
- Heavy-duty rear axle assembly with 4-pinion differential
- Heavy-duty springs and shock absorbers
- 15 inch wheels and nylon tires for more cornering power and better brake cooling
- Wider front brake drums with maximum fade resistant linings

Your high performance Ford is engineered and built to exacting specifications. To attain maximum performance at all times it is your obligation to make sure that your vehicle meets the specification data outlined in this booklet. This, when coupled with your observance of rev limits (red line—6200 rpm) and the recommended lubrication intervals will assure you of thousands of miles of reliable performance from your Ford product.

When making changes such as gear ratios, always follow Ford's recommendations as to proper break-in of gears, proper lubrication (C2AZ-19580-D0), and be sure to steam clean the differential housing every time gear changes are made so as to remove impurities.

For additional information regarding Ford high performance engines and equipment contact your local Ford dealer or write to Ak Miller, Ford Performance Advisor, P.O. Box 627, Dearborn, Michigan.

To the Driveway...

its FORD all the way!

Ford consistently leads Plymouth and Chevrolet over the finish line in open competition.

● JANUARY 20: Riverside, California. Ford wins at Riverside and puts 10 cars over the finish line!

● JANUARY 23: At the Monte Carlo Rallye Falcon V-8 Sprints placed 1st and 2nd in their class . . . no other cars finished.

● JANUARY 27: Ford, over-all winner in economy, acceleration and braking in Class I and Class II in the Pure Oil Performance Trials.

● FEBRUARY 24: Fords proved their ruggedness, endurance and safety—by the numbers 1-2-3-4 and 5 at Daytona.

● MARCH 17: Ford's roadability placed it more than a full lap ahead of its closest challenger to win in Atlanta.

PLYMOUTH   FORD   CHEVROLET

index

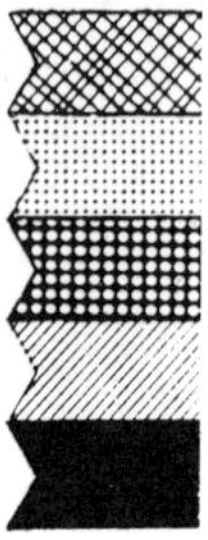

.... frame
.... suspension
.... engine
.... brakes
.... transmission

PLYMOUTH   FORD   CHEVROLET

Frame

Plymouth has a single unit body.

Ford's frame has side rails for stability and protection.

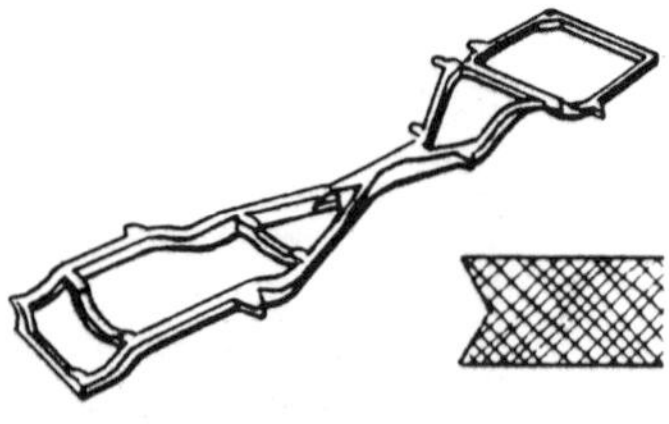

Chevrolet's X-type frame offers little side protection.

PLYMOUTH   FORD   CHEVROLET

Suspension

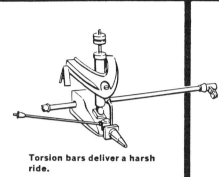

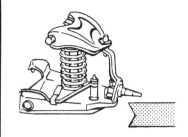

Torsion bars deliver a harsh ride.

"Silent Ride" Smoothes the bumps and cuts road noise.

Full coil suspension does not absorb driving thrusts.

PLYMOUTH   FORD   CHEVROLET

Engine

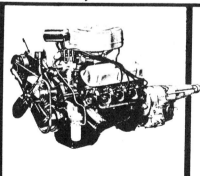

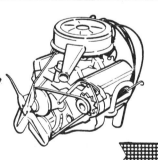

3 basic V-8 engine choices.

5 basic V-8s.

Only 3 basic V-8 engines.

PLYMOUTH　　FORD　　CHEVROLET

Brakes

Smallest brakes . . . 195.2 square inches of lining.

Biggest brakes in its field . . . 212.7 square inches.

Only 200.4 square inches of bonded lining.

PLYMOUTH　　FORD　　CHEVROLET

Transmission

3

Only 3 transmission options.

5

Five transmission choices.

4

Four transmission choices.

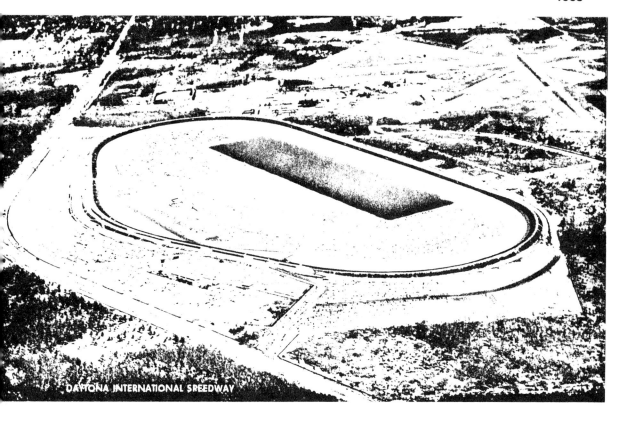

DAYTONA INTERNATIONAL SPEEDWAY

PERFORMANCE PROVING

Daytona, Darlington, Riverside, Charlotte, and Atlanta are all familiar names to every automobile performance enthusiast. On these famous tracks, stock cars are put to extreme tests of power, responsiveness, fuel economy, ease of handling, and roadability. Well-supervised test programs that are in no way competitive or open to the general public are often conducted at these tracks; and, coupled with similar tests at Company proving grounds such as Kingman, Arizona and Romeo, Michigan, significant changes and improvements have found their way into production cars to increase their durability and improve their quality and safety appointments.

In addition, the actual racing events that are held throughout the country each year attract an estimated 32 million spectators to make competition automobile events one of today's most popular sports. Of course, proper governing bodies, safety devices, and expeienced personnel have complete control over such events.

To the owners and drivers of the cars, victory means prize money and prestige as the cars move to the winner's circle, and their thoughts may well be of a chance in the near future for additional challenges and more lucrative conquests.

To the automotive engineers who have observed the event, it is a chance to evaluate products of interest within their engineering area, because a well-supervised competitive high-performance event is actually an accelerated test program. In fact, continuous running for 500 miles or more at speeds up to 160 mph could easily be the equivalent of 100,000 miles of average customer use. The speed of stock cars in a race is well above what an average owner could or would expect from his own car in everyday use on modern highways.

Professional racing teams are allowed to make certain modifications, depending upon the group sanctioning the race. Most common among the modifications are heavy duty suspension systems, fade-resistant brakes, larger wheels, super-premium tires, and heavy duty rear axles with revised axle ratios. These items provide an additional margin of safety for the benefit of the spectators as well as the drivers of the stock cars.

POWER FOR IMPROVED PERFORMANCE...

The 427-cubic-inch High-performance and Super High-Performance engines are the most powerful passenger car engines ever produced for retail sales by Ford Motor Company. An experimental engine of the same basic design, but with a displacement of 483-cubic-inches, broke 46 national and international land records in 1962. From the experience gained in the construction and operation of this engine, and the knowledge obtained from observing engines of this type in competition events, Ford has been able to produce the "427" engine to meet the seven liter class requirements.

Standard equipment on the 427-cubic-inch engine includes a high-pressure oil pump for the specially designed high-volume lubrication system . . . solid valve lifters . . . valve spring dampeners . . . impact extrusion pistons . . . special alloy exhaust valves . . . free-flow aluminum intake manifold . . . and low-restriction header-type exhaust manifolds.

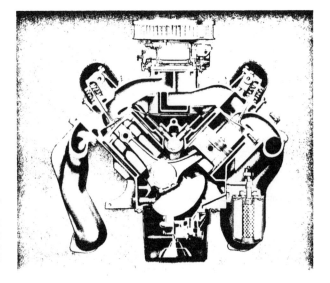

SPECIAL FEATURES OF THE "427" ENGINE

The 427-cubic-inch engine offers many special features which enable it to withstand the stress of high-performance operation and for long life in everyday driving.

CROSS-BOLTED MAIN BEARING CAPS

The cylinder block of the "427" is made in accordance with Ford's advanced foundry techniques and

is reinforced for precise bearing alignment by the cross-bolting of the main bearing caps. Engine speeds that were believed impossible to maintain in large displacement engines are now practical because of the greater crankcase rigidity.

IMPACT EXTRUSION PISTONS AND SPECIAL CONNECTING RODS

Pistons are impact-extruded for a tighter grain structure and cam ground for superior resistance to

heat and the stress set up by the high-performance characteristics of this engine. The piston heads feature forged-in "eyebrows" and two raised pads which can contact the valve heads in case of valve "floating" at extremely high engine rpm. This helps to eliminate the possibility of bent valve stems with resultant engine failure.

The special connecting rods were developed through experience gained in observing competitive events. The rods feature reinforcement contours that are based on the strain pattern of the rods during high speed operation. The connecting rod bearing cap bolt heads and nut faces are a controlled gage finish for precise contact pressure on the rod to help maintain torque specifications.

The crankshaft is electronically balanced to within 1/2 oz./in. at 6000 rpm before the bearing surfaces are individually gaged to select-fit the steel-back precision-type bearings.

ELECTRONICALLY BALANCED CRANKSHAFT

WEDGE-SHAPE COMBUSTION CHAMBERS

The performance-proven wedge-shape combustion chambers of the "427" provide the means for complete and uniform burning of the fuel-air mixture. The turbulence set up within the chambers results in controlled combustion and also helps to clear exhaust gases after each power stroke.

HIGH-PERFORMANCE CAMSHAFT

The specially contoured cam profiles permit high-lift valve opening and greater valve overlap for the optimum engine torque characteristics.

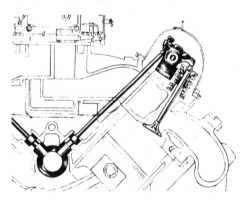

SOLID VALVE LIFTERS

Positive valve action for lively acceleration and durability at sustained high speeds is possible with the solid valve lifters in the "427." The valves are adjustable to provide the "fine tuning" that is so desirable in a performance-type engine.

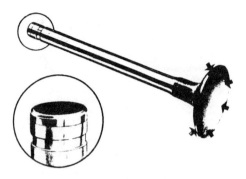

VALVES FOR THE "427"

Exhaust valves are manufactured of 214 N forged steel. For the high-performance application of the "427," the valves feature chrome plated stems to reduce valve guide wear, and hard silchrome tips on the valve stems assist in retaining valve clearance adjustments. The tops and seating surfaces of the intake valves are aluminized for protection against burning and pitting.

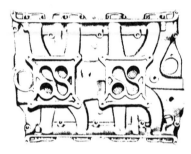

FREE-BREATHING INTAKE SYSTEM

The aluminum intake manifold directs the fuel-air mixture through low-restriction passages for maximum efficiency of distribution. The aluminum construction allows up to 49 pounds reduction in weight over cast iron manifolds.

HEADER-TYPE EXHAUST SYSTEM

Individual headers from each cylinder carry the exhaust gases into the dual exhaust pipes for efficient evacuation of the combustion chambers and a minimum of back pressure.

CARBURETION OF THE "427" ENGINE

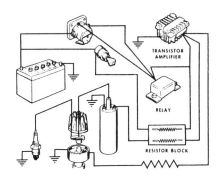

4-VENTURI CARBURETOR

The "427" engine is offered with either a single 4-venturi carburetor or with two 4-venturi carburetors. Each carburetor employs a primary and a secondary fuel system. The primary fuel system functions alone when the engine is operating below full power. The secondary fuel system is controlled by manifold vacuum, and it automatically comes into operation when rapid acceleration or sustained high speed is called for.

OPTIONAL TRANSISTORIZED IGNITION

In the transistorized ignition system, the current to the distributor breaker points is comparatively low, while the current to the ignition coil is high due to the fact that the two are fed by separate circuits. In a conventional ignition system, the breaker points and coil are in the same circuit, and the coil primary current is limited by the amount of current the points can withstand. With the stronger current throughout the entire primary circuit in the conventional system, there is greater metal transfer from contact-to-contact which causes pitting and results in a shorter service life for the points. This optional transistorized system improves the over-all efficiency of the ignition by increasing the voltage to the spark plugs at all engine speeds and by reducing oxidation of the distributor breaker points for longer point life.

ALTERNATOR CHARGING SYSTEM

TWO 4-VENTURI CARBURETORS

When two 4-venturi carburetors are installed, the systems of each carburetor operate in parallel with progressive linkage to provide increased fuel delivery during peak power requirements.

The high-performance engines are equipped with an alternator to provide more positive charging and to improve the over-all efficiency of the electrical and ignition systems. The use of a simplified, more reliable voltage regulator is possible with the alternator charging system because it requires less voltage control than a generator system.

SPECIFICATIONS FOR THE
427-CUBIC-INCH ENGINE

	427 — 4V	427 — 8V
GENERAL		
Type	8 - Cylinder, 90 - Degree Vee, Overhead Valves	
Displacement	427 Cubic Inches	
Bore and Stroke	4.2346" x 3.784"	
Compression Ratio	11.5:1	
Brake Horsepower	410 at 5600 rpm	425 at 6000 rpm
Maximum Torque	476 lbs.-ft. at 3400 rpm	480 lbs.-ft. at 3700 rpm
Valve Lifters	Solid	
Carburetor	One 4 - Venturi	Two 4 - Venturi
Fuel	Super Premium	
Exhaust	Dual	
Cylinder Block Material	Precision - Cast Iron	
Cylinder Head Material	Precision - Cast Iron	
CRANKSHAFT		
Material	Precision - Molded Alloy Cast Iron	
Main Bearings (5)	Steel - Back Copper - Lead Alloy Replaceable Inserts	
Main Bearing Journal Diameter	2.7488"	
Thrust Bearing	No. 3	
Crankpin Journal Diameter	2.4380" - 2.4388"	
CAMSHAFT		
Material	Precision - Molded Special Alloy Iron	
Bearings (5)	Steel - Back Babbitt Inserts	
Camshaft Gear Material	Molded Nylon on Aluminum Die Cast	
VALVE SYSTEM		
Operating Tappet Clearance	0.028" - 0.025" (hot)	
Intake Valve Opens	15°30' ATC at 0.100 Camlift	8°30' ATC at 0.100 Camlift*
Intake Valve Closes	29°30' ABC at 0.100 Camlift	36°30' ABC at 0.100 Camlift*
Duration	194°	208°*
Exhaust Valve Opens	32°30' BBC at 0.100 Camlift	39°30' BBC at 0.100 Camlift*
Exhaust Valve Closes	18°30' BTC at 0.100 Camlift	11°30' BTC at 0.100 Camlift*
Duration	194°	208°*
Valve Opening Overlap	48°	96°*
INTAKE VALVES		
Material	Special Alloy Valve Steel — With Aluminum - Coated Head	
Over - all Length	5.446"	
Over - all Head Diameter	2.082" - 2.097"	
Angle of Seat and Face	121° - 121°30'	
Lift	0.500" at Valve	
Spring Pressure and Length	80 - 90 lbs. at 1.82" (valve closed)	
	255 - 280 lbs. at 1.32" (valve open)	
EXHAUST VALVES		
Material	214 N Forged Steel with Chrome - Plated Stem and Silchrome Tip	
Over - all Length	5.426"	
Over - all Head Diameter	1.645" - 1.660"	
Angle of Seat and Face	91°30' - 91°	
Lift	0.500" at Valve	
Spring Pressure and Length	80 - 90 lbs. at 1.82" (valve closed)	
	255 - 280 lbs. at 1.32" (valve open)	
PISTONS		
Material	Extruded Aluminum, Cam Ground	
Weight	24.41 - 24.62 oz.	
PISTON RINGS		
No. 1 and 2 Compression	Cast Iron Alloy, Chrome Plated	
No. 3 Oil Control	Multi - Piece — Two Chrome Plated Steel	
	Rails and One Blued Steel Expander	
PISTON PINS		
Material	SAE 5015 Alloy Steel, Heat Treated	
Length	3.212 - 3.202"	
Diameter	0.9750 - 0.9753"	
Bushing	Full - Floating, Tubular Bronze	
CONNECTING RODS		
Material	Forged Steel with Separately Forged Caps	
Weight	24.64 - 27.20 oz.	
Length	6.486 - 6.490" Center - to - Center	
CONNECTING ROD BEARINGS		
Material	Steel Back Copper - Lead Alloy Inserts	
Over - all Length	0.736 - 0.746"	

* With optional camshaft

THE HIGH-PERFORMANCE DRIVE LINE FOR THE "427"

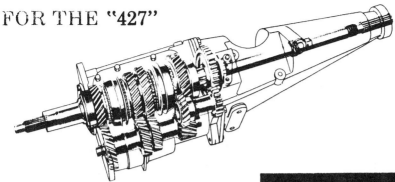

4-SPEED TRANSMISSION

The ultraflexible 4-speed manual shift transmission used with the 427-cubic-inch engine features full synchronization of all forward gears with closely spaced gear ratios that are fitted to the torque curve of the engine. This engine-transmission combination allows rapid upshifts for lively acceleration and split second downshifts for maximum performance and control in passing and engine braking.

The gears and bearings in this performance-type transmission are designed for extended operation in any ratio. All gears are manufactured of tough 9310 steel, with second gear coarse-pitched to withstand the stress of the torque multiplication while running at high engine rpm in second.

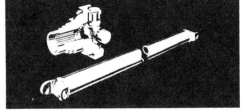

PERFORMANCE-PROVEN DRIVESHAFT AND "U" JOINTS

The 3-inch driveshaft used with the "427" engine is a one-piece tubular type with a forged steel yoke at either end. Particular care is given to the dynamic balancing of the shaft to provide vibration free operation at high rpm.

The front and rear universal joints have low-friction needle bearings for smooth operation and high load-carrying ability.

	Standard Ratio	Optional Ratio
First	2.36:1	2.36:1
Second	1.78:1	1.66:1
Third	1.41:1	1.23:1
Fourth	1.00:1	1.00:1
Reverse	2.42:1	2.42:1

HEAVY DUTY REAR AXLE

The Ford rear axle and differential in the performance package features a 9-inch ring gear and a 4-pinion differential. The pinion drive gear is straddle-mounted with two heavy duty tapered roller bearings ahead of the gear and a straight roller bearing behind.

This provides precise alignment of the ring gear and pinion for extended gear and bearing life. Heavier rear wheel bearings are also used in high-performance vehicles for an extra margin of safety.

The gear shift lever is floor-mounted, and the shift pattern is in the international standard arrangement.

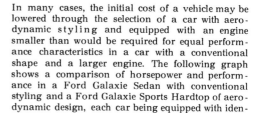

AIR FLOW ON FORD GALAXIE SPORTS HARDTOP

The performance-design of the Ford Galaxie 500 and 500/XL Sports Hardtop models is based on an aerodynamic concept. The practicability of the design has been proven in competition at several of the nation's most difficult road and track events and under conditions that duplicated normal driving on modern freeways.

It is known that power and performance are directly related to the engine power output less the power loss caused by the frictional resistance of rotating parts such as the transmission, rear axle, bearings, oil seals, and tires — plus the further depletion of engine power caused by "body drag," which results in reduced performance because of wind pressure on frontal areas, windshield, and rear deck.

In many cases, the initial cost of a vehicle may be lowered through the selection of a car with aerodynamic styling and equipped with an engine smaller than would be required for equal performance characteristics in a car with a conventional shape and a larger engine. The following graph shows a comparison of horsepower and performance in a Ford Galaxie Sedan with conventional styling and a Ford Galaxie Sports Hardtop of aerodynamic design, each car being equipped with identical power teams.

AIR FLOW ON CONVENTIONAL BODY

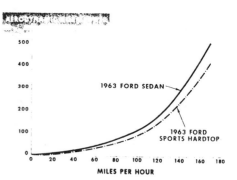

**AERODYNAMIC HORSEPOWER VS
VEHICLE PERFORMANCE**

There are many advantages in aerodynamic styling to make driving more safe by improving stability . . . more economical by reducing fuel consumption . . . and more enjoyable by reducing wind noise . . . and the rakish appearance of the aerodynamic shapes are more pleasing to the eye, as well.

The Ford Galaxie 500 Sports Hardtop offers power availability from 138 to 425 horsepower, and the range of the 500/XL model is from 195 to 425 horsepower to meet the power requirements for all transportation needs.

THE VERSATILE POWER TEAMS OF THE
FORD GALAXIE SPORTS HARDTOPS

ENGINE	TRANSMISSION	REAR AXLE#
138 Horsepower 223-Cubic-Inch-Six +	3-Speed Manual+	3.50:1 3.89:1*
	Overdrive***	3.89:1
	Fordomatic***	3.50:1 3.89:1* 3.25:1*
195 Horsepower 289-Cubic-Inch V-8** (164 Horsepower 260-Cubic-Inch V-8 may be substituted on option basis)	3-Speed Manual+	3.50:1 3.89:1*
	Overdrive***	3.50:1 3.89:1*
	Fordomatic***	3.25:1 3.00:1* 3.50:1*
	Cruise-O-Matic**	3.25:1 3.00:1* 3.50:1*
220 Horsepower 352-Cubic-Inch V-8*	3-Speed Manual+	3.50:1
	Overdrive***	3.50:1 3.89:1*
	4-Speed Manual*	3.50:1 3.89:1*
	Cruise-O-Matic**	3.00:1 3.50:1*
300 Horsepower 390-Cubic-Inch V-8*	3-Speed Manual+ (Constant-mesh)	3.50:1 3.89:1* 4.11:1*
	4-Speed Manual*	3.50:1 3.89:1* 4.11:1*
	Overdrive***	3.50:1 3.89:1* 4.11:1*
	Cruise-O-Matic**	3.00:1
410 and 425 Horsepower 427-Cubic-Inch V-8*	4-Speed Manual	3.50:1 3.00:1* 4.11:1*

#Equa-Lock Differential Options available in the same axle ratios (For all engines except 427 CID).
*Optional
**Optional on Galaxie 500, standard on Galaxie 500/XL

***Optional on Galaxie 500, not available on Galaxie 500/XL
+Standard on Galaxie 500, not available on Galaxie 500/XL

THE FORD TEAM THAT QUALIFIES ...
Performance... Stamina... Safety...

THE CAR . . .

The Ford Galaxie Sports Hardtop. When equipped with the 427-cubic-inch engine, this aerodynamically-styled action car can provide the optimum in performance.

THE ENGINE . . .

410 and 425 Horsepower — Powerful, with stamina and durability combined for any desired performance characteristic.

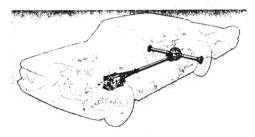

THE DRIVE LINE . . .

The rugged ultraflexible 4-speed transmission, the heavy duty drive shaft, and the rear axle with a 9-inch ring gear combine for precision control and durability.

THE SUSPENSION . . .

Heavy duty front and rear springs and shocks contribute to Ford's superb handling on turns and excellent stability with increased safety.

THE BRAKES . . .

Molded asbestos linings that are "tailored" for the best thermal conductivity make the heavy duty brake assemblies fade-resistant.

DEALER SERVICE HIGH-PERFORMANCE OPTIONS

Additional extra heavy duty and high performance equipment for specialized operations is available from authorized retail Ford Dealer service facilities.

EXTRA HEAVY DUTY EQUIPMENT—

* Front Springs
* Spindles — Right and Left
* Extra-Capacity Oil Pan
* Steering Idler Arm
* Steering Linkage
* Rear Axle Shafts
* Stabilizer Bar
* Pitman Arm
* Seven Optional-Ratio Rear Axle Carriers
* Oil Cooler

THE WHEELS AND TIRES . . .

15-Inch wheels for fewer wheel turns per mile, and better brake ventilation; and 7.10 x 15 nylon premium tires that resist ply separation and damage from impact.

1963 Mercury

Mercury for 1963 was a totally new car, with a totally new design concept. Offering more luxury than in recent years, Mercury also offered the more unusual, the Breezeway. This model, reminiscent of earlier Lincolns, had a reverse-slanted, retractable rear window. Mid-year saw the introduction of the Marauder fastback hardtop.

Engines offered for 1963 were the 390 cid V-8 (2-bbl) rated at 250 hp, the 390 cid V-8 (4-bbl) rated at 300 hp, the 427 cid V-8 (4-bbl) rated at 410 hp and the 427 cid V-8 (dual 4-bbl) rated at 425 hp. The transmissions offered were the 3-speed manual, the 4-speed manual and the 3-speed Multi-drive Merc-O-Matic automatic.

Production amounted to 120,046 units, with the model breakdown as follows. Prices follow each model in ()'s: MONTEREY 4-dr sedan 18,177 ($2,887), 2-dr sedan 4,640 ($2,834), 2-dr fastback Sport Coupe hdt. (quantity unknown, $3,083), 2-dr hdt. coupe 2,879 ($2,930), 4-dr hdt. sedan 1,692 ($2,995); MONTEREY CUSTOM 4-dr sedan 39,542 ($3,075), 2-dr fastback coupe 7,298 ($3,083), 2-dr hdt. coupe 10,693 ($3,083), 4-dr hdt. sedan 8,604 ($3,148), convertible 3,783 ($3,333), 4-dr Station Wagon, 6-pass, 6,447 ($3,295), 4-dr Colony Park Station Wagon 7,529 ($3,365); MONTEREY S-55 2-dr fastback coupe 2,317 ($3,650), 2-dr hdt. coupe 3,863 ($3,650), 4-dr hdt. sedan 1,203 ($3,715), convertible 1,379 ($3,900).

Sixteen exterior colors were offered with 26 two-tones available at extra cost. Vinyl roofs were offered in black, white or blue. Interiors were available in black, red, blue, turquoise, beige, rose, white or gold on bench or bucket seats.

Literature offered for 1963 consisted of the full-line color catalogue, the Monterey color catalogue (see page 85), the Marauder color folder (see page 86), the "Breezeway" die cut color mailer catalogue, the "Mercury is on the move!" folder featuring quotes from leading car magazines (see pages 80-84), the Maurader color postcard, and the three series oversize color postcard. The big cars were included in the full-line press kit.

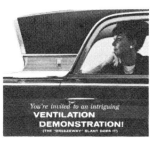

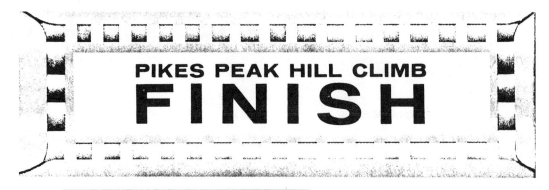

PIKES PEAK HILL CLIMB
FINISH

PARNELLI JONES SETS NEW STOCK CAR RECORD!

News Flash—COLORADO SPRINGS, Colo., July 4—In No. 15 Sachs and Sons 1963 Mercury, Parnelli Jones posted a time of 14:17.4 to crack the Pikes Peak stock car mark of 14:55.1 set a year ago by Curtis Turner.

The stock car record for the Pikes Peak Hill Climb was smashed Thursday by Parnelli Jones, veteran race driver and Indianapolis 500 champion.

Jones, driving a 1963 Mercury, dropped the stock car record by 37.7 seconds, beating out the 1962 champion Curtis Turner by the narrow margin of 2.9 seconds.

Take nothing away from Jones, however; he was at his best. It was only his second visit to this torturous 4700-foot Peak climb of 12.42 miles. He handled it like a 10-year veteran!

The Torrence, California resident who set a new time trials record of 6:11.5 on Tuesday, drove an almost flawless race in this Fourth-of-July classic. He said he was in trouble a couple of times but the big Mercury ran and handled perfectly.

MECHANIX ILLUSTRATED.

TOM McCAHILL CALLS IT...

❝A Car that will make tigers out of tired accountants❞

It was tossed together for the Go, Man! boys —to be used on drag strips, race courses or for friendly dicing with the local gendarmes at a stoplight grand prix.

The styling is a hardtop fastback developed by the engineers for better streamlining at speeds of 100 mph or more—so you can tool to the post office with less resistance, especially if it's two states away.

Anyway you approach this new car it spells special equipment. It's a barge for very special use—mainly; creaming all opposition under most circumstances. The car will be built in several horsepower versions but the hot job is a 427-cubic-inch V-8 engine that develops 425 horsepower.

"It's all male." It has more hair on its chest than a middled-aged yak and is a conversation piece that will keep any owner talking until he's blue in the face. Under duress it will serve for going to the movies or even for city shopping—but watch your foot, Buster. One wrong twitch and you might plow up eight cars in front of you. This job is about as gentle as a barracuda in a goldfish bowl . . .

Here is a car that will end nearly all saloon arguments, turn a tired accountant into a tiger and cop quite a bit of silverware at local drag strips when equipped with a positive-traction rear axle.

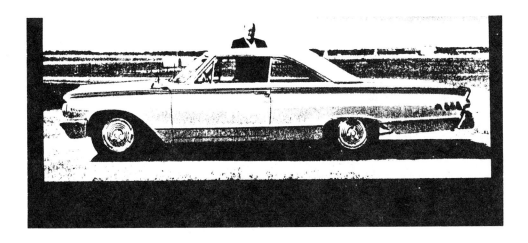

CARS

Test car could burn rubber in any gear. Potent 427 engine sports latest FoMoCo power changes.

MERC MARAUDER'S GOT SPEED TO BURN

Excerpts from a Report by Melvin Jacolow

❝All the speed goodies ...and could it go!❞

About Performance . . .

It's amazing how Detroit has been able to turn out ultra-hot powerplants which remain perfectly docile unless you call upon them for all-out performance. Stop-and-go city driving was absolutely effortless. The car idled quietly and smoothly at about 800 rpm, and the engine ran at normal operating temperature (180° F) consistently, thanks to the large radiator and six-bladed fan standard with 427 engines.

This baby had all the speed goodies available in Ford Division HP cars . . . and could it go for a 4,200 pound car! (We mention the weight at this point because this car uses the same power train as the similarly-equipped '63½ Ford Galaxies.)

A number of changes distinguish this solid lifter powerplant from the 406 which previously constituted Merc's top performance engine. To assure greater durability during sustained high rpm operation, the main bearing caps are cross-bolted at the No. 2, 3, and 4 caps to reinforce the crankcase and gain extra rigidity and more precise bearing alignment. Ribs increase wall thickness in the cylinder block's bulkhead area to carry the higher compression load.

Mandatory options which form part of the 427 package included heavy duty brakes, shocks and springs, an extra strong rear end, heavy duty transmission output shaft and 15-inch wheels.

We recorded corrected acceleration times of 2.9 seconds, 0-30 mph; 7.3 seconds, 0-60 mph; and 13.4 seconds for the quarter-mile at 105.7 mph using First-Third only. Both the 0-60 and 0-30 times were recorded using First only.

About Handling . . .

Handling and ride were fully up to the Merc's power capabilities in terms of cornering, hard stops and normal high speed road driving.

Braking was certainly adequate, with three quick panic stops from 70 mph resulting in some fade, but leaving the driver with sufficient usable pedal for most conditions.

. . . we can truthfully report that this Merc Super Marauder is an extremely desirable piece of machinery. The car's interior noise level was extremely low given the ultra powerful engine it was packing.

About Price . . .

Our specifications box will indicate that this Marauder is not an inexpensive automobile in terms of dollars. However, in terms of quality we could not, in all honesty, consider it expensive.

❝Mercury's fast backed S-55 Marauder is a moving machine!❞

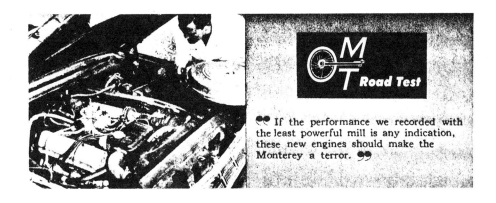

> If the performance we recorded with the least powerful mill is any indication, these new engines should make the Monterey a terror.

MERCURY
GOES RACING

Excerpts from a Motor Trend Road Test Report by Wayne Thoms

About Performance . . .

(As an example of how strong the big Marauder engine is in comparison to Merc's smallest, a Monterey equipped with the new engine has been clocked in excess of 160 mph.) At fast cruise, we found wind and engine noise quite low.

About Size . . .

As big cars go, the Monterey is right in league with the biggest. It hit us as a big automobile—and at 215 inches overall, it is. But size is relative. It's within an inch of the length of all this year's Chryslers, a fraction shorter than the Buick LeSabre, and actually two inches longer than the Continental. Aside from the parking that go with length, it's a very desirable car if interior space is important.

About Price . . .

We felt that the price is fair for a roomy, solidly built family sedan that offers so much comfort and performance. It is a car with qualities that should strike a responsive chord with motorists who appreciate outstanding products.

About Handling . . .

Actually, the ride was excellent, although on the soft side, which was the main reason for the poor cornering. Stiffer shock absorbers should work a healthy transformation on the Monterey's road manners without adverse effect on the ride. The fact that the Merc can be made into a formidable racing car with fantastically good handling indicates what can be done.

427 Super Marauder
MERCURY

❝427 cu. in. engine just doesn't take no for an answer❞

. . . A pair of 427 cu. in. units of positively brutal horsepower, 410 bhp for the single 4-barrel model and 425 for the twin 4-barrel. These, of course, are the racing engines—for drag strip, round track and road course, and for the driver who wants every little bit of performance he can get.

On the other hand, the racing engines are stressed to operate all day in the upper register, as well they must in NASCAR's form of competition. Although drag racers turn their Ford 427's as high as 6500 rpm on occasion (but only for an instant in each run), the round-trackers seldom exceed 6000. Instead, they gear the car so that it will lap Daytona, for instance, at 161-162 mph without exceeding that rpm, longevity usually paying better than absolute speed.

At any rate, the 427's are highly refined engines. Their torque output is nearly as impressive as their bhp rating—476 lb. ft. @ 3400 rpm and 480 @ 3700, respectively. And their performance characteristics leave nothing to be desired.

Nonetheless, a 427 cu. in. engine just doesn't take no for an answer, and the Super Marauder S-55 is startlingly quick. Although neither specially tuned nor equipped for maximum acceleration, it would accomplish the standing quarter mile in 16.1 sec. and do 0-100 in 20.5 sec. Compare this with the performance we measured for the 300-bph, 390 cu. in. automatic-equipped S-55, and that which we obtained from testing a 406 cu. in. S-55 last year.

PERFORMANCE COMPARISON

	390	406	427*
Transmission	auto	4-spd.	4-spd.
Axle ratio	3.00	3.56	4.11
Acceleration, sec. e. t.			
0-40	6.0	4.4	3.8
0-60	10.0	8.0	7.0
0-80	18.0	14.1	12.4
0-100	28.8	25.1	20.5
Standing ¼ mile	16.4	16.1	15.1
Speed at end, mph	75	85	87

(*not equipped for dragging!)

Stylish roof cuts down on drag and front and rear end lift at higher speeds.

On the open road, the Mercury S-55 Super Marauder showed respectable manners and proved a nice combination of firm ride and good handling. The non-power steering is a bit stiff around town, but a blessing on the open road. And having all that power on tap under one's right foot—well, that makes passing a pleasure and hill-climbing fun.

S·55

gets off the beaten track
...in a big way

**TRANSMISSIONS,
REAR AXLE RATIOS**

3-Speed Manual	3.50:1 (3.89:1 opt.)	—	—	—
4-Speed Manual	3.50:1 (3.89:1 opt.)	350:1 (options 3.89:1 or 4.11:1)	3.50:1 (options range from 3.00:1 to 4.11:1)	
Multi-Drive Merc-O-Matic	3.00:1 (3.50:1 opt.)		—	—

*Limited production option

And how the exciting S-55 gets off the beaten track! Engine choices are Mercury Marauder Super 390 V-8 with 4-barrel carburetor (standard) or Marauder 390 V-8 with 2-barrel carburetor (no-cost option). Or go all the way with dual four-barrel Mercury Marauder Super 427 V-8. Transmission choices at no extra cost include: Multi-Drive Merc-O-Matic or optional 4-speed manual, both floor-mounted. Optional tachometer also available. You can count on it: luxury plus performance in 1963 adds up to the year's most exciting big-car member . . . S-55.

total V-8 power throughout the '63 Mercury line-up

ENGINES	Marauder 390 V-8	Marauder Super 390 V-8	Marauder 427 V-8*	Marauder Super 427 V-8*
Displacement (cu. in.)	390	390	427	427
Carburetor	2-barrel	4-barrel	4-barrel	Dual 4-barrel
Bore and stroke	4.05 x 3.78	4.05 x 3.78	4.23 x 3.78	4.23 x 3.78
Compression ratio	8.9 to 1	10.8 to 1	11.5 to 1	11.5 to 1
Exhaust	Single (Dual for convertible)	Dual	Dual	Dual
Adv. horsepower @ rpm	250 @ 4400	300 @ 4600	410 @ 5600	425 @ 6000

*Transmissions? **The 4-speed manual,** a sports car favorite with floor-mounted stick shift, is available with all Mercury engines and mandatory with big Marauder 427 engines. It gets maximum performance out of any engine, adapts quickly to versatile driving situations. **Multi-Drive Merc-O-Matic** is available with both Marauder 390 engines. This flexible dual-range automatic transmission provides two forward drives in addition to low, reverse, park and neutral positions. Fully synchronized **3-speed manual** available only with standard Mercury Marauder 390 V-8.*

luxury...the kind that opens a whole new world of elegance

There's no mistaking the S-55, a sizzler that delivers the luxury of the Monterey Custom series plus sports car features—individually adjustable bucket seats, bright-metal floor console with shift lever and storage compartment, padded instrument panel and exclusive red and white safety-courtesy lights inside of doors. Open one of those doors. But once you do, be prepared for a new brand of beauty, a new kind of driving excitement.

On every S-55, you'll find spacious comfort in addition to deep carpeting, paddle-type door handles, unique emblems on steering wheel and glove box, and a new leather-soft upholstery material of expanded vinyl. For convertibles: vinyl-fabric top in your choice of black, white or blue, with padded cover boot.

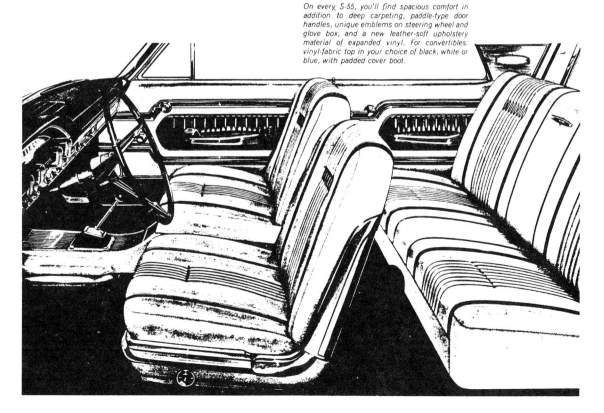

Bucket-seat beauty and sports-car flair go hand in hand in the Marauder S-55 with console-mounted shift lever and console storage space. And, the luxurious bucket seats are individually adjustable.

Even the styling says "go." Note that slim, racy, new hardtop roof. It's not only beautiful, its aerodynamic styling cuts air resistance. Choose from two dashing models: The Marauder with a big 390 V-8 standard...or the sporty Marauder S-55, with console-mounted transmission selector (either Multi-Drive Merc-O-Matic or 4-speed manual), luxurious bucket seats, and 4-barrel Marauder Super 390 V-8 standard engine. Optional engines range up to a special high-performance Marauder Super 427 V-8. Talk about hot! Talk to your Mercury dealer.

"Total Performance" continued to be the password for Ford for 1964. The basic body shell was retained, but the exterior design was totally redesigned and received "Motor Trend's" "Car of the Year" award. The grille was of a clean design, with side spears running from the headlights to the rear fenders. The rear design again featured the traditional round taillights. As if to complement its winning appearance, Ford performance was winning races through out the country.

The engines offered for 1964 were the 223 cid six (1-bbl) rated at 138 hp, the 289 cid V-8 (2-bbl) rated at 195 hp, the 352 cid V-8 (4-bbl) rated at 250 hp, the 390 cid V-8 (4-bbl) rated at 300 hp, the 427 cid V-8 (4-bbl) rated at 410 hp and the 427 cid V-8 (dual 4-bbl) rated at 425 hp. The transmissions offered were the 3-speed manual, the 3-speed manual with overdrive, the 4-speed manual and the 3-speed Cruise-O-Matic.

Production amounted to 923,232 units, with the following model breakdown (sixes and V-8's totals combined). Prices follow each with ()'s, with V-8's costing $109 more: CUSTOM 4-dr sedan 57,964 ($2,404), 2-dr sedan 41,359 ($2,350); CUSTOM 500 4-dr sedan 68,828 ($2,507), 2-dr sedan 20,619 ($2,453); GALAXIE 500 4-dr Town Sedan 198,805 ($2,667), 2-dr Club Sedan 13,041 ($2,613), 4-dr Town Victoria 49,242 ($2,739), 2-dr Club Victoria 206,998 ($2,674), convertible 37,311 ($2,936); GALAXIE 500XL 4-dr Town Victoria 14,661 ($3,287), 2-dr Club Victoria 58,306 ($3,222), convertible 15,169 ($3,484).

Thirteen exterior colors were offered with two-tones optional at extra cost. Vinyl roofs were offered in black or white. Interiors were available in blue, beige, red, turquoise, black, silver, white, or palomino in vinyl or vinyl and cloth on bench or bucket seats.

Literature offered for 1964 consisted the full-line color catalogue dated 8-63 and revised 2-64 (see specs on page 99), the Galaxie color catalogue dated 8-63 and revised 1-64, "The cars we build for two kinds of Sunday driving" color mailer catalogue (see pages 88-89), the accessories color folder, the "Car of the Year" reprint from Feb. '64 "Motor Trend," the "Ford performance tips from Ak Miller" catalogue (see pages 101-112), the "Ford wins Atlanta 500! Score 1-3 finish!!!" folder, the "Total performance since 1903" catalogue (see pages 91-100), and the "Buyer's Digest" booklet, filled with facts and figures. The Galaxies were also included in the full-line press kit.

1964 FORD
the big total performance car

THIS IS THE 1964 FORD ...ford in open competition ...built for total performance...hundreds of pounds stronger than any other car in its field

FORD PERFORMANCE TIPS FROM AK MILLER
COBRA ENGINE PERFORMANCE KITS

The TOTAL PERFORMANCE Cars for Ford
FORD

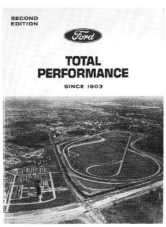
SECOND EDITION
Ford
TOTAL PERFORMANCE
SINCE 1903

lucky Sunday for Tiny

Tiny Lund, winner of this year's Daytona 500, didn't even have a car to drive when he went to the track. But at the last minute, he was offered another driver's Ford and Tiny was off for 500 miles . . . with 50 others . . . in the biggest stock car race in the country! For the first few laps Tiny was well back in the pack. But one by one his competition blew their engines or overheated . . . and before long there were *all Fords in front*. Hours later Tiny was holding on to third place when the leading Fords stopped for gas. He saw his chance. If he could make it on the gas in his tank, he'd win. On the final turn, the gas ran out . . . but not his luck! Tiny rolled across the finish line . . . first . . . followed by *four* other Fords! It was an unprecedented parade of Ford's strength and reliability. This year Fords have entered . . . and won . . . event after event. But speed alone didn't do it. It took sturdy engines, precise handling and rugged durability as well.

In Sunday traffic, or any other day, '64 Fords deliver the kind of superb roadability that helps resist skidding . . . the reliable braking power that permits smoother, straighter-line stops . . . the almost effortless steering . . . exceptional visibility . . . a smooth ride that soaks up road shock and limits wheel bounce. This is *total* performance . . . *durability* that keeps Fords going strong . . . *responsiveness* that delivers whatever the driver asks.

Did you notice: the luxury throughout the '64 Fords you saw in the showroom? Did you see the newly designed shell bucket seats in the Ford Galaxie 500/XL . . . the foot-light and traffic warning light in the door which go on automatically when you step inside? Did you *take a test drive?* If you did you *know* what total performance is!

Some race courses make winding country lanes look almost straight . . . like the Riverside 500 road race circuit, for instance. There are over 2,035 fast turns—and it takes a car that can *corner* to win. Sports car driver Dan Gurney drove a Ford around the tough, twisting 500 miles at Riverside as if his Ford *were* a sports car . . . and he *did* win . . . hands down over all comers. Sports car handling helped Ford take the corners, alright, but it took ruggedness and durability to keep taking corners for 185 laps. (Only 21 out of 44 entries made it through the entire race!)

Superior Ford durability also shows up in the '64 Fords in your dealer's showroom. A Ford has more road-hugging strength . . . more steel in the frame . . . and a tougher suspension than any of its traditional competitors. No sports car ever rode more smoothly at Riverside—or anywhere—than the '64 Ford! A newly developed compliance link makes the big difference. Ford's exclusive suspension system absorbs road shock horizontally—away from the passenger—as well as vertically. Ordinary suspensions can only move up and down, but Ford's suspension "rolls with the punches" like a boxer, to soften the blow. A few years ago, only a millionaire could buy a car that rides as smoothly as a '64 Ford. But Ford spent $10 million to bring you a new suspension that makes you feel as comfortable as a millionaire on his way to the bank.

Did you notice: the '64 Ford's amazing cornering ability . . . its incredibly smooth ride? Did you know that along with a smoother ride, the 1964 Ford is quieter riding too? One of the reasons is that there is much more insulation used throughout the '64 Ford than you'll find in other cars in its class. By the way, have you taken your test ride yet?

1964 FORD SPECIFICATIONS

COLOR AND UPHOLSTERY SELECTIONS: You have a choice of 13 '64 Ford single tone colors or 14 two-tone combinations (except Custom Sedan, Country Squire) in durable, brilliant Diamond Lustre Enamel. There are 35 upholstery choices: 13 cloth and vinyl combinations; 22 all-vinyl trims in wagons, convertibles and 500/XL's; including 5 as options in Galaxie 500 (5 for hardtops, 3 for sedans). Your Ford Dealer will be happy to show you actual samples of '64 Ford colors and upholsteries.

TWICE-A-YEAR (or 6,000-mile) MAINTENANCE: The '64 Super Torque Ford goes 36,000 miles (or 3 years whichever comes first) between major chassis lubes; 6,000 miles (or 6 months) between oil changes and minor lubes. In fact, Ford for 1964 needs so little service it's just good sense to see that it gets the best—at your Ford Dealer's. His factory-trained mechanics and special tools add up to a great service combination you can get nowhere else! Other '64 Ford service savings include: engine coolant-antifreeze, installed at the factory, for 36,000 miles (or two years); self-adjusting brakes; aluminized muffler; galvanized vital underbody parts to resist rust and corrosion.

FORD DESIGN: The way new Fords are built, plus the many features built into new Fords, you'll find add greatly to your enjoyment of any '64 Ford you choose. Among many highlights: Fully Insulated and Weather-Sealed Body; Wide-Contoured, Safety-Type Frame; Electronically Mass-Balanced Engines; Parallel Action Single-Speed Electric Windshield Wipers; Double-Swivel, Shatter-Resistant Rearview Mirror; Deep-Dish Steering Wheel with Chrome Horn Ring; Seat Side Shields; Front Seat Belt Anchors; Step-On Parking Brake; Dual Sun Visors with Retention Clips; Crank-Adjusted Vent Windows; Lined and Illuminated Trunk Compartment; Center-Fill Fueling (except wagons); Quick-Converting, Torsion Spring-Assisted Second Seat (6-pass. wagons); Ribbed Vinyl Loadspace Floor (wagons); Counterbalanced Tailgate (wagons).

ENGINES: *138-hp Mileage Maker Six* (std. on all except 500/XL's)—223 cu. in. displ.; 3.62" bore x 3.60" stroke; 8.4 to 1 comp. ratio; reg. fuel; single-barrel carb.; manual choke; self-adj. valves; oil cap'y. with filter change, 5 qt.

195-hp Challenger 289 V-8 (std. on 500/XL's, opt. on other models)—289 cu. in. displ.; 4.00" bore x 2.87" stroke; 9.0 to 1 comp. ratio; reg. fuel; 2-barrel carb.; auto. choke; self-adj. valves with hydraulic lifters; oil cap'y. with filter change, 5 qt.

250-hp Thunderbird 4V/352 V-8 (opt.)—352 cu. in. displ.; 4.00" bore x 3.50" stroke; 9.3 to 1 comp. ratio; reg. fuel; 4-barrel carb.; auto. choke; self-adj. valves with hydraulic lifters; oil cap'y. with filter change, 6 qt.

300-hp Thunderbird 4V/390 V-8 (opt.)—390 cu. in. displ.; 4.05" bore x 3.78" stroke; 10.1 to 1 comp. ratio; prem. fuel; 4-barrel carb.; auto. choke; self-adj. valves with hydraulic lifters; oil cap'y. with filter change, 6 qt.; dual exhausts.

425-hp Thunderbird 8V/427 High Performance V-8 with 11.2 to 1 comp. ratio and 8-barrel carb. also avail. for all models except wagons. Included in package required with high performance V-8; 40-amp. alternator, 70 amp-hr battery, heavy-duty brakes, 15-in. wheels (including simulated knock-off hub wheel covers on 500/XL models), 6.70 x 15 4-ply black sidewall tubeless tires (7.10 x 15 convertibles), chrome engine dressup kit, heavy-duty springs, shock absorbers and rear axle. Other high performance options: transistorized ignition system, "power pipes" (exhaust bypass). For further details consult your Ford Dealer.

ENGINE FEATURES: For greater economy and long life, Ford engines have short-stroke, low-friction design; full-flow disposable-type oil filter; crankcase emission control system (std. on all except Six, but available special order); 12-volt electrical system; weatherproof ignition with constant-resistance wiring and air-cooled distributor points; 66-plate, 55 amp-hr battery (78-plate, 65 amp-hr with 352 or 390 V-8's with automatic transmission); fully aluminized single muffler (dual mufflers of aluminized and stainless steel).

CLUTCH AND MANUAL TRANSMISSION: Semi-centrifugal clutch with full-weighted levers for more positive engagement. Face diameter 9½" with Six, 10" with 289 V-8, 11" with other V-8's. *New Synchro-Smooth Drive Transmission* (std.) with synchronized manual shifting in all three forward speeds.

4-Speed Manual (avail. on all except wagons)—fully synchronized with console-mounted stick shift on 500/XL models, floor-mounted stick shift on all other models; avail. on 390 or 427 V-8. *Overdrive* (avail. on all except 500/XL's)—conventional 3-speed transmission plus an automatic 4th gear which cuts in above 28 mph, cuts out below 21 mph (approx.). Downshift to direct by flooring accelerator. Lockout control on instrument panel.

CRUISE-O-MATIC DRIVE (std. in 500/XL's with 289 V-8, opt. on others except with 427 V-8): Features lightweight construction with cast-aluminum converter housing. Two selective drive ranges provide a choice of starts; 3-speed range starting in low for all normal driving, or 2-speed range starting in intermediate for more sure-footed driving on slippery surfaces. Three forward gear ratios, one reverse. Vacuum throttle control provides smooth, precise and permanently coordinated-with-engine shifting. Selector sequence: 500/XL's: P-R-N-D$_2$-D$_1$-L; all others: P-R-N-DRIVE-L. Effective engine braking in "L" position.

REAR AXLE: Semi-floating type with deep-offset hypoid gears. Straddle-mounted drive pinion. Optional heavy-duty axle for cars (std. on wagons; any model with 390 V-8) with higher capacity wheel bearings, larger diameter shafts.

WIDE-CONTOURED FRAME: Strong box-section design with tuned frame, butyl body mounts and other refinements to reduce harshness and vibration for more luxurious ride. Convertible has 4 crossmembers plus X-member, others have 5 crossmembers. Siderails extend outside passenger area for increased side protection.

FRONT SUSPENSION: Swept-Back, Angle-Poised Ball-Joint type with wide-base coil springs for softer ride, easier steering. New design feature allows front wheels to "roll with the punch" (move rearward slightly), thus diminish effects of bumps and road faults. Ball joints packed with special 36,000-mile lubricant retained by full life seals. Front end has rubber-bushed ride stabilizer to control roll on turns. Tapered roller wheel bearings with 24,000-mile check interval (repack as required).

REAR SUSPENSION: Asymmetrical, variable-rate design with rear axle located forward from center of springs for anti-dive and anti-squat on braking and acceleration. Extra-long leaf-type springs with wide spring base provide a soft, stable, levelized ride.

STEERING: Recirculating-ball type steering gear with anti-friction bearings throughout plus high numerical ratio for easier steering. Flexible coupling in steering shaft insulates steering wheel. Nylon bearings in tie rod and pitman arm pivots are packed with special 36,000-mile lubricant retained by full life seals. Over-all steering ratio 30 to 1; with power steering, 23 to 1. Turning diameter approximately 41 ft.

BRAKES: Self-adjusting, self-energizing design. Brakes adjust automatically when applied while car is moving backwards. Easy-operating suspended pedal. Dash-mounted master cylinder. Grooved 11-in. composite drums. Total lining area is 234 sq. in. on wagons, 212 sq. in. on other models. Foot-operated parking brake. Optional power brakes have special low pedal.

TIRES: 4-ply rating, black tubeless with Tyrex rayon cord. White sidewall tires optional. Safety-type rims. Basic sizes: Ford Custom—7.00 x 14 4-pr. on 5½" rims with Six. Wagons—8.00 x 14 4-pr. (8-pr. opt.) on 6" rims. For other models, 7.50 x 14 and 8.00 x 14 sizes are determined in part by engine choice and special equipment such as air conditioning. See your Ford Dealer for specifics.

PRICES: Metal-to-web front seat belts, heater and defroster are installed in production on all models unless otherwise specified. If deleted an appropriate price reduction is made. All Power Assists, Optional Equipment and Accessories as well as some items illustrated or referred to as options, optional or available are at extra cost. For the price of the model with the equipment you desire, see your Ford Dealer.

Comparative information in this catalog was obtained from authoritative sources, but is not guaranteed. The specifications contained herein were in effect at the time this catalog was approved for printing. Ford Division of Ford Motor Company reserves the right to discontinue models at any time, or change prices, specifications or designs without notice and without incurring obligation.

PRODUCTS OF  MOTOR COMPANY

POWER...
FOR PROVEN PERFORMANCE

The 427-cubic-inch High-Performance V-8 engines are the most powerful passenger car engines ever produced for retail sales by Ford Motor Company. During 1963, "427" engines powered Ford cars to many important wins on the stock car and drag race circuits. Beginning early in the year, "427"-equipped Fords dominated the longer distance closed circuit events, where toughness and durability, as well as speed, were required—where "Total Performance" brings a car into the winner's circle.

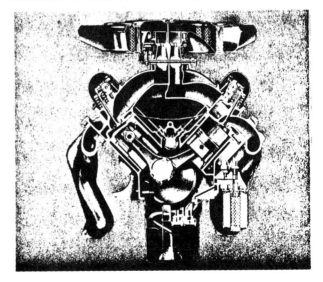

The "427" High-Performance engine is available in three configurations, one version as a regular production option for normal street use, and two versions as limited production options for competition. Standard equipment on all 427-cubic-inch engines includes a high-pressure oil pump for the specially designed high-volume lubrication system . . . solid valve lifters . . . valve spring dampeners . . . impact extrusion pistons . . . special alloy exhaust valves . . . free-flow aluminum intake manifold . . . and low-restriction header-type exhaust manifolds.

SPECIAL FEATURES
OF THE '427' ENGINE

The 427-cubic-inch engine offers many special features which enable it to withstand the stress of high-performance operation and for long life in everyday driving.

CROSS-BOLTED MAIN BEARING CAPS

The cylinder block of the "427" is made in accordance with Ford's advanced foundry techniques, and is reinforced for precise bearing alignment by the cross-bolting of the main bearing caps. Engine speeds that were believed impossible to maintain in large displacement engines are now practical because of the greater crankcase rigidity.

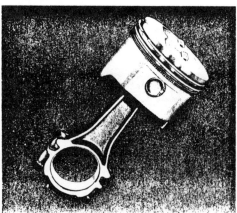

IMPACT EXTRUSION PISTONS AND SPECIAL CONNECTING RODS

Pistons are impact-extruded for a tighter grain structure, and cam ground for superior resistance to heat and stress set up by the high-performance characteristics of this engine. The piston heads have forged-in "eyebrows" and two raised pads which can contact valve heads in case of the valves "floating" at high engine rpm. Also, crown-type pistons are available on special order, and are often used in competitive events.

The special connecting rods were developed through experience gained in observing competition events. The rods feature reinforcement contours that are based on the strain pattern of the rods during high speed operation. The connecting rod bearing cap bolt heads and nut faces are a controlled gage finish for precise contact pressure on the rod to help maintain proper torque.

PRECISION CRANKSHAFT

The precision crankshaft is fully counterweighted and carried in five main bearings. Its short length and the large overlap between main and crankpin journals provide the extra stiffness needed for high-performance durability and long bearing life. All crankshaft oil holes are drilled extra large to provide a generous supply of oil to the bearings under high rpm operation.

The main and connecting rod bearings are of the precision, replaceable, steel-backed insert-type. The bearing material is a copper-lead alloy that provides extra load capacity and greater reliability for high-performance usage. The bearings are lead-tin plated for faster break-in.

The crankshaft is electronically balanced to within 1/2 oz/in. before the bearing surfaces are individually gaged to select-fit the bearings. Like all Ford engines, the "427" is balanced as a complete assembly while running on a special balancing machine.

'427' ENGINE FEATURES

FREE-BREATHING AIR INTAKE SYSTEM

A unique free-breathing air intake system for the "427" engine is available on special order, and it is usually used only for competitive events. The installation differs between the 4- and 8-venturi engines in that on the single-carburetor, 4-venturi engine the air cleaner is attached to an opening in the body cowl to admit cool air through the cowl air intake for greater volumetric efficiency. This is also a benefit at higher car speeds as the air pressure tends to increase in the cowl area to force air into the engine for a slight supercharging effect. On the two-carburetor, 8-venturi engine, pressurized air is admitted through two ducts that extend from behind the grille to the engine air inlet.

Each of the special air intake systems utilize unique high-riser aluminum intake manifolds with low-restriction passages. The high-riser construction reduces restrictive bends and curves to permit maximum air flow and efficiency. The intake manifolds of all "427" engines are of lightweight cast aluminum which allows a great reduction in weight over conventional cast iron manifolds.

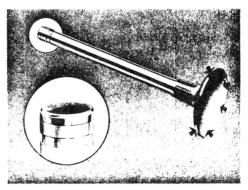

VALVES FOR THE "427"

Exhaust valves are manufactured of 214 N forged steel. For the high-performance application of the "427," the valves feature chrome-plated stems to reduce valve guide wear, and hard silichrome tips on the valve stems assist in retaining valve clearance adjustments. The tops and seating surfaces of the intake valves are aluminized for protection against burning and pitting.

HEADER-TYPE EXHAUST SYSTEM

Cast iron exhaust manifolds feature individual headers from each cylinder. The headers provide efficient evacuation of the combustion chambers by reducing exhaust back pressure and interaction or "pulse" between adjoining cylinders. The headers empty into the dual exhaust pipes, providing a complete low-loss exhaust system.

HIGH-PERFORMANCE CAMSHAFT

The specially contoured cam profiles permit high-lift valve opening and greater valve overlap for the optimum engine torque characteristics. The camshaft actuates the valves through mechanical valve lifters that have cast-in holes for lightness; helping to provide more positive valve action at all speeds.

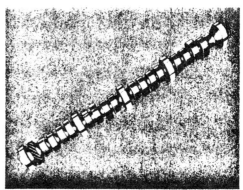

CARBURETION OF THE '427' ENGINE

4-VENTURI CARBURETOR

The "427" engine is offered with either a single 4-venturi carburetor or with two 4-venturi carburetors. Each carburetor employs a primary and a secondary fuel system. The primary fuel system functions alone when the engine is operating below full power. The secondary fuel system is controlled by manifold vacuum, and it automatically comes into operation when rapid acceleration or sustained high speed is called for.

TWO 4-VENTURI CARBURETORS

When equipped with two 4-venturi carburetors, the primary fuel system in both carburetors operate in parallel with a progressive mechanical linkage system. The two carburetor system provides increased fuel delivery during peak power requirements, and is normally the system used when the "427" is installed in a drag strip competition car.

ALTERNATOR CHARGING SYSTEM

The high-performance engines are equipped with an alternator to provide more positive charging and to improve the overall efficiency of the electrical and ignition systems. The use of a simplified, more reliable voltage regulator is possible with the alternator charging system because it requires less voltage control than a generator system.

OPTIONAL TRANSISTORIZED IGNITION

For competition use, the optional transistorized ignition system is highly desirable, providing an increase in combustion efficiency through greater spark plug voltage, especially at the higher engine speeds.

In the transistorized ignition system, the current to the distributor breaker points is comparatively low, while the current to the ignition coil is high due to the fact that the two are fed by separate circuits. In a conventional ignition system, the breaker points and coil are in the same circuit, and the coil primary current is limited by the amount of current the points can withstand. With the stronger current throughout the entire primary circuit in the conventional system, there is greater metal transfer from contact-to-contact which causes pitting and results in a shorter service life for the points.

In addition to providing greater overall efficiency, the optional transistorized ignition system reduces oxidation of the distributor breaker points for longer point life, and helps prevent spark plug fouling through the hotter spark.

SPECIFICATIONS FOR THE
427-CUBIC-INCH ENGINE

	427 – 4V	427 – 8V
GENERAL		
Type	8 - Cylinder, 90 - Degree Vee, Overhead Valves	
Displacement	427 Cubic Inches	
Bore and Stroke	4.2346" x 3.784"	
Compression Ratio	13:1	14:1
Brake Horsepower	410 at 5600 rpm	425 at 6000 rpm
Maximum Torque	476 lbs.-ft. at 3400 rpm	480 lbs.-ft. at 3700 rpm
Valve Lifters	Solid	
Carburetor	One 4-Venturi	Two 4-Venturi
Fuel	Super Premium	
Exhaust	Dual	
Cylinder Block Material	Precision-Cast Iron	
Cylinder Head Material	Precision-Cast Iron	
CRANKSHAFT		
Material	Forged Steel	Precision-Molded Alloy Cast Iron
Main Bearings (5)	Steel-Back Copper Lead Alloy Replaceable Inserts	
Main Bearing Journal Diameter	2.7488"	
Thrust Bearing	No. 3	
Crankpin Journal Diameter	2.4380" - 2.4388"	
CAMSHAFT		
Material	Precision-Molded Special Alloy Iron	
Bearings (5)	Steel-Back Babbitt Inserts	
Camshaft Gear Material	Molded Nylon on Aluminum Die Cast	

	427 – 4V	427 – 8V	
VALVE SYSTEM			
Operating Tappet Clearance	0.028" - 0.025" (hot)		
Intake Valve Opens +	15°30' ATC	8°30' ATC*	0°30' ATC*
Intake Valve Closes +	29°30' ABC	36°30' ABC*	28°30' ABC*
Duration	306° Theoretical	324° Theoretical*	324° Theoretical*
Exhaust Valve Opens +	32°30' BBC	39°30' BBC*	31°30' BBC*
Exhaust Valve Closes +	18°30' BTC	11°30' BTC*	3°30' BTC*
Duration	306° Theoretical	324° Theoretical*	324° Theoretical*
Valve Opening Overlap	78° Theoretical	96° Theoretical*	112° Theoretical*

INTAKE VALVES		
Material	Special Alloy Valve Steel - With Aluminum - Coated Head	
Overall Length	5.446"	
Overall Head Diameter	2.082" - 2.097"	
Angle of Seat and Face	30°	
Lift	0.500" at Valve	
Spring Pressure and Length	80 - 90 lbs. at 1.82" (valve closed)	
	255 - 280 lbs. at 1.32" (valve open)	
EXHAUST VALVES		
Material	214 N Forged Steel with Chrome - Plated Stem and Silichrome Tip	
Overall Length	5.246"	
Overall Head Diameter	1.645" - 1.660"	
Angle of Seat and Face	45°	
Lift	0.500" at Valve	
Spring Pressure and Length	80 - 90 lbs. at 1.82" (valve closed)	
	255 - 280 lbs. at 1.32" (valve open)	
PISTONS		
Material	Extruded Aluminum, Cam Ground	
Weight	23.75 oz.	23.31 oz.
PISTON RINGS		
No. 1 and 2 Compression	Cast Iron Alloy, Chrome Plated	
No. 3 Oil Control	Multi - Piece — Two Chrome Plated Steel	
	Rails and One Blued Steel Expander	
PISTON PINS		
Type	Full - Floating, Tubular	
Material	SAE 5015 Alloy Steel, Heat Treated	
Length	3.212 - 3.202"	
Diameter	0.9750 - 0.9753"	
Bushing	Bronze	
CONNECTING RODS		
Material	Forged Steel with Separately Forged Caps	
Weight	26.85 - 27.30 oz.	
Length	6.486 - 6.490" Center - to - Center	
CONNECTING ROD BEARINGS		
Material	Steel Back Copper - Lead Alloy Inserts	
Overall Length	0.736 - 0.746"	

* With optional camshaft   + At 0.100" camshaft

'427' ENGINE PACKAGE FEATURES PERFORMANCE. . .STAMINA. . . SAFETY

All Ford vehicles equipped with "427" engines also include certain heavy-duty mandatory options, which are combined with the engine into one high-performance package. This is in the interest of safety and in keeping Ford the foremost in satisfying the trend toward Total Performance vehicles.

THE SUSPENSION . . .

Heavy duty front and rear springs and shocks contribute to Ford's superb handling on turns and excellent stability with increased safety.

THE WHEELS AND TIRES . . .

15-inch wheels for fewer wheel turns per mile, and better brake ventilation; and 7.10 x 15 nylon premium tires that resist ply separation and damage from impact.

THE BRAKES . . .

Molded asbestos linings that are "tailored" for the best thermal conductivity make the heavy duty brake assemblies fade-resistant. The large 11-inch brake drums have 381 square inches of swept area, and the brake lining gross area is 234 square inches.

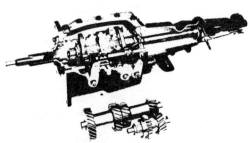

THE TRANSMISSION . . .

The ultraflexible, Ford-built 4-speed manual shift transmission used with the 427-cubic-inch engine features full synchronization of all forward gears. This engine-transmission combination allows rapid upshifts for lively acceleration and split-second downshifts for maximum performance and control in passing and engine braking.

The gears and bearings in this performance-type transmission are designed for extended operation in any ratio.

THE REAR AXLE AND DRIVE SHAFT . . .

The Ford rear axle and differential in the performance package features a 9-inch ring gear and a 4-pinion differential. The pinion drive gear is straddle-mounted with two heavy duty tapered roller bearings ahead of the gear and a straight roller bearing behind. Heavier rear wheel bearings are also used with high-performance vehicles.

The 3-inch driveshaft used with the "427" engine is a one-piece tubular type with a forged steel yoke at either end. Particular care is given to the dynamic balancing of the shaft to provide more vibration-free operation at high rpm.

The front and rear universal joints have low-friction needle bearings for smooth operation and high load carrying ability.

THE TOTAL PERFORMANCE DESIGN OF THE FORD FASTBACKS

The design of the Ford Galaxie 500 and 500/XL Sports Hardtop models is based on an aerodynamic concept. The practicability of the design has been proven in competition at several of the nation's most difficult road and track events and under conditions that duplicated normal driving on modern freeways.

It is known that power and performance are directly related to the engine power output less the power loss caused by the frictional resistance of rotating parts such as the transmission, rear axle, bearings, oil seals, and tires — plus the further depletion of engine power created by "body drag" caused by increased wind pressure on frontal areas, and also increased "drag" characteristics caused by vacuum at the rear deck and back of the car.

There are many advantages in aerodynamic styling to make driving more safe by improving stability, more economical by reducing fuel consumption, and more enjoyable by reducing wind noise — and the rakish appearance of the aerodynamic shapes are more pleasing to the eye, as well.

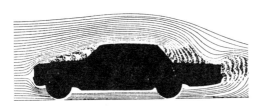

AIR FLOW ON CONVENTIONAL BODY

AERODYNAMIC HORSEPOWER VS VEHICLE PERFORMANCE

It is conceivable that the initial cost of a vehicle may be lowered through the selection of a body style with aerodynamic styling. This is true because a smaller engine can often be used for equal performance with a car of conventional body style. The following graph shows a comparison of horsepower and performance in a sedan with conventional styling and a Ford hardtop of aerodynamic design, each car being equipped with identical power teams.

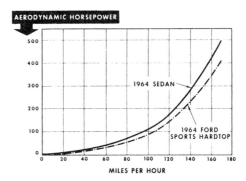

The Ford Galaxie 500 Sports Hardtop offers power availability from 138 to 425 horsepower, and the range of the 500/XL model is from 195 to 425 horsepower to meet the power requirements for all transportation needs.

HORSEPOWER, PERFORMANCE, AND SAFETY

Horsepower and performance are often correlated, but in actual application, horsepower is often a secondary measure of performance, with horsepower being a variable depending upon operating conditions.

The gross horsepower of an engine, as measured on a dynamometer, is reduced by the installation of items such as air filters, mufflers, automatic spark advances, heated intake manifolds, radiator cooling fans and other engine operating accessories. Part of the engine output may be used to operate accessories such as air conditioning and power steering. All mechanical or electrical devices that receive their energy from the engine use engine horsepower while they are operating. Also, operation under conditions of extreme heat or at high altitudes will cause a considerable reduction in available horsepower to drive the vehicle. The horsepower remaining after other operational requirements are fulfilled is delivered to the flywheel where it is further reduced by the power required to turn the transmission and rear axle.

The transmittal of power to the road involves the absorption of horsepower by the resistance offered by the transmission, rear axle, bearings, oil seals, and tires; after which the remaining horsepower is applied as thrust to drive the vehicle, and the "road load horsepower," or power required by the vehicle to maintain a given speed is then the sum of the air resistance and vehicle requirements.

HORSEPOWER AND CAR SPEED

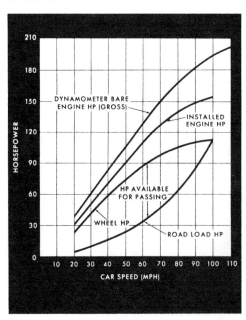

The "wheel horsepower," or the power available, over and above that required to handle the accessory load and to maintain a given speed, is a direct measure of the vehicle's ability to accelerate.

The ability to accelerate may be expressed as the number of seconds required to pass another vehicle which is traveling at a constant speed; allowing six car lengths before and after passing. The effect that the improved acceleration of modern cars has had is shown on the following chart:

PASSING TIME AND TIME EXPOSED TO DANGER

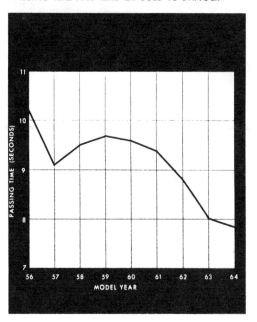

The time required to pass another vehicle at any speed is actually the time of exposure to possible hazard on many two-lane highways. Any reduction of this time may be considered a direct measure of increased safety resulting from high-performance availability.

In the comparison of horsepower, acceleration, and maximum speed, it is known that as maximum speed is approached, the loads on various components are also increased. Therefore, to withstand the stress of the higher loads, many parts of high-performance vehicles are made with greater precision, they are stronger, more durable. As a result, there is a far greater margin of safety at all lower loads and speeds.

STOCK CAR EVENTS

Competitive stock car events in particular have aided in the development of some of the most important contributions to the safety of modern cars — four-wheel brakes . . . pneumatic tires . . . precise steering geometry . . . rigid frames and underbody structures . . . hydraulic shock absorbers — all were developed for and proven in intense competitive events to provide more rapid, more comfortable, and safer motoring.

Ford's interest in competition stock car racing events increased from 1955 through 1957. During this period Ford cars ran at the largest and most difficult events in the country, and the grueling tests of the speedway proved to be a prime factor in the research and development of more reliable and safer cars for the general market.

In the engine area, more-durable cylinder blocks, camshafts, and valves were engineered even though the difficulties encountered at sustained high speed may never have shown up under normal operation or even in a proving ground durability program. Nevertheless, these refinements were incorporated in Ford production vehicles to provide additional performance and stamina.

Today, the testing and search for improvement continues. In preparation for major stock car events, cars are put through exhaustive runs by professional drivers. Accurate records are kept of time, tire wear, and fuel and oil consumption. Company engineers as well as engineers and technicians representing manufacturers of various components are in attendance during the trial runs. Every attempt is made to obtain maximum performance from the cars; and modifications, as permitted by the group santioning the race to be entered, are made to help increase the performance and durability. Shown below is an actual test record of a car being engineered to compete in the 1964 Daytona 500-mile race.

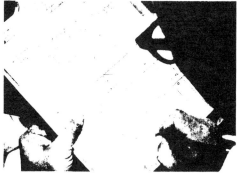

The advance of the Ford Total Performance image started in 1962 when Ford cars placed 1st, 3rd, 5th, and 8th in the rugged 600-mile event at Charlotte, N. C. Since that time, up to April of 1964, results of competitive automotive events the world over have been compiled to add up to eleven out of twelve major victories for Ford cars in sanctioned stock car competition. Of great importance is the fact that all of the events were of 500-mile duration where stamina and design features were prime factors along with the ability for sustained high speed.

Although the "stock cars" of all manufacturers are modified and highly-tuned versions of cars available through a local dealership, the great majority of the parts in each car are standard equipment. The success or failure of a car in a "stock" event is often dependent on a single item such as a simple bolt, or a piston, or an axle — any one of a thousand things can break down and force the car out of competition. Therefore, through the observance of these events, Ford engineers are assisted in the design and development of new and more durable parts in the new Fords for the general public.

In 1963, Ford entered European competition with special compact Falcon models. This proved to be another display of inherent Ford performance and stamina when two V-8 powered Falcon Sprints successfully finished the 71-hour, 2500-mile endurance run in the world-famous Monte Carlo Road Rallye.

Ford returned to Monte Carlo for the 1964 event finishing first in two classes and second overall. The driver of one special Falcon Sprint received five trophies for his victories in Class VIII, one of which was the NASCAR trophy for the highest-placed American car in the Rallye.

FORD RESULTS IN STOCK CAR EVENTS

DATE	TRACK	FORD PLACE
4/5/64	Atlanta, Ga. — 500 Miles	1,3
2/23/64	Daytona Beach, Fla. — 500 Miles	4,8,11,13,14,17, 18,19,20,21
1/19/64	Riverside, Calif. — 500 Miles	1,2,3,5,8,11,17
9/2/63	Darlington, S.C. — 500 Miles	1,2,3,4,8
7/28/63	Bristol, Tenn. — 500 Miles	1,4,7,10
6/2/63	Charlotte, N.C. — 600 Miles	1,6,7,10
3/17/63	Atlanta, Ga. — 500 Miles	1,5,10
2/24/63	Daytona Beach, Fla. — 500 Miles	1,2,3,4,5,10
1/20/63	Riverside, Calif. — 500 Miles	1,6
9/3/62	Darlington, S.C. — 500 Miles	1,3,7
6/10/62	Atlanta, Ga. — 500 Miles	1,8
5/27/62	Charlotte, N.C. — 600 Miles	1,3,5,8

FORD PERFORMANCE TIPS FROM AK MILLER

COBRA ENGINE PERFORMANCE KITS

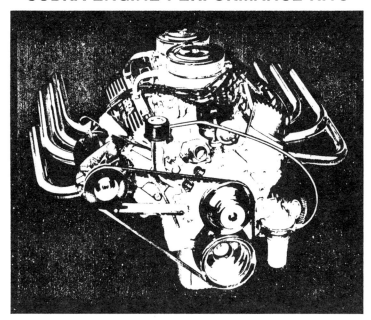

Cobra Kits on Fairlane 289 V-8 with special exhaust header pipes.

Ak Miller, one of America's top authorities on high performance equipment, gives his views and answers questions for those in need of expert advice on the selection and installation of engine modification components. Ak Miller's opinions and advice are his own and do not necessarily represent recommendations of the Ford Motor Company.

New Ford Power With a Custom Look

Own a Falcon powered by a 260 C.I.D. engine? Or a Fairlane with a 221, 260, or 289 2-V? Want more power and sparkle? Check out the new Cobra Kits shown on these pages. Inspired by the championship performance of Ford-powered Cobras, these kits are designed to give your engine stepped-up performance, plus a gleaming, customized appearance.

Read what Ak Miller has to say about Ford's new V-8s and the new Cobra Kits . . .

INSIDE AND OUTSIDE FORD'S NEW V-8s

by Ak Miller

In recent years Ford Fairlane V-8's have been accepted and admired by the motoring world like no other engine in the past. A broad statement admittedly, but one that's backed by the records these fine engines have set for reliability and power output, and their wide popularity with performance-minded car owners.

The Fairlane V-8 has literally stunned the racing world by its consistent winning ways. In 1963, Cobra with its performance-modified 289 became the first sports car to win the coveted Manufacturer's category of the U. S. Road Racing Championship. The final tally in this newly established series of races showed the winning Cobra team with four times as many points as its nearest competitor.

Also in 1963, an aluminum version of the Fairlane engine design shattered records galore in the Indianapolis 500 Memorial Day classic. Installed in a Lotus chassis, this little engine completely changed the established pattern at the Speedway. In late summer, special adaptations of the Fairlane engine racked up three new class records at the 1963 Bonneville Speed Trials. All this in one short year of competition!

Reasons for the Fairlane V-8's success as a pace-setter are many. For example: the basic Fairlane engine is a natural for power-increase modifications because it's designed for high volumetric efficiency and has the advantages of low piston speeds, and short-stroke compactness. The strength and rigidity inherent to Fairlane engine design has permitted output to be boosted to a fantastic 375 horsepower!—a dramatic demonstration of its built-in strength. Remember, these amazing boosts in power were made by modifying without altering the engine's basic compact dimensions.

Along with setting new records, the engine's applications in racing provided a tough proving ground for testing special engine modification parts developed for high speed operation. Because this testing proved these components more than suitable for general use, they are now being offered to enthusiasts who want to get more power and performance from their standard 221-, 260- or 289-cubic-inch V-8 engine. These competition-bred parts are sold in kit form, ranging from special, high-compression cylinder heads to a low-restriction exhaust system.

The performance-minded motorist who doesn't want to go all-out on these kits will find it possible to get a substantial power increase by using just the equipment appropriate to his budget or driving needs. For instance, if one wanted only a moderate 10- to 14-horsepower boost, the single 4-V induction kit would probably do the job. On the other hand, if you were after all-out performance, the ultimate, of course, would be the Weber induction kit. Horsepower carries a price tag, but by careful selection one can pick out kits that will produce the performance desired at a reasonable cost.

In addition to parts that deliver better performance, there are items for your safety and your engine's, too: The high-carbon, cast-steel scatter shield is designed to provide increased protection for you and your passengers. The increased capacity of a competition oil pan provides an extra safety margin for proper lubrication of a high performance engine. Appearance hasn't been forgotten, either. Cobra dress-up kits can make your car's engine a real eye-catcher.

Cobra Kit variety, and the sturdy reliability of the basic design of these engines, facilitate custom modification of Fairlane V-8's to almost any degree of performance and appearance desired.

The opportunity to obtain additional power from your engine without going to the cost of radical machining is given to you through Ford's wide selection of tested and proven Cobra Kits—all you have to do is install them, tune 'er up, and enjoy winning performance with a touch of the throttle.

When it comes to developing competition-winning performance from a Fairlane V-8, the Shelby-American organization has had plenty of experience. Here's how Shelby-American has taken a Fairlane 260 and built it up to obtain various horsepower increases by adding Cobra Kits.

Modifying the 260 CID Engine

Since you determined your engine's displacement when you chose your car, let's consider increasing its horsepower by other means (un-

In developing their winning Cobras, Shelby engineers conducted extensive dynamometer tests of Fairlane V-8's with various modifications. Engine shown has Weber induction system used on King Cobras.

less you want to run for the boring bar). With Cobra Kits, extra power is easily bolted on— no radical machining is necessary. Basically, this additional power output is obtained by increasing the amount of fuel/air mixture and combustion efficiency, and raising the engine speed.

Here are some basic steps requiring little time or money that you can take to make your 260 operate efficiently above the usual passenger car range.

Cobra Distributor Kit

With dual points and mechanically controlled spark advance, the heavy-duty distributor kit delivers reliable spark in the high RPM range. The heavy-duty spark plug leads included in the kit combine with the distributor for an immediate gain of about five horsepower if colder Autolite BF 32 spark plugs are used. (Emission tube removed for competition.)

Cobra Camshaft Kit

Better performance can be had from any engine in which high-RPM "breathing" ability is improved, so let's look at your 260's respiratory system. Except for the distributor kit, the high-lift camshaft and solid lifter kit is the least

expensive path to power. Used with compound valve springs, it can provide a 20-hp jump from the stock 141 rating.

Cobra 4-V Induction Kit

With a change in valve timing allowing better breathing, it makes sense to increase the induction capacity. Replacement of the stock 2-V carburetor with the new 4-V induction kit (carburetor and manifold) can produce an amazing power boost to 220, using racing-type exhaust headers.

Cobra Cylinder Head Kit

The 289 High Performance cylinder head kit, with bigger, stronger valves and heavy-duty springs and rocker arm studs, using a single 4-V carb, pushes power ceiling up to the 225 mark! Total increase? About 85 hp—and no machining necessary.

Cobra 6-V Induction Kit

Prefer the three 2-V induction system? With distributor, cam and cylinder head kits, triple carbs preside over a package capable of providing well over 200 hp.

Cobra Clutch Kit

Getting your performance dollar's worth means full utilization of power at the driving wheels. If a boost to 200 horses or more appeals to you, better start thinking about a clutch that will help handle all that power—the Cobra heavy-duty disc assembly and pressure plate.

Cobra Scatter Shield

Recommended for your own safety in competitive full-throttle operation is the high-carbon cast-steel scatter shield—a good idea for any high-RPM setup.

Cobra Combination Engine Performance Kit

If you want to go all-out from the beginning, the cylinder heads (with complete valve assemblies) and camshaft kits are available as a package that includes a set of matched pistons with heads designed for valve clearance. Top this combination off with the induction system of your choice for a real screamer!

Some notes on the 260...

- The stock 289 4-V High Performance camshaft and solid valve lifters can be used with 260 cylinder heads, and the 289 4-V heavy-duty valve springs can be used with the stock 260 retainers. Screw-in rocker arm studs are not necessary if operation is held below 6000 RPM.

- Caution, the 260 CID cylinder block cannot be bored-out to equal the four-inch bore of the 289 CID block.

- The Cobra Induction Kits should be used in combination with the 289 4-V camshaft kit and heavy-duty valve springs to best obtain maximum engine speed, power and reliability.

... 289 CID Engine

Although the High Performance 289 V-8 is delivered with a 4-V carburetor, additional carburetion is available if premium performance is desired. Since many performance features are a part of this engine's standard equipment, modification is largely restricted to choosing the proper induction system for the type of operation planned for the car.

Tests of power increases from the 289 engine were made for the all-out race preparation of Carroll Shelby's King-Cobras. The horsepower figures shown on the chart on page 6 reveal the results of these tests.

... 221 CID Engine

Cobra Kits and other 289 High Performance equipment can be installed on the 221 CID engine to produce better than 200 horsepower. However, the smaller displacement of this engine will not allow the power boosts obtainable from highly modified 260 or 289 CID engines.

Tips and Precautions for all engines

Although the Cobra Kit line is actually a series of kits, they have been designed for maximum compatibility with each other. The kits provide a wide choice and also separate the equipment into *Street and Competition* or *All-Out Competition* packages. Development emphasis, however, has been for the enthusiast who uses his car for both normal street driving and occasional competition.

Dynamometer tests of Fairlane V-8 engines modified with Cobra Kits have shown their performance ability under a great variety of conditions. Therefore, it will benefit the prospective buyer to check the chart on page 6. It illustrates the combinations of equipment used to obtain various horsepower increases at different engine speeds.

Factory clearances, stock High Performance camshaft and conventional mechanically operated distributor are used to obtain significant power increases. Nevertheless, certain preparations—as well as specific precautions—are desirable, no matter which engine you're working with.

- The Cobra dual-point distributor kit with solid wire spark plug leads should be installed to draw the best performance from any of the other Cobra Kits.

- For all-out performance, compound valve springs are necessary and should be matched as closely as possible using a spring tester and shim stock.

- A substitute or altered crankshaft assembly should be rebalanced before installation. If the heavy-duty clutch kit is used, it should be attached before rebalancing.

- For top efficiency, a dual exhaust system should be installed in place of the single one.

- The 289 High Performance connecting rods are desirable for modified 221, 260 and 289 2-V engines (rebalancing of the crankshaft assembly is required).

- The 289 4-V cylinder head and valve assembly may be used without the specially designed "eyebrow-ed" pistons if the correct stock head gaskets are used.

• When fitting 289 4-V cylinder heads to a 289 2-V, 260- or 221-inch block, be sure to use the stock gasket for the engine block, not the heads.

• The 289 4-V camshaft can be used in all other engines, and without the 4-V cylinder heads, but care must be taken to use the proper head gasket (proper for the block) to provide sufficient valve clearance.

• The 4-V High Performance cylinder heads are stock, production line parts and are not ported, relieved or polished, but may be machined if desired.

• 289 High Performance exhaust manifolds are not recommended for Falcon installations; extensive reworking of the engine compartment is required.

• In assembling your improved engine, remember to use standard head gaskets designed for your engine block. Thinner ones can cause serious valve and piston damage.

• Torque sequence and ratings are extremely important to proper installation of both manifold and cylinder heads.

• The Weber carburetor induction system is recommended for "competition-only" application.

• The Cobra Combination Engine Performance Kit should not be used in cars equipped with automatic transmissions.

Get additional advice on your High Performance Kit or power problems. Write to Ak Miller, Ford Performance Advisor, P.O. Box 627, Dearborn, Michigan.

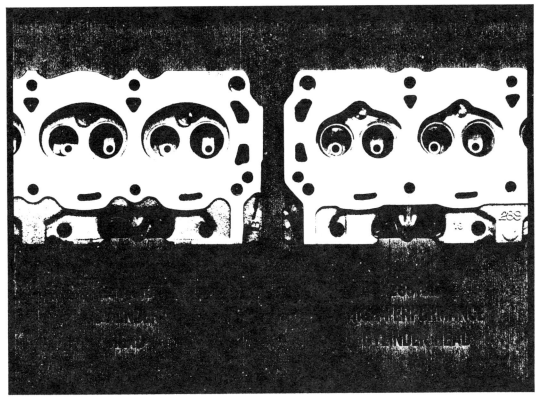

Larger, better breathing valves, reworked combustion chamber of 289 high-performance heads raise 260 engine's compression ratio to 10.5 to 1. These heads can also be used to help boost power on a 221 CID engine.

DYNAMOMETER TEST RATINGS
BY SHELBY-AMERICAN

HOW TO USE CHART BELOW: Choose engine from top of columns at left if you are interested in horsepower—260 engine, Col. A—289 4-V engine, Col. B. Read down left hand column to select HP increase. Then determine components used to gain HP increase by reading across to right. Code letter "A" indicates component listed above was used on 260 engine—code letter "B", component was used on 289 4-V engine.

Columns at far right give peak torque obtained using same equipment.

MODIFICATIONS WITH COBRA KITS

STOCK RATING HORSEPOWER @ RPM — A 260 CID	B 289 CID (4-V)	Heavy-duty Distributor, Pg. 8 spark plug leads	Autolite BF-32 spark plugs	Emission valve plugged	Cobra Cam Kit, Pg. 8	Compound valve springs	Cobra Cylinder Head Kit, Pg. 7	Reworked 4-V heads: ported, enlarged comb. chambers	Steel shim cyl. head gaskets	289 4-V High Performance Exh. Manifolds	Competition (tubing) exh. headers	4-V (1-4V) Induction Kit, Pg. 10	8-V (2-4V) Induction Kit, Pg. 11	6-V (3-2V) Induction Kit, Pg. 10	8-V (4-2V) Weber Kit, Pg. 11	Generator disconnected	STOCK RATING PEAK (lbs.-ft.) TORQUE @ RPM — A 260 CID	B 289 CID (4-V)
141 @ 4500	232 @ 5500		B								B					AB	227 @ 2500	282 @ 4000
145 @ 4500	242 @ 6000	AB	AB[1]	AB							B					AB	228 @ 2500	289 @ 3500
161 @ 5000	247 @ 5500	AB	AB[1]	AB	A	A			B		B					AB	217 @ 3000	295 @ 3500
	249 @ 5500	B	B[1]	B					B	B	B					B	228 @ 4000	296 @ 3500
205 @ 5500	276 @ 6000	AB	AB[1]	AB	A	A			B		AB		B	A		AB	232 @ 3500	285 @ 4000
220 @ 5500	286 @ 6500	AB	AB[1]	AB	A	A		B	B		AB	AB				AB	228 @ 3500	286 @ 4500
211 @ 5500	314 @ 6500	AB	AB[1]	AB	A		A	B	B		AB			A		AB	230 @ 4000	286 @ 4500
207 @ 6000	345 @ 6500	AB	A	AB	A		A	B	B	A	B			A	B	AB	232 @ 3500	286 @ 4500
213 @ 6000		A	A	A	A		A				A			A		A	230 @ 3500	313 @ 5000
222 @ 5500		A	A	A	A	A				A	A						240 @ 4000	
225 @ 5500		A	A	A	A		A			A	A						244 @ 4000	

1. The 289 4-V engine used Autolite type BTF-1 spark plugs up to 276 hp; higher readings were obtained using type BF-603.

COBRA ENGINE AND DRESS-UP KITS ARE AVAILABLE THROUGH YOUR FORD DEALER. FOR ADDITIONAL DETAILS CHECK AT YOUR DEALER'S PARTS DEPARTMENT.

COBRA COMBINATION ENGINE PERFORMANCE KITS

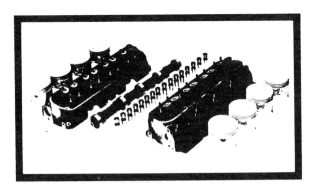

Each of these Performance Kits includes the Cam Kit on page 8, and the Cylinder Head and Valve Kit on this page. Also included are eight matched pistons, designed with extra clearance for the larger valve size and higher lift. Performance Kits can be easily installed on the engines listed below without extra machining. They should be used with manual-shift transmissions only.

ENGINE	PERFORMANCE KIT NO.
221 CID V-8	C40Z-6A044-A
260 CID V-8	C40Z-6A044-B
289 CID V-8	C40Z-6A044-C

Each $342.70*

COBRA CYLINDER HEAD AND VALVE KIT

These cylinder heads have heavy-duty threaded rocker arm studs to resist loosening . . . spring seat ridges to help keep valve springs and dampers aligned . . . solid valve spring retainers and oil-controlling valve stem seals. Intake valve head diameter is 1.665"; exhaust, 1.445". Both are aluminized and have polished chrome-plated stems. Exhaust valves are forged, heat-resistant chrome-manganese alloy. For 221, 260, and 289 CID V-8's. **Cobra Cylinder Head and Valve Kit No. C40Z-6C056-A—$221.50***

KIT INCLUDES:

Cylinder Heads (2)
Intake Valves (8)
Exhaust Valves (8)
Spring Assemblies—
Valve Damper (16)

Stem Seals (16)
Valve Spring Retainers (16)
Key—Valve Spring
Retainer (32)

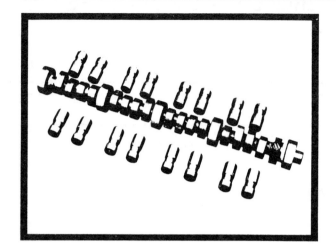

COBRA HIGH PERFORMANCE CAM KIT

This is the same high-lift design cam-shaft used in the High Performance 289 V-8 which powers the latest Cobra model. Cam lift is .289″ and the timing duration is 306°. For 221, 260 and 289 CID V-8's.

Cobra High Performance Cam Kit No. C40Z-6A257-A—$72.55*

Kit includes: Camshaft (1) and Tappets (16)

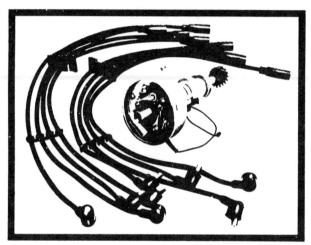

COBRA DISTRIBUTOR KIT

This heavy-duty unit features dual contact points, centrifugal spark advance control. Specially calibrated for best spark timing in the high speed range to produce maximum possible engine speed. For 260 and 289 CID V-8's.

Cobra Distributor Kit No. C4DZ-12050-A—$49.80*

Kit includes: Distributor Assembly with distributor rotor, cap, and spark plug cables.

COBRA HEAVY-DUTY CLUTCH KIT

Complete clutch assembly of heavy-duty construction and semi-centrifugal design in a smooth-working unit with low slip characteristics and a firmer grip at all RPM; especially effective at high speeds. For 221, 260, and 289 CID V-8's.

Cobra Heavy-Duty Clutch Kit No. C30Z-7A537-A—$51.45*

Kit includes: Disc (1) and Pressure Plate (1)

COBRA COMPETITION OIL PAN

Sturdy, cast-aluminum competition-type oil pan features air cooling fins for improved oil temperature control. Also has large 6½ qt. capacity for added engine protection. For 221, 260, and 289 CID V-8's.

Cobra Competition Oil Pan Kit No. C40Z-6675-A

(Available Soon)

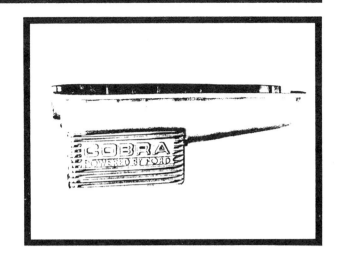

COBRA DUAL EXHAUST KIT

All you'll need to change a single exhaust layout to a dual system. The 4" heavy-duty glass-pack mufflers are of straight-through design to minimize back pressure. For 1963-64 Falcon 260 CID V-8's (Available soon for Fairlane 260 and 289 V-8's).

Cobra Dual Exhaust Kit (Falcon 260 only)

No. C4DZ-5210-A—$69.95*

Kit includes: Glass-Pack Muffler (2) • Exhaust Pipe (1) • Clamps (4)

Pipe, shown separated, is of one-piece construction.

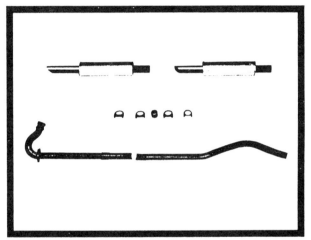

COBRA SCATTER SHIELD

Made of high-carbon cast steel, this housing is designed to give extra protection for occupants and car especially at high engine speeds. Replaces cast-aluminum housing. For 221, 260, and 289 CID V-8's. (Not available for automatic transmissions.)

Cobra Scatter Shield Kit No. C40Z-6394-A—$106.75*

*Manufacturers' suggested retail price. Installation charges and state or local taxes, if any, are extra. All prices subject to change without notice.

SINGLE 4-V INDUCTION KIT

Consisting of production parts, this simple kit will boost engine power at reasonable cost. 4-V kit replaces standard 2-V induction system without major changes to basic system layout. For 221, 260, and 289 CID V-8's.

Single 4-V Induction Kit No. C40Z-6B068-D—$120.30*

Kit includes: Intake Manifold (1) • Carburetor (1) • Air Cleaner (1) • Spacer (1) • Plus miscellaneous seals, gaskets, studs and screws.

6-V INDUCTION KIT

Combines three 2-venturi carburetors on the precision-cast-aluminum intake manifold. Uses center carburetor for starting, low and medium speeds. Front and rear carburetors act as secondaries, cut in at higher engine speeds, or during maximum acceleration demand periods. For 260 and 289 C1D V-8's.

6-V Induction Kit No. C40Z-6B068-A and B (complete)—$210.00*

Kit includes: Intake Manifold (1) • Carburetors (3) • Air Cleaner (1) • Fuel Manifold (1)

3–2-V Linkage Kit—1963 Falcon C3DZ-9B843-A.
3–2-V Linkage Kit—1964 Falcon C4DZ-9B843-A.
3–2-V Linkage Kit—all Fairlane C4OZ-9B843-A.

8-V INDUCTION KIT

This kit features two 4-venturi carburetors mounted on a specially designed cast-aluminum intake manifold. Primary sections of both carburetors operate progressively from throttle linkage for starting, low and medium speeds. Both secondaries are velocity-flow-operated to cut in for acceleration and high speed use. For 221, 260, and 289 CID engines.

8-V Induction Kit No. C40Z-6B068-E—$243.00*

Kit includes: Intake Manifold (1) • Carburetors (2) • Air Cleaner(2)(Appropriate throttle linkage available separately)

8-V WEBER INDUCTION KIT

The ultimate induction system for "all-out" competition. Four 2-V Weber carburetors mounted on a special intake manifold for wide-open running. This is the same kind of high-output system used in the Lotus Fords at Indianapolis and the Cooper Cobra that won at Riverside and Laguna Seca. Not recommended for street use. For 221, 260, and 289 CID V-8's.

8-V Weber Induction Kit No. C40Z-6B068-C—$1230.70*

Kit includes: Intake Manifold (1) • Carburetors (4) • Water and Fuel Manifold (1) (Appropriate throttle linkage available separately)

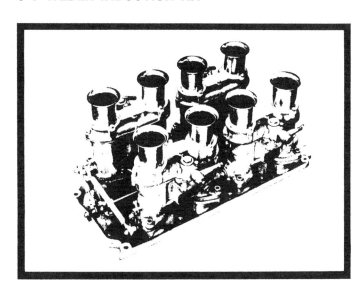

*Manufacturers' suggested retail price. Installation charges and state or local taxes, if any, are extra. All prices subject to change without notice.

1964 Cobra Engine Dress-Up Kit

COBRA ENGINE DRESS-UP KITS

Add the racy "Cobra" look to your engine with bright finned, polished aluminum valve covers; gleaming chrome air cleaner; filler caps and dip stick. For 221, 260, and 289 CID V-8's.

1963 Cobra Engine Dress-Up Kit No. C30Z-6980-A—$72.45*

Kit includes: 1963 Cobra Valve Cover Kit • *Oil Dip Stick • *Radiator Cap • *Oil Filler Cap • *Master Cyl. Cap • *Air Cleaner Cover and Filler.

Chrome Plated

1964 Cobra Engine Dress-Up Kit No. C40Z-6980-A—$78.35*

For 260 and 289 CID V-8's is the same as above except for:

1964 Cobra Valve Cover Kit C40Z-6A547-A.

1964 Cobra Valve Cover Kit

COBRA VALVE COVER KITS

Start your engine dress-up project with a pair of handsome finned, polished aluminum valve covers. For 221, 260, and 289 CID V-8's.

1963 Cobra Valve Cover Kit No. C30Z-6A547-A—$42.00*

Kit includes: Valve Cover Assembly (2) • Chrome Bolts (12) • Chrome Washers (12).

1964 Cobra Valve Cover Kit No. C40Z-6A547-A—$47.85*

For 260 and 289 CID V-8's is the same as above except for:

1964 Valve Cover Assemblies (1 each).

COBRA ENGINE AND DRESS-UP KITS ARE AVAILABLE THROUGH YOUR FORD DEALER. ASK FOR ADDITIONAL KIT DETAILS AT HIS PARTS DEPARTMENT.

*Manufacturers' suggested retail price. Installation charges and state or local taxes, if any, are extra. All prices subject to change without notice.

The Mercury for 1964 was a continuation of the 1963 design with more emphasis on luxury. The styling bore much similarity to the 1959 and 1960 Continentals. For the performance minded there was the Marauder, with its fastback hardtop and high performance engines.

Engines offered were the 390 cid V-8 (2-bbl) rated at 250 hp, the 390 cid V-8 (2-bbl) rated at 266 hp, the 390 cid V-8 (4-bbl) rated at 300 hp, the 390 cid V-8 (4-bbl) rated at 330 hp, the 427 cid V-8 (4-bbl) rated at 410 hp and the 427 cid V-8 (dual 4-bbl) rated at 425 hp. The transmissions available were the 3-speed manual, the 4-speed manual and the 3-speed Merc-O-Matic automatic.

Production amounted to 89,261 units, with the model breakdowns as follows. Price follows each model in ()'s: MONTEREY 4-dr sedan 20,234 ($2,892), 4-dr hdt. sedan 4,143 ($2,957), 2-dr sedan 3,932 ($2,819), 2-dr hdt. Maurader Fastback 8,760 ($2,884), 2-dr hdt. coupe 2,926 ($2,882), convertible 2,592 ($3,226); MONTCLAIR 4-dr sedan 15,520 ($3,116), 4-dr hdt. sedan 8,655 ($3,181), 2-dr hdt. Maurader Fastback 6,459 ($3,127), 2-dr hdt. coupe 2,329 ($3,127); PARK LANE 4-dr sedan 6,230 ($3,348), 4-dr hdt. sedan 3,658 ($3,413), 2-dr hdt. Maurauder Fastback 2,721 ($3,359), 2-dr hdt. coupe 1,786 ($3,359), 4-dr hdt. sedan 2,402 ($3,413), convertible 1,967 ($3,549); STATION WAGON 4-dr Commuter, 6-pass. 3,484 ($3,236), 4-dr Colony Park, 6-pass. 4,234 ($3,434), 4-dr Commuter, 9-pass. 1,839 ($3,306), 4-dr Colony Park 5,624 ($3,504).

Sixteen exterior colors were available with two-tones an extra cost option. Interiors were offered in six colors of cloth and vinyl or six colors of vinyl.

Literature offered for 1964 consisted of the full-line color folder, the full-line color mailer folder with the same cover as above, and the big cars color catalogue (unrevised and revised, see pages 114-116). The big Mercury was also included in the full-line press kit.

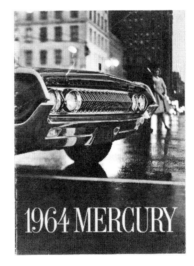

The price is medium ... the action maximum ... the car is Mercury

Mercury

Pikes Peak Champion

Park Lane Marauder two-door hardtop also available on four-door hardtop.

One look is enough to tell you that this is an action car. The slender, racy roof is one reason. The thrusting spear-shaped profile is another. And Marauder keeps the promise of its "let's go" look. A brilliant Marauder Super 390 cu.-in. four-barrel V-8 is standard in the Park Lane series (shown). You can have up to an 8-barrel 427 cu.-in. V-8. All are new editions of the engine that powered Marauder to the championship in the most recent Pikes Peak climb. Options include the special Sports Package with bucket seats, console-mounted transmission selector, and fully synchronized 4-speed transmission or Multi-Drive Merc-O-Matic.

MERCURY V-8 POWER TEAMS

Engines	Marauder 390 V-8	Marauder 390 V-8	Marauder Super 390 V-8*	Marauder Interceptor 390 V-8*	Marauder 427 V-8*	Marauder Super 427 V-8*
Adv hp @ rpm	250 @ 4400	266 @ 4400	300 @ 4600	330 @ 5000	410 @ 5600	425 @ 6000
Monterey	Standard	N.A.	Optional	Optional	Optional	Optional
Montclair	Standard	Standard†	Optional	Optional	Optional	Optional
Park Lane	N.A.	N.A.	Standard	Optional	Optional	Optional
Commuter	Standard	N.A.	Optional	Optional	N.A.	N.A.
Colony Park	Standard	Standard†	Optional	Optional	N.A.	N.A.
Displacement	390 cu in	390 cu in	390 cu in	390 cu in.	427 cu in	427 cu in
Adv torque @ rpm	378 @ 2400	378 @ 2400	427 @ 2800	427 @ 3200	476 @ 3400	480 @ 3700
Bore & stroke (in)	4.05 x 3.78	4.05 x 3.78	4.05 x 3.78	4.05 x 3.78	4.23 x 3.78	4.23 x 3.78
Carburetor	2-V	2-V	4-V	4-V	4-V	Dual 4-bbl.
Compression ratio	9.4	9.4	10.1	10.1	11.5	11.2
Fuel	Regular	Regular	Premium	Premium	Super Prem.	Super Prem.
Exhaust	Single(a)	Single	Dual	Dual	Dual	Dual
Valve lifters	Hydraulic	Hydraulic	Hydraulic	Mechanical	Mechanical	Mechanical
Transmissions						
3-speed manual	●			●	●	
4-speed manual	●			●	●	●	●
Multi-Drive Merc-O-Matic	●	●		●	●	

(a) Dual exhaust for convertible
*Optional at extra cost   N.A.—Not Available

†Std. in Montclair and Colony Park with Multi-Drive Merc-O-Matic
4-speed transmission not available with station wagons

SPECIFICATIONS:

EXTERIOR DIMENSIONS (Inches)

Wheelbase	120.0
Tread, Front	61.0
Rear	60.0
Length, over-all, Sedan	215.5
Station Wagon	210.3
Width, over-all, Sedan	80.0
Station Wagon	80.0
*Height, over-all, Sedan	56.7
Station Wagon	57.8
Convertible	55.7
Curb weight (lbs), 4-door Sedan	4174 lb.
Colony Park, 2-seat	4464 lb.

CAPACITIES

Fuel tank	20 gallons
Cooling system	20 quarts, with heater
Engine oil	6 quarts, with filter change

*With passengers

MANUAL TRANSMISSIONS

All-synchronized 3-speed, steering column lever

Ratios—1st	2.42:1
2nd	1.61:1
3rd	1.00:1
Reverse	2.33:1

4-speed, floor- or console-mounted lever

Ratios—1st	2.36:1
2nd	1.78:1
3rd	1.41:1
4th	1.00:1
Reverse	2.42:1

MULTI-DRIVE MERC-O-MATIC TRANSMISSION

Type .... Torque converter with automatic planetary gear train

Ratios—LO	2.40:1
D2	1.47:1; 1.00:1
D1	2.40:1; 1.47:1; 1.00:1
Reverse	2.00:1

1965 Ford

For 1965 Ford again did a total ground up redesign of its big car series. Comfort and luxury were of the utmost concern, with the new flow-thru ventilation system, first time ever coil spring rear suspension, and luxurious new interiors. The body featured straight lines with little or no curves. The LTD was the new series this year and Ford did extensive advertising announcing that tests proved it quieter than the Rolls-Royce. This car was indeed a low-priced luxury car, being both smooth riding and quiet. Mid-year Galaxie models added chrome stripes on each side of the deck lid emblem to denote the spring models.

Engines offered for 1965 were the 240 cid six (1-bbl) rated at 150 hp, the 289 cid V-8 (2-bbl) rated at 200 hp, the 352 cid V-8 (4-bbl) rated at 250 hp, the 390 cid V-8 (4-bbl) rated at 300 hp, and the 427 cid V-8 (dual 4-bbl) rated at 425 hp. Transmissions offered were the 3-speed manual, the 3-speed manual with overdrive, the 4-speed manual and the 3-speed Cruise-O-Matic automatic.

Production amounted to 978,519 units, with the following model breakdown (sixes and V-8's totals combined). Prices follow each in ()'s, with V-8's costing $116 more: CUSTOM 4-dr sedan 96,393 ($2,366), 2-dr sedan 49,034 ($2,313); CUSTOM 500 4-dr sedan 71,727 ($2,467), 2-dr sedan 19,603 ($2,414); GALAXIE 500 4-dr sedan 181,183 ($2,623), 4-dr hardtop 49,982 ($2,708), 2-dr hardtop 157,284 ($2,737), convertible 31,930 ($2,889); GALAXIE 500XL V-8 2-dr hardtop 28,141 ($3,167), convertible 9,849 ($3,426); GALAXIE 500 LTD V-8 4-dr hardtop 68,038 ($3,245), 2-dr hardtop 37,691 ($3,167); STATION

WAGON 4-dr Ranch Wagon 6-pass. 30,817 ($2,707), 4-dr Country Sedan 6-pass. 59,693 ($2,797), 4-dr Country Sedan 10-pass. 32,344 ($2,899), 4-dr Country Sedan 6-pass. 24,308 ($3,041), 4-dr Country Squire 10-pass. 30,502 ($3,109).

Fourteen exterior colors were offered with two-tones optional at extra cost. Vinyl roofs were available in black, white, brown, blue or ivy gold. Interiors were offered in black, white, red, ivy gold, turquoise or palomino, in vinyl or vinyl and cloth on bench or bucket seats.

Literature for 1965 consisted of the full-line color catalogue dated 8-64 and revised 4-65 (see specs on page 126), the Galaxie color catalogue dated 8-64 and revised 2-65, the Station Wagons color catalogue dated 8-64, the "Double Take..." color mailer catalogue, "The many worlds of total performance for 1965" color mailer catalogue, the "Fact: the 1965 Ford actually tested quieter than a Rolls-Royce!" color mailer catalogue, the "Special Report to 1962 Ford owners" color mailer catalogue, the "ideas that brighten Station Wagon living" color mailer catalogue, the accessories color catalogue (see pages 124-125) and the green spring supplement to the same, the "1964-65 Ford facts and figures on high performance engines by Ak Miller" booklet, dealer item (see pages 118-123), the "Buyer's Digest" booklet filled with facts and figures, the colors selector folder, the full-line string of color postcards, the LTD 4-dr hardtop color postcard, and the 500XL convertible color postcard. Galaxies were also included in the full-line press kit.

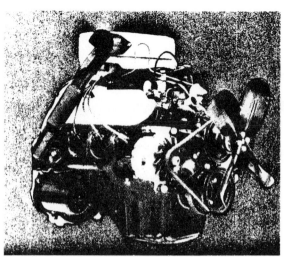

AK MILLER

THE FORD HIGH PERFORMANCE ENGINE STORY

Akton Olson Miller was chosen as Ford's Performance Advisor because of his distinguished career in the performance field.

Ak is a co-founder of the oldest hot rod club in America—The Road Runners founded in 1937. Also he was instrumental in the establishment of the Southern California Timing Association. This organization, with Ak as president, staged the first hot rod show in America. This show was held in Los Angeles Armory in 1948. He also initiated the first annual Bonneville Speed Trial in 1948.

Ak was also a founder of the National Hot Rod Association, and is currently serving as a Vice President.

Ak has participated in almost every type of performance driving from the Pikes Peak Hill Climb, the Bonneville Speed Trials, and the Mexican Road Race to the Mobil Economy Run.

The FORD 289 and 427 high performance engines covered in this booklet have a long and distinguished record of performance and reliability unequalled by any present-day, mass-produced automotive engine.

This is due mainly to the high degree of sophistication achieved in such areas as crankshaft assemblies, valve train assemblies, manifolds, and casting and machining techniques.

Many of the components in these two fine engines were designed strictly for the performance-minded public. It is, therefore, of interest to note that almost without exception these same parts can be readily transferred to the standard production engines with very satisfactory results in horsepower increases coupled with a high order of reliability.

In this booklet, therefore, in addition to giving general specifications on our high performance units, we have set about to acquaint you with the parts numbers of some of these interchangeable components for those of you desiring to obtain a high horsepower rating from your standard production engine.

Generally speaking, the 427 components will adapt to engines of 332, 352 and 390 cubic inch displacement. By taking advantage of the parts listed herein, the owner of any of these production engines can assure himself of horsepower gains with complete reliability by using standard Ford parts that have been proven in competition the world over.

It is also true that 289 high performance engine components will adapt to smaller Ford engines such as the 221, 260 and standard 289. Along this line, we have added the frosting to the cake by offering the very popular Cobra Kit items, designed specifically to enhance the performance of these smaller engines with the highest degree of reliability.

When undertaking such modifications, it is very important that one go about it in a logical and scientific manner. In other words, do not install components that will not readily adjust to your particular every-day needs or that are not compatible with your particular engine or drive train. For example, we do not recommend high performance camshafts with automatic transmissions. Also, we do not recommend the competition Weber setup for general street usage.

In this area, Ford Motor Company is very unique in offering the services of a Performance Advisor to aid in the proper selection and application of items that will be compatible with your particular vehicle and your personal driving requirements. Therefore, we invite you to take advantage of this service by writing to:

AK MILLER
FORD PERFORMANCE ADVISOR
P. O. BOX 627
DEARBORN, MICHIGAN

SPECIFICATIONS

DESCRIPTION	HIGH PERFORMANCE 289-4V	HIGH PERFORMANCE 427-8V
Bore	4.00	4.23
Stroke	2.87	3.78
Firing Order	1-5-4-2-6-3-7-8	1-5-4-2-6-3-7-8
Maximum Brake Horsepower	271 @ 6000 RPM	425 @ 6000 RPM
Maximum Torque	314 ft. lbs. @ 3400	480 ft. lbs. @ 3700
Compression Ratio (cranking compression)	11.6:1 maximum	13:1 maximum
	10.5:1 nominal	12:1 nominal
Camshaft	C3OZ-6250-C	C3AZ-6250-K
Duration	306°	324°
Intake Opens	44° BTC	8° 30' ATC
Intake Closes	82° ABC	36° 30' ABC
Exhaust Opens	92° BBC	39° 30' BBC
Exhaust Closes	34° ATC	11° 30' BTC
Valve Overlap	78° Theo.	96° Theo.
Valve Lash	.020	.025-.028
Valve Lift	.4774	.524
Ignition Timing	36° to 38° at 5000 RPM	39° at 5000 RPM
Contact Point Settings	.018 to .022	.018 to .022
Cam Angle	26° to 28.5°	26° to 28.5°
Breaker Arm Tension	27 to 32 oz.	27 to 32 oz.
Sparkplug Recommendations	BF-32 Autolite for street	BF-32 Autolite for street
	BF-22 Autolite for dragstrip	BF-22 or BTF-1 for dragstrip
Sparkplug Gap	.025-.028 dragstrip	.025-.028 dragstrip
	.032 to .036 street	.032 to .036 street
Fuel Pump Pressure	5½ to 6½ lbs.	5½ to 6½ lbs.
Recommended RPM REDLINE	6500 to 7000	6200 to 6400
Carburetor Jets	To be Added	To be Added
Valve Spring Pressure	88 lbs. at 1.77	80 to 90 lbs. at 1.82
	247 lbs. at 1.32	255 to 280 at 1.32
Clearances		
Pistons	.0030 to .0036	.007
Rod Bearings	.009 to .0029	.0025-.003
Main Bearings	.006 to .0027	.0025 to .003
Rod End Play	.014 to .024	.014 to .025

1964 FORD 427 HIGH PERFORMANCE SERVICE PARTS

The following is a listing of parts most frequently used for servicing or modifying Ford 332, 352, 390 & 406 Engines:

ENGINE	
PART NUMBER	DESCRIPTION
C3AE-6007-HE-361-T	Engine Assembly—427 CI—8V
C3AZ-6009-M	Cylinder Assembly 427 CI—8V
C3AZ-6010-K	Cylinder Block 4V and 8V
C3AZ-6049-J	Cylinder Head Assy. 4V—8V
C3AZ-6200-C	Rod Assy.—Connecting 4V—8V
C3AZ-6200-F	Rod Assy.—Connecting Reinforced Cap 4V—8V
C3AZ-6250-D	Camshaft (306") 4V—8V
C3AZ-6250-K	Camshaft (324°) 4V—8V
C3AZ-6256-A	Sprocket—Camshaft (4V and 8V)
C3AZ-6265-A	Spacer Cam Sprocket (4V and 8V)
B8A-6268-A	Chain—Timing (Link-Belt) (4V and 8V)
C3AZ-6269-A	Plate Camshaft Thrust (4V and 8V)
C3AZ-6303-G	Crankshaft—Roller Fillets (4V and 8V)
B8A-6306-A	Sprocket, Crankshaft (4V and 8V)
C3AZ-6312-B	Damper Assy.—Crankshaft Vibration
C3AZ-6375-E	Flywheel Assembly (4V and 8V)
B9TE-6500-A	Tappet Assy. Valve (4V and 8V)
C3AZ-6505-E	Valve, Exhaust (4V and 8V)
C3AZ-6507-J	Valve Intake Bumper Type (4V and 8V)
C3AZ-6513-A	Spring Assy. Valve Damper (4V and 8V)
C3AZ-6514-A	Retainer—Valve Spring (4V and 8V)
C1SE-6524-A	Baffle, Valve Spring Oil (4V and 8V)
C3AZ-6A536-A	Seat Valve Spring 4V—8V
B8A-6564-B	Arm Assy. Valve Rocker 4V—8V
B8A-6565-C	Rod—Valve Push 4V—8V
B8A-6571-B	Seal—Valve Stem 4V—8V
C3AZ-6600-A	Pump Assy. Oil 4V—8V
C1AZ-6A642-A	Oil Cooler
C0AE-6675-F	Pan Assy. Oil 4V—8V
C1AE-6675-F	Pan Assembly—Oil (1962/63 406 & 427 CI)
C2AZ-6675-A-SO	Pan Assembly—Oil—8 Quart (4V and 8V)

TRANSMISSION & CLUTCH	
C3AZ-7003-H	4-Speed Transmission with Steel Casing 4V—8V
C3AZ-7006-D-SO	Transmission, Case 4-Spd. Alum.
C3AZ-7007-B	Plate Assy. Engine Rear Cover
C3AZ-7A039-D-SO	Extension Housing Alum. 4-Speed
C3AZ-7550-M	Disc Assy. Clutch
C3AZ-7550-N	Disc Assy.—Clutch (Drag Racing)
C3AZ-7563-D	Pressure Plate Assy. (Drag Racing)
C3AZ-7563-C	Pressure Plate—Clutch

FUEL PUMP	
PART NUMBER	DESCRIPTION
C0AE-9350-E	Pump Assy.—Fuel 4V—8V

MANIFOLDS	
C3AZ-9424-J	Manifold Assy.—Intake 4V
C4AZ-6B068-A	8V Intake
	3-2V Intake Manifold Assy.
C3AZ-9430-C	Manifold Assy. Exhaust R.H. 4V—8V
C3AZ-9431-F	Manifold Assy. Exhaust L.H. 4V—8V
	Police option Exhaust Manifolds

CARBURETOR	
C3AZ-9510-S	Carb. Assy. 8V 540 CVM 8V
C4AZ-9510-A	Carburetor Assy. 600 CFM 8V Primary & Secondary
C3AZ-9510-K	Carburetor Assy. Std. 4V

ELECTRICAL	
C3AZ-12127-AE	Distributor Assembly (Except with Transistorized System) (4V and 8V)
C3AZ-12127-AF	Distributor Assembly (Transistor) (4V and 8V)

REAR AXLE	
C1AW-4209-E	Kit—Diff. Gear and Pinion (5.83)
WAB-4209-C	Kit—Diff. Gear and Pinion (5.67)
WAB-4209-D	Kit—Diff. Gear and Pinion (5.43)
WAB-4209-E	Kit—Diff. Gear and Pinion (5.14)
WAB-4209-F	Kit—Diff. Gear and Pinion (4.86)
WAB-4209-G	Kit—Diff. Gear and Pinion (4.71)
WAB-4209-H	Kit—Diff. Gear and Pinion (4.57)
WAB-4209-J	Kit—Diff. Gear and Pinion (4.29)
WAB-4209-K	Kit—Diff. Gear and Pinion (3.40)
C0AW-4234-D	Shaft—Rear Axle Right Hand
C0AZ-4235-C	Shaft—Rear Axle Left Hand
C2AZ-4880-A	Kit—Locking Differential

C4AZ-6980-A	ENGINE DRESS-UP KIT—	*Includes:* Valve Covers • Air Cover Cleaner • Oil Breather Cap • Brake Master Cyl. Cover • Dip Stick • Radiator Cap • Fuel Filter & Fan Guard Shroud

COBRA KIT ITEMS
For Modifying Ford 221, 260 and 289 CID Engines

DESCRIPTION	PART NUMBER
Performance Kit (including cam kit, cylinder head and valve kit, 8 matched pistons designed with extra clearance for larger valve size and higher lift)	C4OZ-6A044-A for 221 CID V-8 C4OZ-6A044-B for 260 CID V-8 C4OZ-6A044-C for 289 CID V-8
Cobra Cylinder Head and Valve Kit	C4OZ-6C056-A
Cobra High Performance Cam Kit	C4OZ-6A257-A
Cobra Distributor Kit	C4DZ-12050-A
Cobra Heavy-Duty Clutch Kit	C3OZ-7A537-A
Cobra Competition Oil Pan	C4OZ-6675-A
Cobra Dual Exhaust Kit	C4DZ-5210-A
Cobra Scatter Shield	C4OZ-6394-A
Single 4-V Induction Kit	C4OZ-6B068-D
6-V Induction Kit	C4OZ-6B068-A (260 CID) C4OZ-6B068-B (289 CID)
8-V Induction Kit	C4OZ-6B068-E
8-V Weber Induction Kit	C4OZ-6B068-C

Cobra Engine Dress-Up Kits... C3OZ-6980-A for 1963 Falcon 260 CID—1963 Fairlane 221, 260, 289 CID
C4OZ-6980-A for 1964 Falcon 260 CID—1964 Fairlane 260, 289 CID
Cobra Valve Cover Kits...... C3OZ-6A547-A for 1963 Falcon 260 CID, 1963 Fairlane 221, 260, 289
C4OZ-6A547-A for 1964 Falcon 260 CID, 1964 Fairlane 260, 289 CID

SERVICE PARTS LIST

New Ford 4V 289 High Performance V-8

PART NUMBER	DESCRIPTION
C4OE-6007-E-563-A	Engine Assembly 289 CI-4V
Following 6 parts are required when installing C4OE-6007-E-563-A engine:	
C3OZ-8600-C	Fan
C3OZ-8620-E	Fan Belt
C3AZ-9350-M	Fuel Pump
C4AZ-9600-E	Air Cleaner
C1TZ-10002-A	Generator
C2OZ-11002-A	Starter
C3OZ-6009-D	Cylinder Assembly 289 CI-4V
C3OZ-6010-D	Cylinder Block 4V (Mechanical Tappets)
C2OZ-6019-D	Kit—Cylinder Front Cover
C2OZ-6020-A	Gasket, Cyl., Front Cover
C3OZ-6049-H	Cylinder Head Assy. Marked C3OE-6090-E or F
C3AZ-6051-C	Cylinder Head Gasket
C2OZ-6065-B	Bolt—Cylinder Head (Long)
C3OZ-6108-K	Piston, Standard
B2AZ-6135-A	Pin—Piston—Standard
B2AZ-6135-B	Pin—Piston—.001 O/S Blue
B2AZ-6135-C	Pin—Piston—.002 O/S Yellow

PART NUMBER	DESCRIPTION
C3AZ-6140-B	Retainer, Piston Pin
C3AZ-6148-B	Partial Ring Set
C3OZ-6200-A	Rod Assy.—Connecting
C3OZ-6211-A	Bearing, Connecting
C1TE-6212-A	Nut—Connecting Rod
C1AE-6214-A	Bolt—Connecting Rod
C3OZ-6250-C	Camshaft
C3OZ-6256-A	Sprocket—Camshaft
C2OZ-6261-B	Bearing—Camshaft—Front
C2OZ-6262-B	Bearing—Camshaft—Center
C2OZ-6263-B	Bearing—Camshaft—Rear
C3OZ-6265-A	Spacer Cam Sprocket
C2OZ-6266-A	Plug
C3OZ-6263-A	Chain—Timing—58 Links
C3OZ-6269-A	Plate—Camshaft Thrust
C2OZ-6278-A	Washer—Camshaft Sprocket
C3AZ-6287-B	Eccentric, Cam Fuel Pump Drive
C3OZ-6303-B	Crankshaft
C3OZ-6306-A	Sprocket, Crankshaft—21 Teeth Steel
C3OZ-6310-A	Slinger—Crankshaft Oil
C3OZ-6316-A	Damper Assy.—Crankshaft
C3AZ-6333-B	Bearing Crankshaft Main Front, Rear, Rear Intermediate Front Intermediate
C3AZ-6337-B	Bearing, Crankshaft Main Center
C2OZ-6345-A	Bolt—Crankshaft Main Bearing Cap
C3OZ-6375-C	Flywheel Assembly
373223-S	Bolt—Flywheel
C3OZ-6378-A	Washer—Crankshaft Damper
C2OZ-6384-A	Gear—Flywheel
C3OZ-6392-C	Housing Assembly—Flywheel
C3OZ-6500-A	Tappet Assy. Valve, Mechanical
C3OZ-6505-A	Valve, Exhaust
C3OZ-6507-A	Valve Intake Bumper Type
C3OZ-6513-A	Spring Assy., Valve Damper
C3OZ-6514-A	Retainer—Valve Spring
7HA-6518-A	Key Valve Spring Retainer
C2OZ-6524-A	Baffle, Valve Spring Oil
C3OZ-6A527-A	Stud—Rocker Arm Support
C2OZ-6564-A	Arm Assy., Valve Rocker
C2OZ-6565-B	Rod—Valve Push
C3OZ-6571-A	Seal—Valve Stem
C3DZ-6582-C	Cover Assy.—Valve Rocker Arm RH & LH (2)
C2OZ-6584-A	Gasket, Valve Rocker
C2OZ-6600-A	Pump Assy.—Oil
B8A-6608-A	Rotor & Shaft Assy.—Oil Pump Drive
B8A-6616-C	Cover, Oil Pump
C2OZ-6A618-A	Shaft Assy.—Oil Pump Intermediate
C3OZ-6622-A	Screen & Cover Assy. Oil Pump
C2OZ-6626-A	Gasket, Oil Pump Inlet Flange
B8A-6629-A	Ring, Oil Pump Shaft Retainer
C2OZ-6A630-A	Duct, Crankcase Ventilation
C2OZ-6A631-A	Element, Crankcase Ventilation
C2OZ-6A633-A	Retainer, Crankcase Ventilation
C2OZ-6659-A	Gasket, Oil Pump to Block
C3AZ-6A666-A	Valve Assy.—Crankcase Ventilation Reg.
C2OZ-6670-A	Spring—Relief Valve
C2OZ-6674-A	Plunger—Relief Valve
C3OZ-6675-A	Pan Assy.—Oil
C2AZ-6700-A	Bearing—Crankshaft—Front Oil
C2OZ-6701-A	Seal—Crankshaft—Rear Oil
C3AZ-6730-A	Plug—Engine Oil Pan
C1AZ-6731-A	Element—Engine Oil Filter
C2OZ-6750-B	Indicator Assembly Oil Level
C2OZ-6734-A	Gasket—Engine Oil Pan Drain Plug
C2OZ-6754-A	Tube Assembly—Oil Level Indicator
COAE-6766-E	Cap Assembly—Oil Filler With Decal
C2OZ-6781-A	Gasket Kit—Oil Pan
C2OZ-6870-A	Gasket—Crankcase Ventilation

427—HIGH RISER AND SPECIAL PA

1964½—427 CUBIC INCH HIGH RISER ENGINE SPECIAL PARTS LISTING

4V ENGINE	8V ENGINE	SPECIAL ORDER PART NUMBER	DESCRIPTION	QUANTITY PER UNIT
X	X	C4AE-6010-J	Block Assembly	1
X	X	C4AE-6049-F	Head	2
X		C4AE-6110-S	Piston	8
	X	C3AE-6110-BJ	Piston	8
	X	C3AE-6150-C	Ring Top	8
X		C4AE-6150-A	Ring Top	8
	X	C3AE-6152-C	Ring Compression	8
X		C4AE-6152-A	Ring Compression	8
	X	C3AE-6159-A	Segment Oil Ring	16
X		C4AE-6159-A	Segment Oil Ring	16
	X	C3AE-6161-C	Expander Oil Ring	8
X		C4AE-6161-A	Expander Oil Ring	8
X	X	C4AE-6200-C	Connecting Rod (7000 RPM)	8
X	X	C4AE-6211-A	Bearing Connecting Rod	16
X	X	C4AE-6214-G	Bolt—Connecting Rod—(7000 RPM)	16
	X	C4AE-6250-B	Camshaft	1
X	X	C4AE-6300-C	Crankshaft Assy. (7000 RPM)	1
X		C4AE-6303-G	Crankshaft	1
X	X	C4AE-6333-A	Bearing—Crankshaft—Red—(7000 RPM)	8
X	X	C4AE-6333-B	Bearing—Crankshaft—Blue—(7000 RPM)	8
X	X	C4AE-6333-G	Bearing Crankshaft	8
X	X	C4AE-6337-T	Bearing Crankshaft—Red—(7000 RPM)	2
X	X	C4AE-6337-U	Bearing Crankshaft—Blue—(7000 RPM)	2
X	X	C4AE-6337-AB	Bearing Crankshaft	2
X	X	C4AE-6A338-A	Bearing Crankshaft—Thin Wall—(7000 RPM)	2
X	X	C4AE-6A339-C	Bearing Crankshaft—Thin Wall—(7000 RPM)	2
X	X	C4AE-6500-C	Tappet	16
X	X	C3AE-6505-N	Valve Exhaust	8
X	X	C4AE-6505-E	Valve Exhaust (7000 RPM)	8
X	X	C3AE-6507-J	Valve Intake	8
X	X	C4AE-6507-J	Valve Intake (7000 RPM)	8
X	X	C4AE-6524-B	Baffle	2
X	X	C3AE-6A527-A	Bolt	8
X	X	C3AE-6531-A	Support	8
X	X	C3AE-6563-B	Shaft	2
X	X	C3AE-6571-D	Seal	16
X	X	C4AE-6622-D	Pick-up Tube	1

4V ENGINE	8V ENGINE	SPECIAL ORDER PART NUMBER	DESCRIPTION	QUANTITY PER UNIT
X	X	C4AE-6675-L	Oil Pan	1
X	X	C4AE-6714-A	Oil Filter (7000 RPM)	1
X	X	C4AE-6A829-A	Tab Oil Pick-up	1
X	X	C4AE-6A829-B	Tab Oil Pick-up	1
X		C4AE-9A274-B	Tube Fuel Filter	1
X		C4AE-9424-G	Intake Manifold	1
X	X	C4AE-9A424-A	Seat—Manifold—Rear	1
X	X	C4AE-9A425-A	Seal—Manifold—Front	1
	X	C4AE-9424-F	Intake Manifold	1
X		C4AE-9D281-B	Hose Carburetor Fuel	1
X	X	C4AE-9439-A	Gasket—Intake Manifold	2
X		C4AE-9447-B	Gasket—Carburetor to Manifold	1
X		C4AE-9447-C	Gasket—Carburetor to Manifold—(7000 RPM)	1
X		C4AF-9510-DA	Carburetor	1
X		C4AF-9510-DT	Carburetor—(7000 RPM)	1
	X	C4AF-9510-CU	Carburetor Primary	1
	X	C4AF-9510-CV	Carburetor Secondary	1
X		376545-S	Clamp—Fuel Hose	A/R
X		88376-S8	Stud—Carburetor to Manifold	A/R
X	X	C3AE-6051-BS	Head Gasket—Stainless Steel—Right Hand	1
X	X	C4AE-6051-BS	Head Gasket—Stainless Steel—Left Hand	1

ENGINE ASSEMBLY	APPLICATION
C4AE-6007-H 359-A1	4V Standard Transmission
C4AE-6007-J 359-B1	4V-Standard Transmission (7000 RPM)
C4AE-6007-H 361-A2	8V-Automatic Transmission
C4AE-6007-H 361-A3	8V-Standard Transmission

1964 FORD AND FAIRLANE 427 C I DRAG STRIP REAR AXLE SPECIAL ORDER PARTS

SPECIAL ORDER PART NUMBER	DESCRIPTION
C4OW-4725-A	Axle Shaft—Left Hand
C4OW-4234-A	Axle Shaft—Right Hand
C2AW-4017-A	Carrier Assembly
C2AW-4204-D	Case—Differential Gear
WAB-44205-A	Seat—Differential Pinion Shaft
WAB-44207-A	Shaft—Differential Pinion
WAC-4221-A	Cone & Roller
WAC-4222-A	Cup—Differential Bearing
C4AW-4662-F	Spacer—Pinion Bearing (.466)

RTS AVAILABILITIES

SPECIAL ORDER PART NUMBER	DESCRIPTION
C4AW-4662-G	Spacer—Pinion Bearing (.468)
C4AW-4662-H	Spacer—Pinion Bearing (.470)
C4AW-4662-J	Spacer—Pinion Bearing (.472)
C4AW-4662-K	Spacer—Pinion Bearing (.474)
C4AW-4662-L	Spacer—Pinion Bearing (.476)
C4AW-4662-M	Spacer—Pinion Bearing (.478)
C4AW-4662-N	Spacer—Pinion Bearing (.480)
C4AW-4662-R	Spacer—Pinion Bearing (.482)
AF-4616-A	Cup—Pinion Gear Bearing
C4AW-4630-A	Cone & Roller—Pinion Gear Bearing
WAA-4616-A	Cup—Pinion Gear Front Bearing
WAA-4621-A	Cone & Roller Pinion Gear Front
C4AW-4851-A	Flange Assembly—Universal Joint (Axle End)
C3AW-4010-F	Housing Assembly—Rear Axle
C3OW-4010-J	Housing Assembly—Rear Axle
C4AW-4204-A	Case Assembly—Differential Gear
C4AW-4234-A	Axle Shaft—Right Hand
C4AW-4725-A	Axle Shaft—Left Hand

1964 FAIRLANE AND GALAXIE DRAGSTER SPECIAL ORDER BODY PARTS

SPECIAL ORDER PART NUMBER	DESCRIPTION	FAIRLANE	GALAXIE
GF-3-X	Cooler Line		X
GF-4-X	Cooler Line		X
W-11	Front Vent Window (Plexiglass)	X	
W-21	Front Door Window (Plexiglass)	X	
W-31	Rear Side Window (Plexiglass)	X	
W-40	Rear Window (Plexiglass)	X	
XC-46-688	Clutch Disc—Aluminum Back	X	X
ATL-64-G	Air Tube—Left Hand (Fiberglass)		X
ATR-64-G	Air Tube—Right Hand (Fiberglass)		X
B-64-FF	Front Bumper (Fiberglass)	X	
H-64-FF	Hood—(Fiberglass)	X	
H-64-G	Hood—(Fiberglass)		X
LH-64-FF	Fender—Left Hand (Fiberglass)	X	
RH-64-FF	Fender—Right Hand (Fiberglass)	X	
SR-64-G	Shift Rod		X
427	Engine Gasket	X	
HE-647	Radiator		X

1964 FAIRLANE AND GALAXIE DRAGSTER SPECIAL ORDER BODY PARTS

SPECIAL ORDER PART NUMBER	DESCRIPTION	FAIRLANE	GALAXIE
S-4116	Gasket—Exhaust Manifold	X	
C4AW-4602-G	Driveshaft—Automatic		X
C4OA-4602-B	Driveshaft—Automatic	X	
C4OA-4602-C	Driveshaft—Standard	X	
C3AE-6750-L	Dipstick	X	X
C4AE-6758-C	Breather Tube	X	X
C4AA-7003-E	Standard Transmission		X
C4AE-8620-J	Fan Belt	X	X
C4AF-9600-BD	Air Cleaner (4V)		X
MT-9600-A	Air Box (8V)	X	
C4AF-9601-C	Air Cleaner Element (4V)		X
C4ZF-9654-A	Gasket Air Cleaner (4V)		X
29905-XX	Bucket Seat	X	
XA-560732	Standard Transmission	X	
5071000	Air Box (8V)		X

"HX" AUTOMATIC TRANSMISSION FAIRLANE AND GALAXIE DRAGSTER SPECIAL ORDER PARTS

SPECIAL ORDER PART NUMBER	DESCRIPTION
C4AP-7A256-D	Lever Assembly Manual Control
C4AP-7A096-A	Output Shaft and Ring Gear Assembly
C4AP-7C053-B	Governor Assembly
C4AP-7902-E	Convertor Assembly
C4AP-7A100-F	Main Control Assembly
C4AP-7000-U	Automatic Transmission Assembly

GALAXIE DRAGSTER—FOUR SPEED STANDARD TRANSMISSION C4AA-7003-E SPECIAL ORDER PARTS

SPECIAL ORDER PART NUMBER	DESCRIPTION
SK-4516-QY-8	Countershaft Gear
SK-4516-QY-11	Third Speed Gear
SK-4516-QY-16	Main Drive Gear

ALL OTHER COMPONENTS FOR GALAXIE DRAGSTER TRANSMISSION ARE THE SAME AS THE CATALOGUED FOUR SPEED GALAXIE TRANSMISSION

FAIRLANE DRAGSTER—FOUR SPEED STANDARD TRANSMISSION XA-560732 SPECIAL ORDER PARTS

SPECIAL ORDER PART NUMBER	DESCRIPTION
*C3AZ-7006-DSO	Transmission Case (Aluminum)
*C3AZ-7A039-DSO	Transmission Extension (Aluminum)
T-10K-16B	Main Drive Gear
SK-4516-RB-8A	Countershaft Gear
SK-4516-RB-11A	Third Speed Gear
SK-4516-RB-31A	Second Speed Gear

*CAN ALSO BE USED WITH GALAXIE FOUR SPEED TRANSMISSION. ALL OTHER COMPONENTS FOR FAIRLANE DRAGSTER TRANSMISSION ARE THE SAME AS THE CATALOGUED FOUR SPEED FAIRLANE TRANSMISSION.

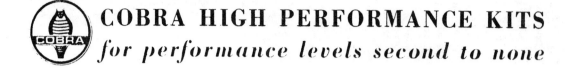

COBRA HIGH PERFORMANCE KITS
for performance levels second to none

With Cobra Kits, extra power is bolted-on . . . no radical machinery is necessary. The additional power obtained will satisfy *any* demand: from normal street driving, to occasional competition, to *all-out competition*.

COBRA ENGINE PERFORMANCE KIT (289 C.I.D.)

Complete kit . . . easily installed—includes cam kit, cylinder head and valve kit, plus 8 matched pistons. For use with manual transmissions.

Part No. C4OZ 6A044-C   Price: 345.55

COBRA CYLINDER HEAD AND VALVE KIT (289 C.I.D.)

Cylinder heads with heavy-duty threaded rocker arm studs, spring seat ridges . . . solid valve spring retainers and oil-controlling valve stem seals.

Part No. C4OZ 6C056-A   Price: 224.25

COBRA HIGH PERFORMANCE CAM KIT (289 C.I.D.)

High-lift design camshaft and 16 special tappets.

Part No. C4OZ 6A257-A   Price: 75.10

COBRA DISTRIBUTOR KIT (289 C.I.D.)

Features dual contact points and centrifugal spark advance control. Gives best spark timing in high range for maximum engine speed.

Part No. C4DZ 12050-A   Price: 49.80

COBRA HEAVY-DUTY CLUTCH KIT (289 C.I.D.)

Heavy-duty, semi-centrifugal clutch assembly . . . smooth-working, low-slip . . . firmer grip at all RPM's—especially in the high range.

Part No. C3OZ 7A537-A   Price: 51.45

Prices shown are manufacturer's suggested retail price. Installation charges and state or local taxes, if any, are extra.

PARTS AND ACCESSORIES WITH *GO*
for the high performance enthusiast

TACHOMETERS

Precision instruments to aid performance enthusiasts in evaluating engine performance. Available for 6 and 8-cylinder engines and 6 or 12-volt systems. Variously calibrated from 0-6000 RPM to 0-9000 RPM. Mounting brackets available for steering column or top of instrument panel installation.

(A) 8-cylinder (6 or 12v) 8000 RPM, 4" with "Zero Knob."
Rotunda—Part No. C2RZ 17A326-B   Price: 31.75

(B) 6-cylinder (6 or 12v) 6000 RPM, 3" with "Zero Knob."
Rotunda—Part No. C3RZ 17A326-A   Price: 35.40

(C) 8-cylinder (6 or 12v) 6000 RPM, 3" with "Zero Knob."
Rotunda—Part No. C3RZ 17A326-B   Price: 35.40

(D) 8-cylinder (12v) 9000 RPM, 4" with "Zero Knob."
Sun—Part No. C4AZ 17A326-A   Price: 60.00

(E) Rally-Pac
Unique twin-pod cluster tachometer and an illuminated, self-regulating clock for the Mustang . . . tach available in 6,000 and 8,000 RPM . . . hooded bezel with "camera case" finish.
MUSTANG
Part No. C5ZZ 10B960-B (6-cyl.)   Price: 75.95
      C5ZZ 10B960-C (8-cyl.)   Price: 75.95

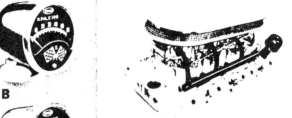

HIGH PERFORMANCE ENGINE KITS

Increased performance for Ford 352 and 390 C.I.D. engines . . . kits include special intake manifold and triple two venturi carburetors plus special air cleaner and other extras for on-the-double action.
FORD
Part No. C5AZ 6B068-A   Price: 206.66

LAKE PIPES

For the performance enthusiast who wants extra horsepower . . . T-type of installation on manifold pipe . . . bright chrome ends . . . universal adapters for all models with 1¾" and 2" pipes.
FORD, FAIRLANE, FALCON AND MUSTANG
Part No. C4AZ 5C246-A   Price: 57.00

LIMITED-SLIP DIFFERENTIAL

(Available on every engine—transmission combination except the 427 C.I.D. engine).
An item particularly suited to competition . . . designed to give in-line faster starts and true solid axle performance on the straightaway . . . minimum power loss on the curves.
Part No. C3AZ 4880-A   Price: 125.00

17

Prices shown are manufacturer's suggested retail price. Installation charges and state or local taxes, if any, are extra.

COLOR AND UPHOLSTERY SELECTIONS: Pick your favorite color from 15 brilliant Diamond Lustre Enamel single tones, or 19 two-tone combinations (single tones only on Convertibles and Country Squires). You have a total of 43 Ford upholstery choices of rich fabrics or handsome vinyls or combinations of the two. Counting standard trims and options, you have 24 choices in new Ford hardtops, 21 choices in Ford sedans, 13 in wagons and 13 in convertibles. (In some cases a trim is offered on more than one model.) Your Ford Dealer will be happy to show you actual samples of new Ford colors and upholsteries.

FORD DESIGN: The Fords for 1965 are completely new from top to tires with an all-new body, frame, and full coil spring suspension to give an ultra-smooth ride with new handling ease and improved roadability. Feature highlights include: advanced frame design with strategically placed body mounts to "tune out" vibration and noise; protective wheelhousings under front fenders; crank-adjusted vent windows; Silent-Flo ventilation system (4-door hardtops); curved side glass; new reversible keys, right-hand ignition, and keyless door locking; suspended accelerator, clutch and brake pedals; step-on parking brake.

CLUTCH AND MANUAL TRANSMISSION: Semi-centrifugal clutch with weighted levers for more positive engagement. Face diameter 10″ with Big Six and Challenger. V-8, 11″ with Thunderbird V-8's. *Synchro-Smooth Drive Manual Transmission* (std. except 500/XL's, LTD's and 425-hp V-8)—provides smooth, fully synchronized shifting in all three forward speeds.

4-Speed Manual Transmission (avail. with 300- and 425-hp V-8's)—fully synchronized with console-mounted stick shift on 500/XL models; floor-mounted on others. *Overdrive* (avail. with Big Six, Challenger V-8 and Thunderbird Special V-8)—conventional 3-speed manual transmission plus automatic 4th gear which cuts in above 28 mph, cuts out below 21 mph (approx.). Downshift to direct by flooring accelerator.

CRUISE-O-MATIC DRIVE (std. on 500/XL's and LTD's with Challenger V-8, opt. on others except with 425-hp V-8)—Features lightweight construction with cast-aluminum converter housing. Three forward ratios, one reverse. Two selective drive ranges provide a choice of starts: 3-speed range starting in low for all normal driving, or 2-speed range starting in intermediate for more surefooted driving on slippery surfaces. Effective engine braking in low range for better control on grades and hilly driving.

REAR AXLE: Semi-floating type with deep-offset hypoid gears. Straddle-mounted drive pinion with 3 roller bearings. Optional heavy-duty axle (std. with 300- and 425-hp V-8's) with higher capacity wheel bearings, larger diameter axle shafts. 425-hp V-8 axle has 4-pinion differential.

NEW DESIGN FRAME: More efficient, torque-box type frame with node-point body mount locations for high combined body-frame strength with superior noise and vibration suppression characteristics.

FRONT SUSPENSION: Wider 62″ tread; new drag-strut, ball-joint type suspension members with mounting feature that allows slight rearward movement of front wheels to reduce the effects of bumps and road faults. Ball joints packed with special 36,000-mile lubricant retained by full-life seals. Rubber-bushed stabilizer helps to control roll on turns. Tapered roller wheel bearings with 30,000-mile check interval (repack as required). Specially calibrated shock absorbers with all-weather fluid.

REAR SUSPENSION: Wider 62″ tread. Three-link, coil spring system with long and short mounting-link arrangement to control dive and squat tendencies in braking and acceleration. Lateral track bar centers axle, resists body sway and roll in turns. All links and track bar rubber-bushed for smooth, quiet operation. Shock absorbers sea-leg mounted to resist body side movement, have all-weather fluid.

STEERING: Recirculating-ball type steering gear with antifriction bearings throughout, plus high numerical ratio for easier steering. Flexible coupling in shaft helps insulate steering column and wheel from road shock. Improved nylon bearings in tie rod and pitman arm pivots reduce steering effort; packed with special 36,000-mile lubricant retained by full-life seals. Overall steering ratio 30.9 to 1; with power steering 23 to 1. Turning diameter, approximately 41 ft. *New Integral Power Steering* locates hydraulic mechanism in engine compartment; has improved pump, longer-lived seals and more compact design.

BRAKES: Self-adjusting, self-energizing design. Brakes adjust automatically when applied while car is moving backwards. Easy-operating suspended pedal, dash-mounted master cylinder. 11-inch composite drums, grooved for better cooling. Total lining area 212 sq. in. Foot-operated parking brake. Optional power brakes have special low pedal position.

TIRES: New low-profile design. 4-ply rating black tubeless tires with Tyrex rayon cord. Safety-type rims. Basic size: 7.35 x 15. Optional: 7.75 x 15 and 8.15 x 15. Tire sizes are determined in part by engine choice and special equipment such as air conditioning. See your Ford Dealer for complete details.

DIMENSIONS AND CAPACITIES: Overall length 210″; width 77.4″; height 55.6″ (sedans), 54.7″ (hardtops), 54.8″ (convertibles); wheelbase 119″; treads 62″ (front/rear); fuel 20 gal.; oil 5 qt. (Six, Challenger V-8), 6 qt. (Thunderbird V-8's); cooling system (with heater) 16 qt. (Six and Challenger V-8), 21.5 qt. (other V-8's).

*For all models except wagons. Complete specifications and other special wagon information is included in the 1965 Ford Wagons Catalog. Ask your Ford Dealer for a copy.

1965 Mercury

Mercury for 1965 again was a newly designed car. Bearing much resemblince to the 1965 Continental, the car featured a horizontal bar grille and vertical taillights.

The engines offered for 1965 were the 390 cid V-8 (2-bbl) rated at 250 hp, the 390 cid V-8 (4-bbl) rated at 300 hp and a 427 cid V-8 (dual 4-bbl) rated at 425 hp. The transmissions offered were the 3-speed manual, the 3-speed manual with overdrive, the 4-speed manual and the Multi-Drive Merc-O-Matic automatic.

Production amounted to 181,701 units, with the model breakdown as follows. Price follows each model in ()'s: MONTEREY 4-dr sedan 23,363 ($2,782), 2-dr sedan 5,775 ($2,711), 2-dr hdt. Maurader Fastback 16,857 ($2,843), 4-dr Breezeway sedan 19,569 ($2,845), 4-dr hdt. sedan 10,047 ($2,918), convertible 4,762 ($3,165); MONTCLAIR 4-dr Breezeway sedan 18,924 ($3,074), 2-dr hdt. Maurader Fastback 16,977 ($3,145), 4-dr hdt. sedan 9,645 ($3,072); PARK LANE 4-dr Breezeway sedan 8,335 ($3,301), 4-dr hdt. sedan 14,211 ($3,372), 2-dr hdt. Maurader Fastback 6,853 ($3,299), convertible 3,008 ($3,526); STATION WAGON 4-dr Commuter, 6-pass. 8,081 ($3,169), 4-dr Colony Park, 6-pass. 15,294 ($3,364).

Seventeen exterior colors were offered with 26 two-tones optional at extra cost. Vinyl roofs were available at extra cost. Interiors were offered in black, blue, Ivy Gold, Palomino, turquoise and white in vinyl or vinyl and cloth on bench or bucket seats.

Literature offered for 1965 consisted of the full-line color folder, the big cars color catalogue (see specs on page 128), and the accessories catalogue The big cars were included in the full-line press kit.

1965 *Mercury*

FULL DETAILS OF THE NEW MERCURY AND MERCURY COMET

SPECIFICATIONS

EXTERIOR DIMENSIONS (INCHES)—Wheelbase . . . 123.0 passenger cars and 119.0 station wagons; over-all length . . . four-door sedans 218.4, station wagons 214.5; over-all height . . . four-door sedans 56.0, station wagons 56.7, two-door hardtops 55.1, convertibles 55.2; over-all width . . . four-door sedans and station wagons 79.6, two-door hardtops and convertibles 79.4; wheel tread (front and rear) . . . 62.0 for all models; curb weight (lbs) . . . four-door sedan 4000, four-door Commuter station wagon 4210. (Weights are for vehicles equipped with automatic transmission.)

CAPACITIES—Fuel tank . . . 21 gallons passenger cars and 20 gallons station wagons; cooling system 20.5 quarts, with heater; engine oil . . . 6 quarts with oil filter; usable luggage capacity . . . 18.6 cubic feet for 4-door sedans.

BRAKES—type . . . 4-wheel hydraulic, self-energizing, self-adjusting; drum diameter . . . 11 inches; total lining area . . . 204.0 square inches for passenger cars and 225.0 square inches for station wagons.

TIRES—size . . . 8.15 x 15 on all models.

SUSPENSION—front . . . Cushion Link with compliance-strut design; rear . . . coil-link with full rubber insulation.

PEAK PERFORMANCE WITH IMPROVED MARAUDER ENGINES

ENGINES		CAR SERIES					TRANSMISSIONS		
	Adv hp @ rpm	Park Lane	Montclair	Monterey	Colony Park	Commuter	3-Speed Manual	4-Speed Manual*	Multi-Drive Merc-O-Matic*
390 V-8	250 @ 4400	N.A.	Standard	Standard	Standard	Standard	•	•	•
390 V-8	266 @ 4400	N.A.	Standard‡	N.A.	Standard‡	N.A.	N.A.	N.A.	•
Super 390 V-8†	300 @ 4600	Standard	Optional	Optional	Optional	Optional	•	•	•
Interceptor 390 V-8*	330 @ 5000	Optional	Optional	Optional	Optional	Optional	•	•	•
Super 427 V-8*	425 @ 6000	Optional	Optional	Optional	N.A.	N.A.	N.A.	•	N.A.

*Optional at extra cost.
†Optional at extra cost for all models except Park Lane.
‡Standard in Montclair and Colony Park with Multi-Drive Merc-O-Matic.

4-speed manual transmission not available with station wagons. Park Lane with optional Special Sports Package includes either 4-speed manual or Merc-O-Matic transmission at no extra cost. N.A.—Not available.

New for the 1966 model year was the 7-Litre, the performance model of the line-up. It featured a 428 cid V-8 rated at 345 hp. The 1966 big cars carried on with the "squared edges" theme of styling. The front end featured grilles that were less luxurious than the 1965 grilles, but the overall theme of the car did offer a more prestigious look. The taillights were now square, instead of the rectangular ones of 1965.

The engines offered for 1966 consisted of the 240 cid six (1-bbl) rated at 150 hp, the 289 cid V-8 (2-bbl) rated at 200 hp, the 352 cid V-8 (4-bbl) rated at 250 hp, the 390 cid V-8 (2-bbl) rated at 275 hp, the 390 cid V-8 (4-bbl) rated at 315 hp, the 428 cid V-8 (4-bbl) rated at 345 hp, the 427 cid V-8 (4-bbl) rated at 410 hp and the 427 cid V-8 (dual 4-bbl) rated at 425 hp. The transmissions offered were the 3-speed manual, the 3-speed manual with overdrive, the 4-speed manual and the 3-speed Cruise-O-Matic automatic.

Production amounted to 1,040,930 units with the following model breakdown (sixes and V-8's totals combined). Prices for sixes follow each model in ()'s, with V-8's costing $115 more: CUSTOM 4-dr sedan 72,245 ($2,415), 2-dr sedan 32,292 ($2,363); CUSTOM 500 4-dr sedan 109,449 ($2,514), 2-dr sedan 28,789 ($2,464); GALAXIE 500 4-dr sedan 171,886 ($2,658), 4-dr hdt. sedan 54,886 ($2,743), 2-dr Fastback hdt. 198,532 ($2,685), convertible 27,454 ($2,914); GALAXIE 500XL V-8 2-dr Fastback hdt. 25,715 ($3,208), convertible 6,360 ($3,456); GALAXIE 500 7-LITRE V-8 2-dr Fastback hdt. 8,705 ($3,596), convertible 2,368 ($3,844); GALAXIE 500 LTD V-8 4-dr hdt. sedan 69,400 ($3,278), 2-dr Fastback hdt. 31,696 ($3,201); STATION WAGON 4-dr Ranch Wagon, 6-pass. 33,306 ($2,793), 4-dr Country Sedan, 6-pass. 55,616 ($2,882), 4-dr Country Sedan, 9-pass. 36,633 ($2,999), 4-dr Country Squire, 6-pass. 27,645 ($3,182), 4-dr Country Squire, 9-pass. 47,953 ($3,265).

Fifteen exterior colors were offered with two-tones optional at extra cost. Vinyl roofs were available in black or white. Interiors were offered in 42 combinations of vinyl or vinyl and cloth on bench or bucket seats.

Literature offered for 1966 consisted of the full-line color catalogue dated 8-65 and dated 1-66, the Big Fords color catalogue dated 8-65 and 1-66, the Station Wagons color catalogue dated 8-65 and 1-66, the "Take a second look at the '66s from Ford" color mailer catalogue and the "Buyer's Digest" booklet filled with facts and figures. Another police options catalogue is included here (see page 130). Galaxies also were included in the full-line press kit.

FORD CUSTOM
FORD CUSTOM 500
AND WAGON

ENGINES: *New 360-hp Police Interceptor V-8* (Interceptor)—428-cu. in. displ.; 4.13" bore x 3.98" stroke; 10.5 to 1 comp. ratio; premium fuel; 4-barrel carburetor with automatic choke; copper-lead main and connecting rod bearings; 5-qt. oil capacity, incl. filter; dual exhausts.* Special features include high-lift camshaft, solid lifters; high performance valve springs with solid retainers and internal dampers; precision-fitted exhaust valves with chromed stems; free-breathing air cleaner plus other hi-speed and long-life features. *315-hp Thunderbird Special V-8* (Cruiser)—390-cu. in. displ.; 4.05" bore x 3.78" stroke; 10.5 to 1 comp. ratio; premium fuel; 4-barrel carburetor with automatic choke; free-turn valves with hydraulic lifters; precision-molded crankshaft; copper-lead main and connecting rod bearings; 5-qt. oil capacity, incl. filter; dual exhausts.* *275-hp Thunderbird V-8* (Guardian)—390-cu. in. displ.; 4.05" bore x 3.78" stroke; 9.5 to 1 comp. ratio; regular fuel; 2-barrel carburetor with automatic choke. Other specifications same as 315-hp V-8. *200-hp Challenger V-8* (Sentinel)—289-cu. in. displ.; 4.00" bore x 2.87" stroke; 9.3 to 1 comp. ratio; regular fuel; 2-barrel carburetor with automatic choke; free-turn valves with hydraulic lifters; precision-molded crankshaft, 5-qt. oil capacity, incl. filter; single exhaust. *150-hp Police Special Six* (Deputy)—240-cu. in. displ.; 4.00" bore x 3.18" stroke; 9.2 to 1 comp. ratio; precision-molded crankshaft with seven main bearings; gear-driven camshaft; regular fuel; single-barrel full economy carburetor with automatic choke; free-turn valves with hydraulic lifters; oil-bath air cleaner; disposable cartridge-type full-flow oil filter; 5-qt. oil capacity, incl. filter; single exhaust.

Dual exhausts not included on wagons

CLUTCHES AND TRANSMISSIONS: *Clutches* in Police Packages have thick facings, and high-capacity pressure-plate springs. All are semi-centrifugal. Face diameter and frictional area is: 11.5" (130 sq. in.) with 428-cu. in. V-8, 11.0" (113.1 sq. in.) with 390 4V V-8, 10.4" (103.7 sq. in.) with 289-cu. in. V-8; heavy-duty 11" (113.1 sq. in.) with Six. Standard sedan clutch face diameter and frictional area: all same as above except 9½" (85.2 sq. in.) on Six. *3-Speed Manual Transmission* (standard; HD type in Deputy) is fully synchronized in all forward speeds, has hardened and shot-peened alloy-steel helical gears, and forged bronze synchronizers.† Police Package includes heavy-duty steering column. *4-Speed Manual Transmission* (optional for 428- and 390-cu. in. 4-barrel V-8's except wagon) is fully synchronized in all forward speeds, floor-mounted shift lever. *Overdrive* (optional with 289 V-8 and 240 Six only) has 3-speed manual transmission plus automatic 4th gear that cuts in above 28 mph and cuts out below 21 mph (approx.), with downshift for passing by flooring accelerator. *Cruise-O-Matic Drive* (optional; HD type in Sentinel and Deputy) is 3-speed automatic transmission with two drive ranges: 3-speed range starting in low for all normal driving, or 2-speed range starting in intermediate for better control on slippery surfaces. *Interceptor Cruise-O-Matic* is specially calibrated for upshifts at higher rpm.

†*Not available on 390 2V or 428 4V engine*

REAR AXLE: *Police Package Heavy-Duty Axle* is semi-floating type with deep-offset hypoid gears and straddle-mounted drive pinion. Also included: fade-resistant brakes, higher capacity wheel bearings with larger diameter axle shafts. For axle ratios see page 6.

ELECTRICAL: 12-volt electrical system with 42-amp. alternator. Police Packages have 66-plate, 70 amp-hr heavy-duty battery. Standard sedan has 54-plate, 45 amp-hr battery. Weatherproof ignition system with Static-Ban constant-resistance wiring and air-cooled distributor points; 18-mm. Turbo-Action spark plugs; positive-engagement starter.

SUSPENSION: *Front*—Wide 62" tread; drag-strut, ball-joint type suspension system with mounting feature that allows slight rearward movement of front wheels to reduce effects of bumps and road faults. Ball joints packed with special 36,000-mile lubricant retained by full-life seals. Rubber-bushed stabilizer helps control sway on turns. Tapered roller wheel bearings with 30,000-mile check interval (repack as required). Specially calibrated shock absorbers with all-weather fluid for better year-round control. *Police Package* same as above with heavy-duty coil springs, shock absorbers and front stabilizer bar.

Rear—Wide 62" tread. Three-link coil spring system with long and short mounting-link arrangement to control dive and squat tendencies in braking and acceleration. Lateral track bar centers axle, resists body sway and roll on turns. All links and track bar rubber-bushed for smooth, quiet operation. Shock absorbers sea-leg-mounted to resist body side-shake, have all-weather fluid for more uniform ride control. *Police Packages* have heavy-duty coil springs and shock absorbers.

STEERING: Precision-control, low-friction recirculating-ball type steering gear with anti-friction bearings throughout plus high ratio for easier steering. Flexible coupling in steering shaft insulates steering wheel. Symmetrical linkage with nylon bearings in tie rod and pitman arm pivots packed with special 36,000-mile lubricant retained by full-life seals. Overall steering ratio 30.9 to 1; with power steering, 23 to 1. Turning diameter approx. 41 feet.

BRAKES: Hydraulic, double-sealed, self-energizing design. Dash-mounted master cylinder. *Police Package Heavy-Duty Brakes* have 225-sq. in. riveted linings and specially grooved 11" dia. composite drums for maximum cooling and fade resistance. Manual or automatic adjustment. Standard sedan brakes have 204-sq. in. (225-sq. in. on wagons) riveted linings, air-grooved 11" composite drums and self-adjustment. Foot-operated parking brake with hand release under panel. New power disc front brakes optional.

TIRES: Low-profile design, 4-ply rating black tubeless tires with Tyrex rayon cord. Safety-type rims. Basic sizes: 7.35 x 15 (sedans); 8.15 x 15 (wagons). See your Ford Dealer for tire options.

DIMENSIONS: Overall length 210"; width 79.0"; height 55.6" (sedans), 56.7" (wagons); wheelbase 119"; treads 62" front and rear; fuel 25 gal. (sedans), 20 gal. (wagons); sedan trunk luggage vol. 19.1 cu. ft.; wagon cargo vol. 91.3 cu. ft.

1966 Mercury

The 1966 Mercury was a redesign of the 1965 Mercury with a much cleaner look. Luxury was still an important part of the big Mercury. Performance was still available in the S-55 series.

The engines offered for 1966 were the 390 cid V-8 (2-bbl) rated at 265 hp, the 390 cid V-8 (2-bbl) rated at 275 hp, the 410 cid V-8 (4-bbl) rated at 330 hp and the 428 cid V-8 (4-bbl) rated at 345 hp. The transmissions available were the 3-speed manual, the 4-speed manual and the 3-speed Merc-O-Matic automatic.

Production amounted to 143,401 units, with the models breakdown as follows. Price follows each model in ()'s: MONTEREY 4-dr sedan, 18.998 ($2,854), 2-dr sedan, 2,487 ($2,783), 4-dr Breezeway sedan, 14,174 ($2,917), 4-dr hdt. sedan, 7,647 ($2,990), 2-dr hdt. coupe, 19,103 ($2,915), convertible 3,279 ($3,237), MONTCLAIR 4-dr sedan 11,856 ($3,087), 4-dr hdt sedan 15,767 ($3,217), 2-dr hdt. coupe 11,290 ($3,144), PARK LANE 4-dr hdt. sedan 19,204 ($3,460), 2-dr hdt. coupe 8,354 ($3,387), 4-dr Breezeway sedan 8,696 ($3,389), convertible 2,546 ($3,608).

Seventeen exterior colors were offered with two-tones optional at extra cost. Vinyl roofs were available in black, white or ivy gold. Interiors were offered in up to thirteen combinations of cloth and vinyl or all vinyl.

Literature offered for 1966 consisted of the full-line color folder, the big cars color catalogue (see specs on page 132), the full-line color roto mailer, and the accessories catalogue. The big cars were included in the full-line press kit.

S-55 Sleek . . . smooth . . . and sassy—that's Mercury's new S-55. Sports-car handling, mixed in with potent thrust and dashes of good looks, add up to excitement-on-wheels. Your choice of two-door hardtop or convertible. Up front is the full-bore scat and staying power of the Super Marauder 428 CID V-8 that packs a 345-hp punch. Dual exhausts for reduced engine back-pressure complete the power package. Ready at hand, a console-mounted 4-speed manual transmission or a special Multi-Drive Merc-O-Matic (your choice: optional at extra cost). Bucket seats are contoured for your comfort and the all-vinyl trim presents the deluxe appearance and "touch" of hand-rubbed leather. Note the deluxe steering wheel, the big-dial full instrumentation, heavy deep-loop carpeting and the bright-metal seat side shields. Styling accents include unique body side-striping, deluxe wheel covers and the distinctive S-55 emblem on rear quarter panel and 428 V-8 emblem on the front fender sides. S-55 . . . with a power personality all its own . . . and everything it takes in looks, appointments and equipment to satisfy the performance-minded.

S-55 2-DOOR HARDTOP (S-55 Convertible also available)

THE POWER OF MERCURY

More power and livelier performance for every model come with the 1966 Mercury engines. A full range of power plants is available from the Marauder 390 V-8 rated at 265 hp up to the Super Marauder 428 V-8 with 345 hp. Big news for '66 is the introduction of the new Marauder 410 V-8 featuring four-barrel carburetion and producing 330 hp. The Marauder 410 is standard for all Park Lane models and optional for other models as shown in Engine Chart, below. "Deep breathing" is a key factor to the high power and efficiency of Mercury engines. Carburetors are more efficient with improved airflow through the cleaner. Intake manifolds are designed for minimum restriction and new camshafts provide increased valve lift and overlap for better breathing. Transmissions are carefully matched to engines for maximum performance. And there is a new Multi-Drive Merc-O-Matic especially designed to be teamed with the Marauder 410 V-8 or Super Marauder 428 V-8. In all, seven new Mercury engine-transmission teams. Availabilities are shown on the chart below.

1966 Mercury regular production engines Engines and transmissions other than standard are optional at extra cost.

	Marauder 390 V-8 (a)	Marauder 390 V-8 (b)	Marauder 410 V-8 (c)	Super Marauder 428 V-8 (f)	
Displacement	390 cu. in.	390 cu. in.	410 cu. in.	428 cu. in.	(a) Standard for all Monterey, Montclair, Commuter and Colony Park models with manual transmission.
Bore and stroke (in.)	4.05 x 3.78	4.05 x 3.78	4.05 x 3.98	4.13 x 3.98	(b) Standard for Monterey, Montclair, Commuter and Colony Park with Multi-Drive Merc-O-Matic.
Adv. hp @ rpm	265 @ 4400	275 @ 4400	330 @ 4600	345 @ 4600	(c) Standard for Park Lane and optional for other models.
Adv. torque lb.-ft. @ rpm	401 @ 2600	405 @ 2600	444 @ 2800	462 @ 2800	(d) Dual exhaust optional at extra cost. Not available for station wagons.
Carburetor	2-bbl	2-bbl	4-bbl	4-bbl	(e) Standard for Park Lane bench-seat models. Not available for station wagons.
Compression ratio	9.5 to 1	9.5 to 1	10.5 to 1	10.5 to 1	(f) Standard for S-55, optional at extra cost for all other models.
Fuel	Regular	Regular	Premium	Premium	
Exhaust	Single	Single	Single (d)	Dual (g)	(g) Dual exhaust not available for station wagons.
Valve lifters	Hydraulic	Hydraulic	Hydraulic	Hydraulic	(h) 4-speed manual transmission not available for station wagons.
Alternator	42-amp	42-amp	42-amp	42-amp	(i) Optional at extra cost. Multi-Drive Merc-O-Matic or 4-speed manual mandatory option for Mercury S-55 and Park Lanes with optional bucket seats.
transmission availabilities					
3-speed manual transmission	■		■ (e)		
4-speed manual transmission (h) (i)			■	■	
Multi-Drive Merc-O-Matic (i)		■	■	■	

1967 Ford

"Totally new" was the way to describe the 1967 full-size Ford. Like its competition, Ford went to the rounded, flowing-lines philosophy of design. The 2-dr hardtops were of the true fastbacks. The sedans now had a less formal roof-line. The 1967 models were the first to use the new government mandated energy-absorbing steering wheels and the dual master brake cylinders. The grille was a new stamped aluminum design with a pointed center. The taillights were now recessed into the rear fenders.

Engines offered for 1967 were the 240 cid six (1-bbl) rated at 150 hp, the 289 cid V-8 (2-bbl) rated at 200 hp, the 390 cid V-8 (2-bbl) rated at 265 (275 with automatic transmission) hp, the 390 cid V-8 (4-bbl) rated at 315 hp, the 428 cid V-8 (4-bbl) rated at 345 hp, the 427 cid V-8 (4-bbl) rated at 410 hp and the 427 cid V-8 (dual 4-bbl) rated at 425 hp. The transmissions offered were the 3-speed manual, the 3-speed manual with over-drive, the 4-speed manual and the 3-speed Cruise-O-Matic automatic.

Production amounted to 877,127 units, with the following model breakdown (sixes and V-8's totals combined). Prices follow each model with ()'s, with V-8's costing $106 more; CUSTOM 4-dr sedan 41,417 ($2,496), 2-dr sedan 18,107 ($2,441); CUSTOM 500 4-dr sedan 83,260 ($2,551), 2-dr sedan 18,146 ($2,596); GALXAIE 500 4-dr sedan 130,063 ($2,732), 4-dr hdt. sedan 57,087 ($2,808), 2-dr Fastback Coupe 197,388 ($2,755), convertible 19,068 ($3,003); GALAXIE 500XL V-8 2-dr Fastback Coupe 18,174 ($3,243), convertible 5,161 ($3,493); LTD V-8 4-dr sedan 12,491 ($3,298), 4-dr hdt. sedan 51,978 ($3,363), 2-dr hdt. coupe 46,036 ($3,362); STATION WAGON 4-dr Ranch Wagon, 6-pass. 23,932 ($2,836), 4-dr Country Sedan, 6-pass. 50,818 ($2,935), 4-dr Country Sedan, 9-pass. 34,377 ($3,061), 4-dr Country Squire, 6-pass. 25,600 ($3,234), 4-dr Country Squire, 9-pass. 44,024 ($3,359).

Fourteen exterior colors were offered with two-tones an extra cost option. Vinyl roofs were available in black or white only. Interiors were offered in 11 colors of cloth and vinyl or all vinyl on bench or bucket seats.

Literature offered for 1967 consisted of the full-line color catalogue dated 8-66 and the same dated 1-67 (see specs on page 134), the big cars color catalogue dated 8-66 and 1-67, the Station Wagons color catalogue dated 8-66 and the same dated 1-67, the accessories color catalogue, the "Buyer's Digest" filled with facts and figures. The full-sized Ford was also included in the full-line press kit.

Ford for 1967...

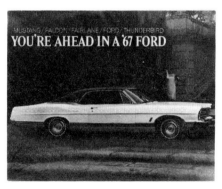

YOU'RE AHEAD IN A '67 FORD

Take a second look at the '67s from Ford

See for yourself...You're ahead in a Ford all the way.

1967 Ford Specifications*

COLOR AND UPHOLSTERY SELECTIONS: Pick your favorite color from 15 brilliant Super Diamond Lustre Enamel single tones, or 25 two-tone combinations (single tones only on Convertibles and Country Squires). You have a total of 52 Ford upholstery choices of rich fabrics or handsome vinyls or combinations of the two. Counting standard trims and options, you have 28 choices in new Ford hardtops, 24 choices in Ford sedans, 14 in wagons and 15 in convertibles. (In some cases a trim is offered on more than one model.) Your Ford Dealer will be happy to show you actual samples of new Ford colors and upholsteries.

ENGINES (see chart for availability): 240-cu. in. FORD BIG SIX—150 hp; 4.00″ bore x 3.18″ stroke; 9.2 to 1 comp. ratio; 7 main bearings; reg. fuel; auto. choke; self-adj. valves; oil cap'y incl. filter, 5 qt.

289-cu. in. CHALLENGER V-8—200 hp; 4.00″ bore x 2.87″ stroke; 9.3 to 1 comp. ratio; reg. fuel; 2-barrel carb.; auto. choke; self-adj. valves; oil cap'y incl. filter, 5 qt.

390-cu. in. THUNDERBIRD V-8—270 hp; 4.05″ bore x 3.78″ stroke; 9.5 to 1 comp. ratio; reg. fuel; 2-barrel carb.; auto. choke; self-adj. valves; oil cap'y incl. filter, 5 qt.

390-cu. in. THUNDERBIRD SPECIAL V-8—315 hp; Same specifications as 390-cu. in. V-8 except 10.5 to 1 comp. ratio; prem. fuel; 4-barrel carb.

428-cu. in. THUNDERBIRD 428 V-8—345 hp; 4.13″ bore x 3.98″ stroke; 10.5 to 1 comp. ratio; prem. fuel; 4-barrel carb.; auto. choke; self-adj. valves; dual exhaust (single on wagons); oil cap'y incl. filter, 5 qt.

427-cu. in. COBRA▲ 427 4V V-8—410 hp; 4.23″ bore x 3.78″ stroke; 11.1 to 1 comp. ratio; 4-barrel carb. available for all models except wagons. Included in equipment package with this engine: transistorized ignition; 42-amp. alternator; 70 amp-hr battery; heavy-duty springs, shock absorbers and rear axle; chrome engine dress-up kit. Your Ford Dealer has complete details.

427-cu. in. COBRA▲ 427 8V V-8—425 hp; Same specifications as Cobra 427 4V V-8 above except dual 4-barrel carbs.

ENGINE FEATURES: 6000-mile (or 6-month) full-flow oil filter; dry-type air cleaner; year-round 190° thermostat; 12-volt electrical system; 42-amp. alternator; 54-plate, 45 amp-hr battery (66-plate, 55 amp-hr with 270- and 315-hp V-8's with automatic transmission); weatherproof ignition with constant-resistance wiring and air-cooled breaker points; positive-engagement starter; fully aluminized muffler. (Dual mufflers of aluminized and stainless steel.)

15 Power Team Selections

ENGINES	TRANSMISSIONS	
	LTD's & XL's	Other Models
240-cu. in. Big Six†		S†,O,C
289-cu. in. Challenger V-8‡	C‡	S§,O,C
390-cu. in. Thunderbird V-8	C	S§,C
390-cu. in. Thunderbird Special V-8	C,4	S§,C,4
428-cu. in. Thunderbird 428 V-8	C,4	C,4
427-cu. in. Cobra 427 4V V-8▲	4	4
427-cu. in. Cobra 427 8V V-8▲	4	4

†Std. engine and trans. all models except LTD's & XL's ‡Std. engine and trans. LTD's & XL's §Std. trans. as indicated, all others optional

Transmission Key:
S—Synchro-Smooth Drive (fully synchronized 3-speed manual)
O—Overdrive C—Cruise-O-Matic Drive 4—4-Speed Manual

*For all models except wagons. Complete wagon information is included in the 1967 Ford Wagons Catalog. Ask your Ford Dealer for a copy.
▲Limited production engines. Available only for special purchase.

CLUTCH AND MANUAL TRANSMISSIONS (see chart for availability): Semi-centrifugal clutch with weighted levers for more positive engagement. Face diameter 10″ with Big Six and Challenger V-8, 11″ with Thunderbird V-8's. Synchro-Smooth Drive Manual Transmission—provides smooth, fully synchronized shifting in all forward speeds.

4-SPEED MANUAL TRANSMISSION—Fully synchronized with console-mounted stick shift on XL models; floor-mounted on others. Overdrive—conventional 3-speed manual transmission plus automatic 4th gear which cuts in above 28 mph, cuts out below 21 mph (approx.). Downshift to direct by flooring accelerator.

SELECTSHIFT CRUISE-O-MATIC DRIVE—Lets you drive fully automatic or shift manually through the gears. Three forward gears, one reverse. Effective engine braking in low gear (1) for better control on grades and hilly driving. Quadrant sequence P-R-N-D-2-1.

REAR AXLE: Semi-floating type with deep-offset hypoid gears. New overhung drive pinion and cast center section with roller bearings for all 240- and 289-cu. in. engines. Straddle-mounted drive pinion with roller bearings for all other engines.

FRAME: Perimeter design consisting of front end assembly, rear end assembly, and four torque box assemblies connected by formed center siderails. The frame is ladder-type construction with five reinforced crossmembers. Node-point body mounting results in superior noise and vibration suppression characteristics.

FRONT SUSPENSION: Wide 62″ tread; drag-strut, ball-joint type suspension components with mounting feature that allows slight rearward movement of wheels to reduce the effects of bumps and road faults. Rubber-bushed stabilizer helps to control roll on turns. Tapered roller wheel bearings.

REAR SUSPENSION: Wide 62″ tread. Three-link, coil spring system with long and short mounting-link arrangement to control dive and squat tendencies in braking and acceleration. Lateral track bar centers axle, resists body sway and roll in turns. All links and track bar rubber-bushed for smooth, quiet operation.

STEERING: Recirculating-ball type steering gear with antifriction bearings throughout, plus high numerical ratio for easier steering. Flexible coupling in shaft helps insulate steering column and wheel from road shock. Nylon bearings in tie rod and pitman arm pivots reduce steering effort. Overall steering ratio 30.9 to 1; with power steering 21.9 to 1. Integral Power Steering locates hydraulic mechanism in steering gear box.

BRAKES: New dual hydraulic brake system with dual master cylinder, separate lines to front and rear brakes. Self-adjusting, self-energizing design. Brakes adjust automatically when applied while car is moving backwards. 11-inch composite drums, grooved for better cooling. Total lining area 203.8 sq. in.

TIRES: New, uniform pressure 4-ply rating black tubeless tires with rayon/polyester cord. Basic sizes 7.75 x 15, 8.15 x 15, 8.45 x 14. Wide-Oval Sports Tires standard on 7-Litre XL's. Tire sizes are determined in part by engine choice and special equipment such as air-conditioning. See your Ford Dealer for complete details.

BASIC DIMENSIONS & CAPACITIES (All Models)—Length—213″. Width—78.6″. Height—55.7″ (sedans), 54.7″ (hdtps.), 54.8″ (convs.). Wheelbase—119″. Tread (front/rear)—62″. Trunk Luggage Vol. (cu. ft.)—18.7 (convs.), 19.1 (others). Fuel—25 gal.

In 1967, Mercury again offered a new car. It still carried on a strong Mercury heritage, but bore a great resemblance to the Ford lineup. New models were the Brougham and the Marquis. Production amounted to 119,411 units.

The engines offered were the 390 cid V-8 (4-bbl) rated at 270 hp, the 410 cid V-8 (4-bbl) rated at 330 hp, the 427 cid V-8 (4-bbl) rated at 345 hp and the 428 cid V-8 (4-bbl) rated at 360 hp. The transmissions offered were the 3-speed manual, the 4-speed manual and the 3-speed Select Shift Merc-O-Matic automatic.

Literature offered for 1967 consisted of the full-line color catalogue dated 9-66 (see page 136), the large full-line color catalogue, the color roto catalogue newspaper insert, and the accessories catalogue. The big cars were included in the full-line press kit.

The 1968 Mercury continued the same basic design as the 1967, but with a bolder look to the grille while retaining the same basic rear end design. Mercury as a performance car was slowly coming to an end. Production amounted to 126,000 units.

The engines offered were the 390 cid V-8 (2-bbl) rated at 265 hp, the 390 cid V-8 (2-bbl) rated at 280 hp, the 390 cid V-8 (4-bbl) rated at 315 hp, the 390 cid V-8 (4-bbl) rated at 335 hp, the 428 cid V-8 (4-bbl) rated at 340 hp and the 428 cid V-8 (4-bbl) rated at 360 hp. The transmissions offered were the 3-speed manual transmission and the 3-speed Select Shift Merc-O-Matic automatic.

Literature offered for 1968 consisted of the full-line color catalogue, the full-line color mailer catalogue, the large full-line color catalogue, the Station Wagons color folder, the Wood-tone color mailer, the Lincoln-Mercury accessories color catalogue. The big cars were included in the full-line press kit.

The big news for 1969 was the Marauder hardtop. This sleek new model sported a tunneled rear window, while the Marauder X-100 featured a matte black tunneled rear window area, a 429 cid V-8, styled steel wheels, fender skirts and much more. Production amounted to 217,132 units.

The engines offered were the 390 cid V-8 (2-bbl) rated at 265 hp, the 390 cid V-8 (4-bbl) rated at the 429 cid V-8 (2-bbl) rated at 320 hp, and the 429 cid V-8 (4-bbl) rated at 360 hp. The transmissions that were available were the 3-speed manual and the 3-speed Select Shift automatic.

Literature offered for 1969 consisted of the full-line color catalogue, the Station Wagons color catalogue, the Lincoln-Mercury contest full-line color catalogue , the "Streep Scene" performance cars color folder, the accessories color catalogue. The big Mercury was also included in the full-line press kit.

The Mercury for 1970 offered a much cleaner look than in 1969 with a front end design that resembled the Continental. The rear design featured larger taillights with a smaller panel separating them. The Marauder and Marauder X-100 retained the same rear design as 1969. Production amounted to 140,079 units.

The engines offered were the 390 cid V-8 (2-bbl) rated at 265 hp, the 429 cid V-8 (2-bbl) rated at 320 hp, and the 429 cid V-8 (4-bbl) rated at 360 hp. The transmissions that were available were the 3-speed manual and the Select Shift automatic.

Literature offered for 1970 consisted of the full-line color catalogue, the big cars color catalogue, the Station Wagons color catalogue. The big Mercurys were also included in the full-line press kit.

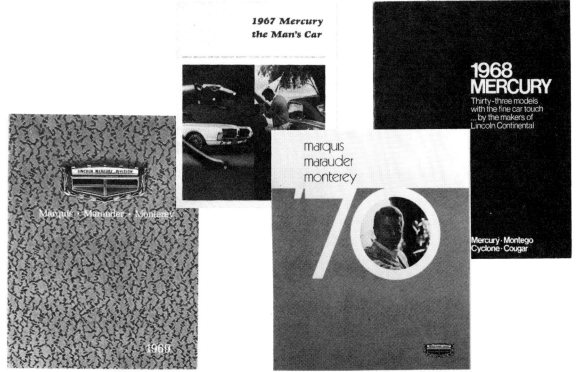

1967 Mercury the Man's Car

1968 MERCURY
Thirty-three models with the fine car touch ... by the makers of Lincoln Continental

marquis marauder monterey

'70

Mercury · Montego Cyclone · Cougar

Marquis · Marauder · Monterey

1969

Mercury S-55

If you want more sport mixed into your Man's Car, try the S-55 Sports Package. Choose from two adventurous-looking models: two-door hardtop or convertible. In the power department there's a husky four-barrel Super Marauder 428 V-8 mustering up 345 horses. Also standard is an engine dress-up kit. It includes: chrome-plated rocker arm covers and air cleaner cover, oil filter cover, oil filler cap, fan guard, radiator cap, master brake cylinder cap, plus a stainless steel oil dip stick. Other

S-55 standard equipment: tuned dual exhausts, the surer stopping of power front disc brakes, a heavy-duty battery and special luxury car body insulation. Outside, the S-55 is easily identified by special ornamentation, sporty striping and deluxe wheel covers with spinners. Your pick of

optional console-mounted transmissions — 4-speed manual or Select-Shift Merc-O-Matic. Inside, deluxe steering wheel, a handy Sports Console and bucket seats of a new design for greater comfort. For the ultimate in luxury, handling and performance . . . get an S-55.

Mercury, the Man's Car

S-55 two-door hardtop (S-55 convertible also available)

Ford continued with the same basic styling as in 1967. The front end design was quite different than the 1967's, but the rest of the car was similar to it. The top of the line models offered hidden headlights. The 289 cid V-8 was replaced with the 302 cid V-8. The 427 cid V-8's with over 400 hp were dropped.

The engines offered for 1968 consisted of the 240 cid V-8 (1-bbl) rated at 150 hp, the 289 cid V-8 (2-bbl) rated at 200 hp, the 390 cid V-8 (2-bbl) rated at 270 hp, the 390 cid V-8 (4-bbl) rated at 315 hp, the 428 cid V-8 (4-bbl) rated at 345 hp, the 427 cid V-8 (4-bbl) rated at 410 hp and the 427 cid V-8 (dual 4-bbl) rated at 425 hp. The transmissions offered were the 3-speed manual, the 3-speed manual with overdrive, the 4-speed manual and the 3-speed Cruise-O-Matic automatic.

Production amounted to 615,929 units, with the following model breakdown (sixes and V-8's totals combined). Prices follow each model with ()'s, with V-8's costing $107 more: CUSTOM 4-dr sedan 45,980 ($2,642), 2-dr sedan 18,485 ($2,584); CUSTOM 500 4-dr sedan 49,398 ($2,741), 2-dr sedan 8,938 ($2,699); GALAXIE 500 4-dr sedan 117,877 ($2,864), 4-dr hdt. sedan 55,461 ($2,936), 2-dr Fastback Coupe 69,760 ($2,881), 2-dr hdt. Coupe 84,332 ($2,916), convertible 11,832 ($3,108); GALAXIE 500XL V-8 2-dr Fastback Coupe 50.048 ($3,092), convertible 6,066 ($3,321); LTD V-8 4-dr sedan 22,834 ($3,135), 4-dr hdt. sedan 61,755 ($3,206), 2-dr hdt. Coupe 54,163 ($3,153).

Fifteen exterior colors were offered with two-tones available at extra cost. Interiors were offered in many color combinations in vinyl or vinyl and cloth on bench or bucket seats.

Literature offered for 1968 consisted of the full-line color catalogue dated 9-67, the big cars large color cars color catalogue undated and revised 12-67, the Station Wagons color catalogue undated and revised 12-67, the accessories color catalogue, the "Here's why Fords are more popular..." color mailer folder, the "Now Ford lowers the cost of high performance..." color mailer folder (see page 138). The Galaxies were also included in the full-line press kit.

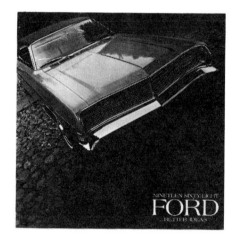

The 1968
Ford XL
Convertible

Ford XL, America's sportiest full-size fastback

heads its field in luxury, too. Standard equipment includes a solid die-cast grille with built-in hidden headlights that not only look great but protect the headlamps from stones and other road hazards during daytime rallies. The grille on Chevrolet's top-of-the-line model is just a thin stamping, pounds lighter, and hidden headlights

are an extra-cost option—$79.00* extra!

Ford's become famous for standard equipment features like a double-edged key that fits into ignition or door locks either side up, fully synchronized 3-speed transmission, courtesy lights, color-keyed, loop-pile carpeting, just to name a few.

But, you have to drive the XL to discover its biggest advantage. It's got the quiet ride, the rugged strength that Ford has made famous, and you can feel it on any kind of road surface, in any driving situation. And talk about handling! Ford's got the kind of "stick" you could expect only on race-bred Italian machinery just a few years back.

The 1968
Ford XL Fastback

1969 Ford

Ford was now settling into a period of full-size luxury cars rather than full-size performance cars, and let the intermediate and pony cars carry the performance honors. The LTD's and the XL's looked the part of true luxury cars, with tastefully designed grilles and hidden headlights.

The engines available for 1969 were the 240 cid six (1-bbl) rated at 150 hp, the 302 cid V-8 (2-bbl) rated at 210 hp, the 390 cid V-8 (2-bbl) rated at 265 hp, the 429 cid V-8 (2-bbl) rated at 320 hp and the 429 cid V-8 (4-bbl) rated at 360 hp. The transmissions offered were the 3-speed manual, the 4-speed manual and the 3-speed Cruise-O-Matic automatic.

Production amounted to 518,530 units, with the following model breakdown (sixes and V-8's totals combined). Prices follow each model with ()'s, with V-8's costing $109 more: CUSTOM 4-dr sedan 45,653 ($2,674), 2-dr sedan 15,439 ($2,632), 4-dr Ranch Wagon, 6-pass. 17,489 ($3,074); CUSTOM 500 4-dr sedan 45,761 ($2,773), 2-dr sedan 7,585 ($2,731),

4-dr Ranch Wagon, 6-pass. 16,432 ($3,138), 4-dr Ranch Wagon, 10 pass. 11,563 ($3,251); GALAXIE 500 4-dr sedan 104,606 ($2,897), 2-dr Fastback Coupe 63,921 ($2,913), 2-dr hdt. Coupe 71,920 ($2,965), 4-dr hdt. sedan 64,031 ($2,966), convertible 6,910 ($3,247), 4-dr Country Sedan, 6-pass. 36,287 ($3,257), 4-dr Country Sedan, 10-pass. 11,563 ($3,373).

Fifteen exterior colors were offered with two-tones optional at extra cost. Vinyl roofs were optional at extra cost. Interiors were available in many color combinations of vinyl or vinyl and cloth on bench or bucket seats.

Literature offered for 1969 consisted of the full-line color catalogue dated 8-68 (see page 140), the big cars color catalogue dated 8-68, the Station Wagons color catalogue dated 8-68, and the "If this isn't your year to move to Cadillac.." color mailer folder dated 2/3/69. The Galaxies were also included in the full-line press kit.

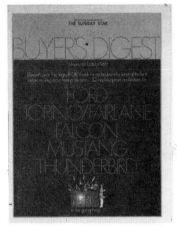

1969 Ford XL GT SportsRoof

Ford XL GT Specifications—*Required engine:* 390 CID 2V V-8, bore and stroke 4.05 x 3.78 in., compression ratio 9.5:1, regular fuel, 265 horsepower at 4400 rpm, 390 lbs-ft torque at 2600 rpm. Single exhaust. *Optional engines:* 429 CID 2V Thunder Jet V-8. Bore and stroke 4.36 x 3.59 in. 10.5:1 compression ratio, premium fuel. 320 hp at 4400 rpm. Torque 460 lbs-ft at 2200 rpm. Single exhaust. 429 CID Thunder Jet V-8, 4V carburetor. Bore and stroke 4.36 x 3.59 in. 10.5:1 compression ratio, premium fuel. 360 hp at 4600 rpm. Torque 480 lbs-ft at 2800 rpm. Dual exhausts. *Transmission:* 3- and 4-speed manual fully synchronized, ratios 2.42:1, 1.61:1, 1.00:1. Optional SelectShift Cruise-O-Matic, ratios 2.46:1, 1.46.1, 1.00:1. "U" handle selector on op-

tional center console with SelectShift. Rear axle ratio 3.25:1, 2.80:1 on 429-4V with automatic transmission. *Brakes:* Power front disc, swept area 217.3 sq. in. *Wheelbase:* 121", overall length 216". *Weights:* Sports-Roof—4160 lb., Convertible—4393 lb. *Suspension:* Maximum handling package. **XL GT options:** 429 CID 2V Thunder Jet V-8 (320 hp) (requires Cruise-O-Matic transmission; 429 CID 4V Thunder Jet V-8 (360 hp) (requires Cruise-O-Matic or 4-speed manual transmission) • SelectShift Cruise-O-Matic Transmission with 390 2V V-8; with 429 2V or 4V V-8 • 4-Speed Manual Transmission • Power Steering • Limited-Slip Differential • Bucket Seats, Console and Comfortweave Knitted Vinyl Trim.

At the time of printing this guide (12/12/68), product information, and specifications were in effect and correct. Ford Division of Ford Motor Company reserves the right to change product specifications and designs at any time, without notice and without incurring obligation.

Products used in Racing Competition are specifically excluded from any Warranty or Guarantee, expressed or implied. Products utilized for Racing Competition shall be deemed "subjected to abnormal use" and do not qualify for Warranty protection.

See your Ford Dealer for a complete list of options and prices.

FORD
XL

Ford XL GT—
the Michigan Strong Boy.

It's the big one. Sleek, solid, and silent—until you crack the throttle on 360 horses in that new 4V Thunder Jet 429 CID V-8. With 480 pounds of torque this optional muscle machine could move a mountain . . . what it does for these sport luxury XL GT's is completely up to your imagination. (If your performance requirements are a shade less than all-out, order your XL GT with the 2V 390 CID V-8 of 265 hp, or the 2V 429 CID V-8 of 320 hp.) With any of these three great engines you get the glued-to-the-ground roadability of Ford's low, wide-tread all-coil spring chassis. And every XL GT, whether SportsRoof or Convertible, carries power front discs, heavy-duty shocks, simulated mag-type wheel covers, extra heavy-duty coil springs front and rear, high-rate front stabilizer bar, H70-15 belted wide-oval white stripe boots, GT stripe and ornamentation. Plus Rim-Blow deluxe steering wheel. Only Ford could give you this much moving luxury.

1970 Ford

As Ford continued to move away from the big car performance market and into the luxury car market, the cars took on a much more luxurious look inside and also on the outside. This year was really the last year that you could say that there were performance models available at all. A new option was the Dual-paint trim offered on the XL series only.

Engines offered for 1970 were the 240 cid six (1-bbl) 150 hp, the 302 cid V-8 (2-bbl) rated at 220 hp, the 351 cid V-8 (2-bbl) rated at 250 hp, the 390 cid V-8 (2-bbl) rated at 265 hp, the 429 cid V-8 (2-bbl) rated at 320 hp and the 429 cid V8 (4-bbl) rated at 360 hp. The transmissions available were the 3-speed manual and the 3-speed Cruise-O-Matic automatic.

Production amounted to 850,315 units, with the following model breakdown (sixes and V-8's totals combined). Prices follow each model with 0's, with V-8's costing $118 more: CUSTOM 4-dr sedan 42,849 ($2,771), 4-dr sedan 41,261 ($2,872), V-8's only, 4-dr Ranch Wagon, 6-pass. 15,086 ($3,305), 4-dr Ranch Wagon, 6-pass. 15,304 ($3,368), 4-dr Ranch Wagon, 10-pass. 9,943 ($3,481); GALAXIE 500 4-dr sedan 101,784 ($3,026), 4-dr hdt. sedan 53,817 ($3,096),

2-dr hdt. coupe 57,059 ($3,094), 2-dr Fastback Coupe 50,825 ($3,043), V-8's only, 4-dr Country Sedan, 6-pass. 32,209 ($3,488), 4-dr Country Sedan, 10-pass. 22,645 ($3,600); FORD XL V-8 2-dr Fastback Coupe 27,251 ($3,293), convertible 6,348 ($3,501); FORD LTD V-8 4-dr sedan 78,306 ($3,307), 4-dr hdt. sedan 90,390 ($3,385), 2-dr hdt. coupe 96,324 ($3,385), 4-dr Country Squire, 6-pass. 39,837 ($3,832), 4-dr Country Squire, 10-pass. 69,077 ($3,909); FORD LTD BROUGHAM V-8 (production included in with FORD LTD) 4-dr sedan ($3,502), 4-dr hdt. sedan ($3,579), 2-dr hdt. ($3,537).

Fifteen exterior colors were offered with two-tones optional at extra cost. Vinyl roofs were available in black, white, blue, green and brown. Interiors were offered in 31 combinations of vinyl or vinyl and cloth on bench or bucket seats.

Literature offered for 1970 consisted of the full-line color catalogue "Buyers Digest" dated 8/69, the big cars color catalogue dated 8/69 (see specs on page 143), the Station Wagons color catalogue dated 8/69, the Performance Buyer's Digest color catalogue dated 8/69 (see page 142), the "Armchair Estimator" folder dated 9/23/69 and reprinted twice. The Big Cars were also included in the full-line press kit.

Ford XL — makes luxury a sporting proposition.
Here's fun in a king-sized package. And what a package! Hideaway Headlamps. Dual accent paint stripes. Special grille. Full wheel covers. Bright vinyl seat trim. Simulated woodgrain appliques. Nylon loop-pile carpeting. You've never seen a sportier luxury car. And it's on the move, too, with a lively 351 V-8 and fully synchronized 3-speed standard. Add all the muscle you want with 390 2V, 429 2V or 429 4V V-8's. The 429's are designed after the famed tunnelport competition engines and they're all muscle all the way. Tailor your XL SportsRoof or Convertible to fit your kind of fun. Get SelectShift (with console-mounted control optional) and go through the gears automatically or manually as you wish. There are new special Class II or Class III trailer towing options, too, if you're pulling a boat or trailer. And the list of other options goes on and on. Ask your dealer for the '70 Ford Catalog.

Ford goes to sea! Ford V-8 conversions are raising the big splash in drag boat racing.

Here's XL, Big Daddy of Ford's Fun Fleet. You can take it with you (or behind you)! With XL's 429 V-8 options you've got the torque for it.

Color and Trim Selections: 15 single tones, 24 (15 Dualtone for XL) two-tone combinations. Upholstery choices: Up to 32 in hardtops, 32 in sedans, 21 in wagons, 10 in the convertible.

Engines (see chart for availability): 240-cu. in. Big Six—150 hp; 4.00" x 3.18" stroke; 9.2 to 1 comp. ratio; 7 main bearings; reg. fuel; auto. choke; self-adj. valves; oil capacity, incl. filter, 5 qt.

302-cu. in. V-8—220 hp; 4.00" bore x 3.00" stroke; 9.5 to 1 comp. ratio; reg. fuel; 2-barrel carb.; auto. choke; self-adj. valves; oil capacity, incl. filter, 5 qt.

351-cu. in. V-8—250 hp; 4.00" bore x 3.50" stroke; 9.5 to 1 comp. ratio; reg. fuel; 2-barrel carb.; auto. choke; self-adj. valves; oil capacity, incl. filter, 5 qt.

390-cu. in. V-8—265 hp; 4.05" bore x 3.78" stroke; 9.5 to 1 comp. ratio; reg. fuel; 2-barrel carb.; auto. choke; self-adj. valves; oil capacity, incl. filter, 5 qt.

429-cu. in. V-8—320 hp; 4.36" bore x 3.59" stroke; 10.5 to 1 comp. ratio; prem. fuel; 2-barrel carb.; auto. choke; self-adj. valves; oil capacity, incl. filter, 5 qt.

429-cu. in. V-8—360 hp; 4.36" bore x 3.59" stroke; 10.5 to 1 comp. ratio; prem. fuel; 4-barrel carb.; auto. choke; self-adj. valves; single exhaust; oil capacity, incl. filter, 5 qt.

Power Team Selections

ENGINES	TRANSMISSIONS		
Cu. In. Displacement	Horsepower	LTD Broughams, LTD's, XL's, Wagons	Other Models
240 Big Six*	150		S*, C
302 V-8‡	220	S, C	S†, C
351 V-8	250	S‡, C	S, C
390 V-8	265	S, C	S, C
429 V-8 2V	320	C	C
429 V-8 4V	360	C	C

*Std. engine and trans. all models except XL's, LTD's and Wagons

†Std. trans. as indicated, all others optional

‡Std. engine and trans. LTD's and Country Squires, LTD Broughams, XL's

Transmission Key:

S—Synchro-Smooth Transmission (fully synchronized 3-speed manual)
C—SelectShift

Engine Features: 6000-mile (or 6-month) full-flow oil filter; dry-type air cleaner; year-round 190° thermostat; 12-volt electrical system; 42-amp. alternator, batteries; 240-cu. in. Six 45 amp.; 302- and 351-cu. in. V-8 55 amp.; 390-cu. in. V-8 45 amp. (55 amp. with auto. trans.), 429-cu. in. V-8's 80 amp.; all with SelectAire Conditioner, exc. 429 V-8's. 70-amp. Autolite Sta-Ful battery; weatherproof ignition with constant-resistance wiring and air-cooled breaker points; positive-engagement starter.

Clutch and Manual Transmissions—(see chart availability): Semi-centrifugal clutch. Face diameter 9.5" with Big Six, 10" with 302- and 351-cu. in. V-8, 11" with 390-cu. in. V-8, 3-Speed Manual Transmission—smooth, fully synchronized shifting in all forward speeds.

SelectShift Cruise-O-Matic Transmission—Shift automatically or manually through the gears. Three forward gears, one reverse. Effective engine braking in low gear (1) for hilly driving. Quadrant sequence: P-R-N-D-2-1.

Frame: Front end assembly, rear end assembly, and four reinforced torque box assemblies connected by center siderails. S-shape front frame rails for energy-absorbing ability. Node-point body mounting with variable rate mounts for superior vibration suppression.

Front Suspension: Wide 63" tread; ball-joint type drag-strut, rubber-mounted to allow slight rearward movement of wheels to reduce effect of road faults. Rubber-bushed stabilizer helps control roll on turns.

Rear Suspension: Wide 64" tread. Three-link to control dive and squat on braking, acceleration. Lateral track bar centers axle, resists body sway. Links, track bar rubber-bushed for smooth, quiet operation.

Steering: Overall steering ratio 30.7 to 1; with power steering ratio of 21.8 to 1.

Brakes: Dual hydraulic system with dual master cylinder, separate lines to front and rear. Self-energizing, self-adjusting (when applied while car is moving rearward), 11-inch composite drums, grooved for better cooling. Lining area 201.6 sq. in., 222.7 sq. in. on Wagons (240 Six, 302 V-8 only), 217.3 sq. in. swept on front power disc brakes.

Tires: Black tubeless with rayon/polyester cord. Basic sizes F78-15, G78-15, H78-15; load-range B, belted bias ply. Belted Wide-Tread Tires optional on all models (except Wagons). Tire sizes determined in part by engine choice and special equipment.

Basic Dimensions & Capacities—Length 213.9" (XL and LTD are 216"), 4-Dr. Wagon 216.9" (LTD Wagon is 219"). Width 79.8" 4-Dr.; 79.7" 2-Dr. Hdtps., SportsRoof and Conv.; Height 54.9" (Sedans), 53.6" 4-Dr. Hdtps., 53.5" 2-Dr. Hdtps. & SportsRoof, 53.8" Conv., 56.8" Wagons. Wheelbase—121". Tread is 63" front, 64" rear. Trunk Luggage Vol. (cu. ft.)—18, 15.9 (Conv.). Fuel 24.5 gal.

Approximate Weights—Custom 4-Dr. Sedan 3700 lb., Custom 500 4-Dr. Sedan 3740 lb., Galaxie 500 2-Dr. Hdtp. 3723 lb., Galaxie 500 SportsRoof 3722 lb., Galaxie 500 4-Dr. Hdtp. 3784 lb., Galaxie 500 Sedan 3713 lb., Ford XL SportsRoof 3931 lb., Ford XL Conv. 4164 lb., LTD 2-Dr. Hdtp. 3908 lb., LTD 4-Dr. Hdtp. 3952 lb., LTD 4-Dr. Sedan 3882 lb., LTD Brougham 2-Dr. Hdtp. 3953 lb., LTD Brougham 4-Dr. Hdtp. 3997 lb., LTD Brougham 4-Dr. Sedan 3927 lb.

Station Wagons: For full details and specifications on Station Wagon models referred to herein, ask for the Ford Wagons Catalog.

Trailer Towing: For trailer towing information, see your Ford Dealer. Ask for a copy of the brochure, 1970 Ford Cars & Trucks for Recreation.

Twice-a-Year Maintenance: 1970 Fords are designed to go 6,000 miles (or 6 months) between oil changes and minor chassis lubrications; 36,000 miles (or 3 years, whichever comes first) between major chassis lubes. Other service-savers include: 2-year engine coolant-antifreeze, self-adjusting brakes, long-life Autolite Sta-Ful battery, and more.

NOTE: Your 1970 Ford comes with factory engineered and approved parts such as the Autolite Sta-Ful battery, Autolite Power-Tip spark plugs, Autolite shock absorbers, an Autolite 6000-mile oil filter. For continued top performance be sure to specify genuine Autolite parts whenever replacement is necessary.

SOURCE BOOKS!